Creating Safer Organis

THE NSPCC/WILEY SERIES
in
PROTECTING CHILDREN
The multi-professional approach

Series Editors: Christopher Cloke
NSPCC, 42 Curtain Road,
London EC2A 3NX

Jan Horwath,
Department of Sociological Studies,
University of Sheffield,
Sheffield S10 2TU

Peter Sidebotham,
Warwick Medical School,
University of Warwick,
Coventry CV4 7AL

This NSPCC/Wiley series explores current issues relating to the prevention of child abuse and the protection of children. The series aims to publish titles that focus on professional practice and policy, and the practical application of research. The books are leading edge and innovative and reflect a multi-disciplinary and inter-agency approach to the prevention of child abuse and the protection of children.

All books have a policy or practice orientation with referenced information from theory and research. The series is essential reading for all professionals and researchers concerned with the prevention of child abuse and the protection of children.

Creating Safer Organisations

Practical Steps to Prevent the Abuse
of Children by Those Working
with Them

Edited by

MARCUS EROOGA

A John Wiley & Sons, Ltd., Publication

This edition first published 2012
© 2012 John Wiley & Sons, Ltd.

Wiley-Blackwell is an imprint of John Wiley & Sons, formed by the merger of Wiley's global Scientific, Technical and Medical business with Blackwell Publishing.

Registered Office
John Wiley & Sons, Ltd, The Atrium, Southern Gate, Chichester, West Sussex, PO19 8SQ, UK

Editorial Offices
350 Main Street, Malden, MA 02148-5020, USA
9600 Garsington Road, Oxford, OX4 2DQ, UK
The Atrium, Southern Gate, Chichester, West Sussex, PO19 8SQ, UK

For details of our global editorial offices, for customer services, and for information about
how to apply for permission to reuse the copyright material in this book please see our website at
www.wiley.com/wiley-blackwell.

The right of Marcus Erooga to be identified as the authors of the editorial material in this work has
been asserted in accordance with the UK Copyright, Designs and Patents Act 1988.

Library of Congress Cataloging-in-Publication Data

Creating safer organisations : practical steps to prevent the abuse of children by those working with
them / edited by Marcus Erooga.
      p.   cm.
   Includes index.
   Summary: 'This is an accessible resource for those seeking to ensure that they have taken all
possible steps to safeguard the children and young people they are responsible for' – Provided
by publisher.
   ISBN 978-1-119-97269-3 – ISBN 978-1-119-97268-6 (pbk.)
1. Child abuse–Prevention.   I. Erooga, Marcus, 1957–
   HV713. C7125 2012
   362.76'7–dc23

                                             2011052857

A catalogue record for this book is available from the British Library.

Wiley also publishes its books in a variety of electronic formats. Some content that appears in print may
not be available in electronic books.

Set in 10/12pt Times Ten by SPi Publisher Services, Pondicherry, India
Printed in Malaysia by Ho Printing (M) Sdn Bhd

1   2012

Dedicated to: Caroline and to Tony Morrison (1953–2010)

Contents

About the Contributors

Debbie Allnock is an independent researcher with over 20 years of quantitative and qualitative research experience and teaching experience in the field of social policy in both the United States and the United Kingdom. Most recently an NSPCC Senior Research Officer, prior to that, she worked on the National Evaluation of Sure Start investigating the implementation of these programmes and has co-authored a number of articles and a book chapter on this experience. She is currently working on a mapping study of therapeutic services for children and young people who have experienced sexual abuse.

Kerry Cleary has extensive experience in Human Resources having previously worked at a senior level in the private sector specialising in recruitment, retention and graduate recruitment, leading the strategic direction of recruitment within the companies she worked for.

For the past nine years Kerry has worked for the NSPCC initially as the HR Safeguarding Manager specialising in organisational safeguarding and for the past two years a more extensive role as the Head of Engagement, which includes responsibility for employee engagement, employee relations, reward and strategic recruitment as well as maintaining her responsibilities for organisational safeguarding. The safeguarding work undertaken by Kerry covers every function across the NSPCC and looks at areas such as vetting and CRB, safer recruitment and selection processes including the development of value based interviews, the involvement of children and young people in recruitment, safeguarding action planning for all functions across the Society, campaigning for change with government and advising and providing training to external organisations on safer recruitment and selection.

In 2004 Kerry was part of the NSPCC team who provided a written submission to Sir Michael Bichard as part of his Enquiry into the deaths at Soham. She was subsequently called to give evidence on the final day of the Enquiry to Bichard and went to on to be a member of a number of the working groups which were responsible for the development of the Independent Safeguarding Authority (ISA) and the Safer Recruitment Training for Head Teachers and Schools Governors which Kerry co-wrote. She has subsequently spoken at a number of national conferences about safer recruitment post Bichard, has written articles in personnel publications and continues to work with the DCSF on the implementation of the ISA.

Kerry has a Masters Degree in Human Resource Management, and is a member of the Chartered Instituted of Personnel and Development.

Marcus Erooga is NSPCC Theme Adviser for Child Sexual Abuse and a Visiting Research Fellow at the University of Huddersfield's Centre for Childhood Studies.

During 2006 and 2007 he was seconded to undertake a review of the literature about staff and volunteers who may present a risk to children in the workplace and subsequently jointly undertook research with people convicted of sexual offences in those settings.

A past editor and current Board member of the *Journal of Sexual Aggression*, Marcus has authored and edited some 25 publications on child protection related issues, including *Children and Young People who Sexually Abuse others – Challenges and Responses*, Routledge, 2006 (edited with Professor Helen Masson)

Marcus is immediate past Chair of the National Organisation for the Treatment of Abusers (NOTA) and NOTA Conference Director & Training Committee Chair elect.

Jo Green is Lead Officer for Safeguarding in Education for Westminster City Council. She has a wide range of experience of working as a practitioner and manager within both the voluntary and statutory sectors and has been a member of consecutive national networks of advisers established by the DCSF to support the implementation of newly created procedures for safeguarding children. Working from the Government Office for London as a Safeguarding Adviser she also provided advice, support and challenge to London Local Authorities and Local Safeguarding Children Boards across a range of Safeguarding policy issues and held the regional policy lead for Serious Case Reviews, Safe Work Force and Education Safeguarding.

Jo has contributed to national training materials for the safer recruitment of adults who work with children and was part of a small subject expert group that revised the materials in 2008. She also contributed to *The Child Protection Handbook Third Edition* (Elsevier, 2007).

Benjamin R. Kaufman has a B.A. in Spanish from the University of Oregon (Eugene, Oregon, USA) in 2009 and a degree in Psychology from Portland State University (Portland, Oregon, USA) in 2011. He was accepted into the doctoral program in Industrial/Organisational Psychology at Old Dominion University (Norfolk, Virginia, USA) beginning in the Fall of 2011. Ben has worked for a number of Industrial/Organisational Psychology Professors at Portland State University as an undergraduate on issues related to occupational safety and work-family balance. He has also assisted in the collection of data and the development of research measures related to the prevention of child sexual abuse.

Dr Keith L. Kaufman has served as a Professor of Psychology at Portland State University (PSU) in Portland, Oregon, USA, since 1998, for the first nine years of which he was Psychology Department Chair. During his time in Oregon, he has served as a member of the Oregon Youth Authority's Advisory Board and as Chair of the Prevention Subcommittee of the Oregon Attorney General's Sexual Assault Task Force. Keith also co-chaired the committee that created Oregon's first statewide sexual violence prevention plan.

He has served on the board of the National Alliance of Sexual Assault Coalitions and is a Past President of the Association for the Treatment of Sexual Abusers (ATSA) as well as chairing ATSA's Ethics and Prevention Committees. Keith is also a member of the National Center for Missing and Exploited Children's Prevention Committee. His clinical work has involved the assessment and treatment of both child sexual abuse victims and juvenile sexual offenders and their families.

Keith's publications include two books and a variety of book chapters and research articles regarding sexual violence and sexual violence prevention. He edited a comprehensive sexual violence prevention handbook *Preventing Sexual Violence: A Practitioner's Sourcebook* (NEARI Press, 2010) and was recently awarded the Vision of Hope grant by the Pennsylvania Coalition to Prevent Rape to develop the situational prevention approach as a self-assessment tool for youth serving organisations.

Dr Ethel Quayle is a lecturer in clinical psychology in the School of Health in Social Science at the University of Edinburgh and Director of the COPINE research which until September 2008 was based at University College Cork, Ireland.

She is a clinical psychologist and as a practitioner worked with both sex offenders and their victims. For the last twelve years has been working in the area of Internet abuse images, collaborating internationally with government and non-government agencies in the context of research, policy and practice. She has published widely in this area and is co-author of *Child Pornography: An Internet Crime (2003)*, *Viewing Child Pornography on the Internet* (2005) and *Only Pictures? Therapeutic Work with Internet Sex Offenders* (2006) as well as academic and professional papers. Her current research relates to the influence of social networks on Internet offending behaviour, an analysis of images depicting the online exploitation of children and qualitative research on children's experiences of online grooming and sexual exploitation.

Jessica M. Schuett earned her B.A. in Psychology from Hamline University (Saint Paul, Minnesota, USA) in 2010. As an undergraduate, she received funding to participate in a collaborative research program at Hamline. She subsequently completed an undergraduate thesis examining the relationship between culture of honour, acculturation and attitudes toward intimate partner violence in Latinos. From the fall of 2011, Jessica will begin graduate study in the doctoral program in Applied Social and Community Psychology at Portland State University (Portland, Oregon, USA).

Dr Joe Sullivan is a registered Forensic Psychologist with the Health Professionals Council (UK) and is on the British Psychological Society (BPS) register of Chartered Psychologists. He is the Director of Mentor Forensic Services Ltd, which is an organisation specialising in Behaviour Analysis, Child Protection and Professional Sexual Misconduct issues. He holds a PhD in Forensic Psychology, a Masters Degree in Criminology, a Post-Graduate Diploma in Psychology, a Bachelor of Arts Degree in applied Social Sciences, and a Certificate of Qualification in Social Work. Dr Sullivan is an honorary lecturer in Forensic Psychology at the University of Birmingham, UK.

Since 1996 he has collaborated with law enforcement He has worked as an independent consultant for several UK and European police forces specialising in assisting investigations into sexually motivated abduction, murder and assault of children and as Consultant Forensic Psychologist in the Behaviour Analysis Unit at the Child Exploitation and Online Protection Centre, UK. He received a Chief Constables Commendation for his contribution to the investigation into the sexually motivated abduction and murder of a child in 2001.

He has published and presented papers to national and international conferences on the techniques he uses for engaging, assessing and interviewing sexual offenders.

Paula Telford is an NSPCC Development Manager, having previously managed and worked in an NSPCC team specialising in work with children and young people with sexually harmful behaviours. Prior to joining NSPCC in 1995 Paula worked for 19 years in statutory children's services dealing with child protection, especially sexual abuse, including enquiries into abuse in children's homes.

Paula has co-authored a number of chapters in the field of sexually harmful behaviour and was a member of the research team interviewing people convicted of sexual offences in professional settings.

Hayley Tews received a Bachelor of Arts degree in Psychology and Criminal Justice from California State University (Fullerton, California, USA) in 2010. She is currently a graduate student at Portland State University (Portland, Oregon, USA) in the Department of Psychology's Applied Psychology doctoral program. Hayley works under the advisement of Dr Keith Kaufman focusing on the prevention of child sexual abuse. Her current research interests focus on the modus operandi of child sexual abusers, specifically the factors that contribute to the construction of an abuser's unique modus operandi patterns.

Preface

'Despite the profusion of official inquiries, remarkably little serious attention has been paid to the possible factors associated with abuse of children in residential institutions' (Colton, 2002, p. 34)

Almost a decade later this comment from Matthew Colton is still as relevant today and as applicable to all workplace settings, not solely residential settings. Considering its potential impact on the lives of children there remains relatively little published about those who might be unsuitable to work with children. A recent review of the literature (Erooga, 2009) identified a relatively small number of studies of sex offenders in workplace settings, either as paid employees or volunteers. The majority were both North American and with samples who were predominantly catholic clergy. Whilst they have possibly attracted the majority of media attention, there is no indication from the literature that clerics are over represented in terms of incidence as offenders in this context. Rather it appears that they have formed the research samples because of their continued institutional links after discovery of abuse which enabled them to gain access to treatment and therefore readily identifiable to researchers.

High profile cases inevitably increase awareness of particular issues. Two such cases are those of childminder and foster carer Eunice Spry (Lock, 2007) and the Little Teds Nursery case in Plymouth. Mrs Spry was convicted in March 2007 for 26 offences involving abuse of three children and sentenced to 14 years imprisonment. The court heard that Mrs. Spry had beaten the children with sticks and metal bars, scrubbed their skin with sandpaper and forced them to eat lard, bleach, vomit and their own faeces. During the five-week trial she denied any wrongdoing, insisting she had simply tried to instil Christian values into them.

The conviction of Vanessa George and others in the Little Teds Nursery case in 2009 caused widespread concern with the revelation not only of female sexual offenders but also that children entrusted to the care of a nursery could be sexually abused in ways most adults find unimaginable (Plymouth SCB, 2010). The additional element of new technologies, in this case photographs on a mobile phone and a social networking website only added to the confusion at the implications for children's safety in a fast changing world felt by many. Those feelings of fear and confusion are undoubtedly compounded by a further case involving a nursery worker, this time in Birmingham (Birmingham SCB, forthcoming)

Another significant development was the public response to the attempted implementation of The *Safeguarding Vulnerable Groups Act, 2006*, intended to introducing a vetting and barring scheme designed to prevent those deemed unsuitable to work with children and vulnerable adults from gaining access to them through their work and the introduction of the Independent Safeguarding Authority. Whilst increasingly requiring the active participation of organisations in safeguarding measures beyond taking up Criminal Records Bureau (CRB) checks when recruiting and selecting staff, the public outcry at (largely misunderstood) aspects of the scheme also indicated the sensitivities in this area and the importance of a nuanced approach to this difficult issue.

This book brings together practitioners, academics and researchers who have informative, practical contributions to make. A range of topic areas are addressed, including the up to date research with people who have committed sexual offences against children in these settings and new developments in interviewing approaches. The book is intended to be an accessible single resource for those seeking to ensure that their organisation has taken all reasonable steps to safeguard the children and young people they are working with or are responsible for.

The authorship reflects the book's firm commitment to the importance of multi-agency and inter-disciplinary collaboration and is relevant in both community and residential settings. Although there are differences in perspective and emphasis between chapters, this is seen as healthy in an area of work where confusion and concern leads many to seek certainty and a message that 'Sex offenders will behave like this'. Regrettably there is no such simple formulation. Those who sexually offend against children are a diverse and heterogeneous population and the approaches taken to protect children must address the range of possible risks across the spectrum from those highly motivated individuals whose primary sexual interest is children and for whom the organisation is a means of accessing them through to those with no known predisposition or sexual interest in children – even to themselves.

It is hoped that the rich mix of theoretical and practical perspectives within the book will offer stimulation, food for thought and practical measures for its readership in dealing with this difficult, disturbing and extremely challenging area of human behaviour.

At the conclusion of this foreword to the book I want to record my grateful thanks to all the chapter contributors for their expertise and their forbearance in the face of some enthusiastic editing. My thanks to the NSPCC for the opportunity to undertake two fascinating pieces of research and to all the offenders who agreed by interviewed for the study discussed in Chapter 4. Their perspectives were invaluable in forming some of the thinking reflected here. Also my heartfelt thanks to my long suffering partner who has, once again, provided all the hidden support without complaint whilst I was absorbed in 'that book'.

This book is dedicated to the memory of Dr Tony Morrison, MBE who died tragically in an accident in February 2010. Tony, as my first manager when I joined NSPCC, opened my eyes to possibilities in myself and others that I fear I may never have otherwise seen. In the intervening years he became a source of wise counsel, a mentor and above all a valued friend. He is sorely missed by the many, many people whose lives he changed, of whom I am only one.

Marcus Erooga
September 2011

REFERENCES

Birmingham Safeguarding Children Board, forthcoming.

Colton, M (2002) Factors associated with abuse in residential child care institutions. *Children and Society*, 16(1), 33–44.

Erooga, M (2009) *Towards safer organisations: A study of the literature about staff and volunteers who may present a risk to children in the workplace and implications for recruitment and selection to organisations where children may be vulnerable*, London, NSPCC.

Lock, R. (2007) *Executive Summary Report of the Serious Case Review 0105 Mrs Spry*, Gloucester, Gloucestershire Safeguarding Children Board.

Mason, S. (2011) *A Common Sense Approach, A review of the criminal records regime in England and Wales*, London, Home Office.

Plymouth Safeguarding Children Board, 2010, *Case Review Overview Report Executive Summary in respect of Nursery Z*, March.

Creating Safer Organisations – An Overview

Marcus Erooga

The protection of children from abuse and neglect has long been a priority for society and the institutions within it. However, during the last decade public concern, particularly about sexual abuse of children by 'paedophiles', has heightened considerably. This has coincided with concerns about children's welfare in organisational settings, ranging from revelations of what appear to be systematic institutional failings by the Catholic Church (Ryan, 2009) to cases of sexual abuse by individuals of both extreme physical abuse, as in the case of Eunice Spry a private foster carer sentenced to 14 years imprisonment for a range of almost unimaginably cruel and violent behaviours toward children (Lock, 2007), to the sexual abuse of very young children in a nursery by Vanessa George (Plymouth SCB, 2010).

It was against this backdrop that in 2009 the Government announced the introduction of the Vetting and Barring Scheme, designed to improve the protection of children in organisational settings. It came in the wake of the launch of the initial pilots of what the News of the World called 'Sarah's Law'. Correctly known as the Child Sex Offender Disclosure scheme, a process whereby members of the public who have concern about specific individuals can report that to the police and potentially receive information about risks that an individual might pose if the applicant is deemed the person best able to protect the child[1]. As such, it could reasonably be expected that the Vetting and Barring Scheme would be broadly welcomed.

In the event it appeared to be a classic case of poor media management leading to a disastrous outcome. Confused explanations of the detail and implications of the scheme led the public to believe that almost any contact with children outside of their family would mean they needed to be checked with the Criminal Records Bureau (CRB). The example on which there was a

---

[1] For more information see http://www.homeoffice.gov.uk/crime/child-sex-offender-disclosure/.

Creating Safer Organisations: Practical Steps to Prevent the Abuse of Children by Those Working with Them, First Edition. Edited by Marcus Erooga.
© 2012 John Wiley & Sons, Ltd. Published 2012 by John Wiley & Sons, Ltd.

consistent lack of clarity in media interviews was of a parent taking neigh-bours' children to a football club and whether they would or would not come under the scheme.

In the event the public outcry was such that the whole scheme was scrapped and the incoming coalition administration announced a rather less intrusive and minimal approach to vetting[2]. An interesting aspect of the outcry was that it appeared to some extent to crystallise a view that a 'Sarah's Law' was needed to keep children safe from 'paedophiles' but that these were 'other', not people like us and that any suggestion that 'we', the public, should be checked or vetted was offensive. In this context there is resonance with the notion referred to by Sir Michael Bichard in his report on the organisational failings surrounding the employment of Ian Huntley that preceded the murders of Jessica Chapman and Holly Wells in Soham (Bichard, 2004). He comments 'where a sufficiently devious person is determined to work their evil … our task is to make it as difficult as possible for them to succeed' (Bichard, 2004, 6.4).

Whilst none would disagree, it is of concern is that attention becomes solely focused on the devious individual determined to work their evil. Highly motivated abusers undoubtedly exist and a proportion will attempt to access organisations in order to abuse. Indeed in exceptional circumstances like Castle Hill School (Brannan, Jones and Murch, 1993) the whole organisation appears to have been established in order to facilitate access to, and abuse of, children. In Chapter Five Joe Sullivan and Ethel Quayle outline the key findings of a research study into professionals who used their work as a cover for targeting, sexually manipulating and abusing the children with whom they worked, with a specific focus on the 'manipulation styles' they used to engender trust and deflect suspicion.

Focusing on organisational processes, Chapter Seven, by experienced HR professional Kerry Cleary, outlines the components of a 'Safer Recruitment' process which may serve to both prevent those who are already known, possi-bly by virtue of a conviction or previous poor performance, to be unsuitable to work with children and families. When reviewing such material a first thought is often 'but we know that & we do it … or most of it'. Public enquiries and reviews after the event, however, repeatedly highlight failings in basic systems, most recently in the case of the Little Ted's Nursery. It may be helpful to take to heart the exhortation by the Chair of the enquiry into the case of paediatric nurse Beverly Allitt, that 'It would not be wise for anyone to approach this report on the basis that it all happened a long time ago and that nothing like it could ever happen again' (Kirkwood, 1993, Para 1.45).

Other chapters, notably Chapter Four where Marcus Erooga, Debra Allnock and Paula Telford discuss their research, suggest that as well as an external facing prevention approach, designed to keep out those who are inappropriate or an actual danger to children, a different perspective is also needed. Amongst the interviewees were a small but possibly representative sample of

[2] For more information see http://www.homeoffice.gov.uk/crime/vetting-barring-scheme/.

people who abused in organisational settings and yet appeared to have no known predisposition or motivation to abuse before taking up those posts. Counter-intuitive though this might appear, it highlights the need to create preventive, as well as protective systems. In Chapter Eight Keith Kaufmann and colleagues review efforts in other areas of activity to create safe environments in order to offer a systematic framework for assessing and addressing child sexual abuse in community based institutions and organisations. Developing the Situational Prevention Model for use in this context, it outlines a process for applying the approach in order to identify risks and to prescribe prevention and risk reduction strategies to address concerns.

It should also be remembered that the issue of allegations against professionals is a highly contested one. Concerns about unfounded allegations about professionals, particularly teachers, are always present and some texts (cf. Sikes and Piper, 2010) suggest that many of the processes to address and deal with such allegations are fundamentally flawed. For children the situation is equally challenging. In the 1980s Roland Summitt, outlining his seminal 'Child Sexual Abuse Accommodation Syndrome' (he is referring to emotional accommodation) commented that 'The small victim of a private crime must search … for the adult who will listen to an unwelcome, offensive account and take action against a trusted peer' (Summit, 1983). No matter how effective systems may be, the challenge for children in disclosing will always be a major one. Chapter Nine considers the difficulties frequently encountered by employers when making judgments about what constitutes inappropriate behaviour. The chapter's author, Jo Green, explores the dichotomy between the need to give paramountcy to the welfare of children and the need to ensure that the careers of workers are not inappropriately blighted. She offers practical examples to illustrate how fairness to adults and the protection of children can be combined through a process underpinned by transparency, information sharing, multi-agency working and rigorous assessment, resulting in a professional judgment that can properly withstand scrutiny.

Elsewhere in the book Chapters One and Two review the literature regarding people who sexually abuse children whilst employed in positions of trust. Chapter One relates primarily to offenders and offending behaviour whilst Chapter Two focuses on organisational issues. Similarly addressing material which forms the basis for what follows, Chapter Three reviews the development of official measures designed to prevent inappropriate people from working with children, and the principles which underlie those approaches. It focuses primarily on arrangements in England and Wales although there are parallels with developments in Scotland and Northern Ireland.

Finally in this summary, in Chapter Six Ethel Quayle considers some of the situations in which technology may be used in ways that are harmful to children in organisational settings, including the production and sharing of abusive images, or 'child pornography'. The chapter further considers the characteristics of people who offend and the organisational contexts that offer opportunity for such offences to take place, concluding with consideration of what can be done to create safer organisations in relation to these new technologies.

One of the challenges in writing for a book such as this is the nagging doubt about whether it is really needed. Surely with so much guidance and the experience over decades of professionals and children being so badly affected by allegations and incidents of abuse, every organisation now functions effectively in relation to procedures and practice? Regrettably the evidence suggests that the situation is far from being so satisfactory. Inquiries (cf. Erooga, 2009) still reveal that organisations, presumably believing their practice and procedures are working well, are in fact failing children and staff.

A recent example is the report of a joint investigation into processes and procedures in Pembrokeshire County Council undertaken by the Care and Social Services Inspectorate (CSSIW) and the Education Inspectorate (Estyn) (HMSO, 2011). Aspects of it are described here as it illustrates the continuing importance of not only attending to the issues discussed in this book, but of organisations continuing to audit their own practice to ensure that they continue to be used effectively.

In June 2011, the joint investigation was begun into allegations of professional abuse and the arrangements for safeguarding and protecting children in education services in Pembrokeshire County Council from April 2007 to March 2011, 25 cases in all.

At that time 642 staff were due to be working with children over the summer holiday period. 18 (2.9%) staff were found to be without an active CRB check and 41 (6.4%) not to have the required written references. The standard is that there should be two references: of these 41 staff, 33 had no written reference at all. Overall therefore 9.2% of staff potentially working with children for the summer period either did not have the required CRB check or written references in place.

When a sample of past cases was reviewed significant concerns were identified, including:

- Managers minimising serious safeguarding concerns.
- The duty to safeguard children being outweighed by consideration of the previous good record of staff.
- Managers inappropriately considered redundancy, resignation or retirement instead of assessing and managing risks.
- After being made redundant, staff were re-employed without any references being sought, despite known concerns within the authority.
- Failing to deal appropriately with subsequent allegations following previous disciplinary action.
- A school provided false information in a reference for a former member of staff stating that they had resigned their post when in fact they had been dismissed for sexual misconduct with a young person. A second reference then minimised the sexual misconduct. A further allegation of sexually inappropriate behaviour was later recorded on file. There was no record of whether these matters had been identified and acted on.

- CRB checks and references not effectively and consistently screened.
- Human resource files incomplete and poorly maintained, disciplinary issues and allegations against professionals not routinely recorded on personnel files in accordance with guidance, thereby limiting management oversight of individuals who might present a risk to children.

Comment has been made above about the problems faced by children in reporting concerns or abuse. In this report comment was made about the credibility given to an allegation made by children against a professional, that the voice of the child was often absent in strategy meetings and children were either not spoken to or their concerns were not given full credence in about 50% of cases. In four of the cases the child's reported 'difficult behaviour' became the focus of the strategy meetings rather than the allegation against the professional. In a proportion of cases there was little or no evidence of a rights-based approach to safeguarding children in education.

A key conclusion of the report is that in fulfilling its responsibilities the local authority should have effective quality assurance systems in place to ensure that the necessary checks and balances are in place to safeguard and protect children. Whilst the report focuses specifically on the local authority, this recommendation is equally applicable to any organisation, large or small.

In increasingly challenging times, with public spending cuts likely to bite ever deeper and an increasing imperative to 'do more with less', effective systems are likely to be ever more at a premium. Having practice and procedures which are embedded in organisational culture rather than being regarded as a burdensome addition, will not only reduce the likelihood of time and effort in retrospective investigations, but also promote protective and safer environments for children and staff.

The chapters that follow are intended to be provide an up to date, accessible resource for professionals from all disciplines to develop those systems and to consider actions they can take to keep the children they work with or are responsible for, and themselves, safe. That, combined with learning the lessons from repeated inquires that a systematic approach and ongoing review and audit is required if systems are to function effectively will hopefully assist the reader in creating what organisations staff and children ultimately desire and deserve, a safe environment.

REFERENCES

Bichard, M. (2004) The Bichard Inquiry Report – *An Independent Inquiry Arising from the Soham Murders*. House of Commons: London, The Stationery Office.

Brannan, C., Jones, J., and Murch, J. (1993) *Castle Hill Report: Practice Guide*, Shropshire County Council.

Her Majesty's Inspectorate for Education and Training in Wales (Estyn) and the Care and Social Services Inspectorate Wales (CSSIW), 2011, Joint Investigation Into the Handling and Management of Allegations of Professional Abuse and the

Arrangements for Safeguarding and Protecting Children in Education Services in Pembrokeshire County Council (HMSO).

Lock, R. (2007) Executive Summary Report of the Serious Case Review 0105 Mrs Spry, Gloucester, Gloucestershire Safeguarding Children Board.

Plymouth Safeguarding Children Board, 2010, Case Review Overview Report Executive Summary in respect of Nursery Z, March.

Ryan, S. (2009) The Commission to Inquire into Child Abuse.

Sikes, P. and Piper, H (2010) Researching Sex and Lies in the Classroom: Allegations of Sexual Misconduct in Schools, Routledge/Falmer, London.

Summit (1983) The child sexual abuse accommodation syndrome. *Child Abuse and Neglect*, 7(2), 177–193.

1 Understanding and Responding to People Who Sexually Abuse Children Whilst Employed In Positions of Trust: An Overview of the Relevant Literature – Part One: Offenders

Marcus Erooga

The starting point for understanding any issue is to review the existing knowledge. Chapters One and Two therefore outline key aspects from the literature regarding people who sexually abuse children whilst employed in positions of trust. This chapter relates primarily to offenders and offending behaviour, Chapter Two to organisational issues.

PEOPLE WHO SEXUALLY ABUSE CHILDREN IN ORGANISATIONAL POSITIONS OF TRUST – A DEFINITION

For the purposes of this review of the literature this population was defined as anyone working with children who had sexually offended against a child or young person in a context directly related to their paid work or volunteering activity. Working with children here is used to include people working with children in health, social welfare, education, residential accommodation, leisure, sporting, religious activities and criminal justice systems and extends to the voluntary and private sectors (Beyer *et al.*, 2005). The term is further extended to include managers. Worker will be used as a generic term to describe anyone in this category.

Creating Safer Organisations: Practical Steps to Prevent the Abuse of Children by Those Working with Them, First Edition. Edited by Marcus Erooga.
© 2012 John Wiley & Sons, Ltd. Published 2012 by John Wiley & Sons, Ltd.

Inevitably the literature regarding this population relates primarily to those whose offending has come to the attention of law enforcement agencies, usually those who have been convicted. The literature relating to people who have abused but not been detected tends to focus, for obvious practical and ethical reasons, on a desire or willingness to abuse (Briere and Runtz, 1989; Freel, 2003) rather than on the modus operandi of unconvicted offenders. The findings from the literature must therefore be regarded with that potential limitation or bias.

HOW PREVALENT ARE SEXUAL OFFENCES COMMITTED AGAINST CHILDREN IN PROFESSIONAL OR WORKPLACE SETTINGS?

One of the striking features of an issue about which there has been so much publicity is that there are no definitive figures relating to incidence. What is known about the prevalence of organisational, or institutional, abuse comes from disparate sources as there are no national figures collated on the basis of the context of sexual abuse (Kendrick, 1997). Press coverage will inevitably distort public perception with the issue gaining awareness following the murders of Holly Wells and Jessica Chapman by Ian Huntley in Soham in 2002 and more recently the sexual abuse of children in nursery by Vanessa George (Plymouth SCB, 2010). However, statistical information is far more difficult to obtain. One indicator of the increase in official interest in the issue is public inquiries, of which there were 20 between 1967 and 2000, with 14 of those during the 1990s.

In the United States, a recognised expert in the field suggests that the most reliable estimate is that 9.6% of U.S. school students experience sexual abuse by an education professional (Shakeshaft, 2004). In the UK, the most recent information derived from retrospective studies with adults comes from the 2011 NSPCC study on the prevalence of maltreatment and victimisation of children which found only 0.7% reported sexual abuse by a professional (Radford *et al.*, 2011). In one police force, investigation of institutional abuse in 1994–5 constituted 4% of all Child Protection investigations (Gallagher, 2000). From these figures, it is clear that the precise extent of the prevalence, or indeed incidence, of such abuse is largely unknown.

CHARACTERISTICS AND BEHAVIOUR OF PEOPLE WHO SEXUALLY ABUSE CHILDREN IN ORGANISATIONAL POSITIONS OF TRUST

The literature in relation to organisations and the potential for abuse is sparse and has relatively little to offer in terms of the attributes of those who have sexually abused specifically in professional settings. Nevertheless, this section presents what is known about sexual offending in workplace settings.

There is a single detailed study of people who sexually abuse children in organisational positions of trust carried out in the UK by Sullivan and Beech (2004). Because of the uniqueness of the study, and because of its marked contrast to some of the findings of the current study, it is intended to first review its findings before going on to outline the more general literature about those who sexually offend against children.

FINDINGS FROM A STUDY OF RESIDENTS IN A SPECIALIST TREATMENT SETTING WHO HAD SEXUALLY ABUSED CHILDREN WHILST IN ORGANISATIONAL POSITIONS OF TRUST

Over a five year period a sample of 41 men who admitted sexually abusing children with whom they worked in a professional capacity was drawn from residents in a specialist sexual abuse assessment and treatment centre. The centre also provided a comparison group of residents whose sexual offences had not been in professional settings. Whilst the study is informative, providing information from men admitting their offences and becoming increasingly disclosive as they progressed through a treatment programme, the sample will undoubtedly be skewed by virtue of the selectivity of being resident in such a specialist setting for which funding was required.

Twenty-seven of the participants were Roman Catholic priests, religious brothers, ministers or missionaries, 14 of whom had also worked in teaching roles and three of whom had primary care responsibilities with groups of children, either in residential homes or boarding schools. The religious brothers had also worked in boarding schools. There were two residential social workers, both of whom had also trained as teachers. Ten participants were teachers, two of whom also had carer responsibilities for children within residential school settings and one was a sports coach. The remaining two were a nursery carer, who also worked in a pre-school group and a social worker. A large proportion of the sample group also had voluntary or non-statutory involvement with children through church or children's organisations.

Sullivan and Beech (2004) noted significant differences in the clerics who sexually abused children from other child abusers, being older and having a higher IQ. This supports findings from earlier North American studies (Haywood, Kravitz, Grossman, Wasyliw, and Hardy 1996; Langevin, Curnoe, and Bain, 2000; Plante, Manuel, and Bryant, 1996). Mean age on arrival at the Centre (i.e. post discovery of the abuse) was higher, at 50.71 years, than with the other residents, with the oldest group being the faith community leaders who had a mean age of 53.15 years and the youngest group being the childcare workers with a mean age of 35.25 years. Overall, the sample of professional offenders were less likely to be married, in an adult sexual relationship or have children of their own than the other residents. However, the proportion of Catholic clergy in the sample may render this finding atypical.

The majority (73%) of the professional offender sample were accused of sexually abusing only male children, while 22% were exclusively accused by females and 5% were alleged to have sexually abused both boys and girls. For the general centre population, 58% were accused of abusing girls and 21% were accused by boys and 21% accused by both, consistent with other research in this area (Haywood *et al.*, 1996; Loftus and Camargo, 1993). However, in terms of sexual interests whilst there was an exact correlation between girls being the child alleging the index offence and professional offenders' expressed preference, this was not the case when the child making the allegation was a boy (e.g. males were the victim in 73% of cases but were the offender's primary sexual preference in only 56%). Additionally, 24% of offenders reported an exclusive sexual interest in children.

Abel, Osborn, and Twigg (1993) estimate that around one half of adult sex offenders report an adolescent onset of sexual deviance. When their sample were asked to identify when they were first aware of their sexual arousal to children, Sullivan and Beech found that the overwhelming majority (90%) were aware of their sexual arousal to children prior to undertaking their professional careers. Based on a single study, however, it is not appropriate to generalise this finding to all professional sexual offenders.

Fifteen per cent said that gaining access to children in order to sexually abuse them formed a part of their career choice; a further 42% said abuse was part of their motivation for choosing their job and 25% said it was not. The majority of the sample (76%) reported using emotionally coercive methods to facilitate the abuse, one said he only used physical force and 22% reported using both. Other methods commonly used involved taking children away from the normal work environment: 77.5% arranged to meet children outside work with the specific intention of sexual abuse, and 67.5% reported taking children away overnight in order to sexually abuse them. Typically these were educational or recreational trips involving other professionals also accompanying the children, although some were private arrangements with parents. One participant spoke of abusing children on an annual summer camp where he was responsible for the infirmary and would sexually abuse children who became ill, upset or homesick.

Another common method of identifying children to sexually abuse was as part of their work in children's voluntary organisations. In total, 51.2% of the group admitted they had sexually abused children in voluntary settings. By contrast, in a sample of 207 Australian convicted sex offenders, Smallbone and Wortley (2001) found that of those who abused solely outside of their family settings, 18.9% had found their victims through organised activities such as sporting organisations or scouts.

Widespread use of the internet was just beginning at the time Sullivan and Beech's study was concluding. In 1995, the final year from which data for the study was drawn, the authors noted a new development in that the majority of the professional offenders in the clinic admitted use of the internet either to access pornography or to attempt to contact children for potential sexual contact. Of those who participated in the study, 29.3% admitted using the internet to collect pornography (not specified whether indecent images of children or other pornographic images), whilst 9.8% admitted to also attempting to contact children via the internet to sexually abuse. In addition Sullivan, Beech, Craig, and Gannon (2010) report an emerging trend from current police investigations into internet facilitated sexual abuse of children, with significant numbers of those working with children offending in this way.

Whilst it is clear that children are vulnerable in professional relationships, it is instructive to be reminded of what offenders themselves have said about their offending patterns and particularly to review those issues which are most relevant to the likely context of professional relationships in organisational settings. This section on offender characteristics concludes with a review of what is known about grooming.

GROOMING

Noting Gallagher's (2000) reservations about the term 'grooming' as euphemistic and preference for the term 'entrapment', grooming is used here to mean 'A process by which a person prepares a child, significant adults and the environment for the abuse of this child' (Craven, Brown, and Gilchrist, 2006, p. 297).

There are two widely cited studies in which treated sex offenders, those considered most likely to have an understanding of their own behaviour and be most disclosive, were interviewed about their modus operandi. They differ in that one (Conte, Wolf, and Smith, 1989) is a relatively small North American sample (n=20) with community based offenders whilst the other (Elliott, Browne, and Kilcoyne, 1995) draws on a larger sample (n = 91) of U.K. offenders from a range of community and custodial settings including special hospitals. There are, however, consistent themes which emerge and are illustrated here with quotes from the offenders themselves.

TARGETING VULNERABILITY

The offenders interviewed across both studies claimed a particular ability to identify vulnerable children. This referred either to a child's status, home circumstances or age, or their emotional or psychological state. The interviews demonstrated that they manipulated that vulnerability as a means of gaining sexual access to those children. In Elliott *et al.*'s (1995) sample, for example, 49% reported being attracted to children who seemed to lack confidence or had low self-esteem: 'I would probably pick the one who appeared more needy … Someone who had been a victim before: quiet, withdrawn, compliant' (Elliott *et al.*, 1995, p. 596).

EXPLOITING RELATIONSHIPS

Of note in this context is the proportion of abusers who chose to develop a
relationship which had ascribed authority in order to facilitate the abuse, with
48% of Elliott *et al.*'s sample using babysitting. In the same sample just under
half felt a 'special relationship' was vital to either wishing to, or being able to,
achieve the abuse. 'Unless the child and I like each other and find each other
attractive, it doesn't work' (p. 584).

The majority of the Conte *et al.* (1989) sample described a process of developing a relationship prior to initiating sexual contact. What is possibly of most
significance in this context are the features of the relationships described, and
their similarity to the legitimate features of professional adult / child relationships: 'Playing, talking, giving special attention ... get the child to feel safe to
talk with me ... making the child feel comfortable with me. Early on during the
grooming process I used a lot of conversation ... and spent time alone with her.
I kept telling her how proud I was of her and how special she was' (p. 297).

In an Australian study by Smallbone and Wortley (2001) 55% of the offenders gave the child non-sexual attention as part of the process of enabling the
abuse to take place. In Elliott *et al.*'s sample, 30% used demonstrations of affection, understanding or love. It is indicative of how effective such methods can
be that the Inquiry into sexual abuse of young children by Jason Dabbs in
Nursery classes, where he was a student on placement, reports that a number
of the children, even in the context of disclosing abuse, reported a liking for
him (Hunt, 1994, para. 5.4.8).

The comments from the men in Conte *et al.*'s (1989) sample, when asked
what they would include in a hypothetical manual on 'How to sexually abuse
a child' are similar in theme and again match a number of the features of
populations which will come into contact with professionals: 'Identify a child
who would be looking for help, who is vulnerable..., Target children who
appear to be not close to their parents or children who have already been victimised. Look for some kind of deficiency. I would find a child who doesn't
have a happy home life, because it would be easier to groom them ... Choose
a kid who has been abused. Your victim will think that this time is not as bad.'
(p. 298). And significantly, given the difficulty which other adults frequently
experience in believing that such abuse is possible: 'Get as many people who
are close to the victim to trust you' (p. 298).

These themes are echoed in Smallbone and Wortley's (2001) study of 207
incarcerated sex offenders who reported offences involving 1,010 children,
39% of which had resulted in convictions, which gives an insight into offenders'
modus operandi. For extra-familial offenders, the category which would include
organisational offenders, the most common locations for finding the children
subsequently abused were a friend's home (36.5%) and through organised
activities such as sporting associations or scouts (18.9%). For these offenders,
the most commonly used strategies toward the child's carers were making

friends with them (44.4%) and spending time with the child when carers were also present (44.4%). 64.4% touched the child non-sexually in order to desensitise them, 59.3 % gave the children a lot of attention and 56% spent a lot of time with them doing things the child wanted to do.

Turning to abusers in organisations specifically, Abel *et al.* (1998) suggest that they gradually introduce physical and then sexual touching once a relationship with their victims is established. In Gallagher's (2000) study 43% of cases involved first initiating physical contact with the child. Colton and Vanstone's (1996) study with six organisational sexual offenders indicated that the offender was perceived as a peer, a father figure or a rescuer by his victim. By giving attention and gifts, they managed to develop an emotional relationship into which sexual contact was gradually introduced.

Using a sample of 23 men who had at least one conviction for a sexual offence against a child with whom they were working professionally or as a volunteer, Leclerc, Proulx and McKibben (2005) found that modus operandi was related to their position of trust. Thus they were perceived as non-threatening to the child, could easily build a close relationship with a potential victim and used strategies such as giving attention to gain the child's trust (Table 1.1). The child could then be gradually desensitised, and their compliance in sexual activity gained by way of non-sexual touching. The authors suggest that due to their close relationship with the child, some offenders may believe that they do not need strategies to maintain victim silence. The methods used to gain victims' co-operation are instructive in this context, indicating as it does

Table 1.1 *Strategies used by sex offenders to gain victims' co-operation* (Leclerc *et al.*, 2005)

Strategy	Number (per cent)
Giving the child non-sexual attention	23 (100%)
Touching the child non-sexually	22 (95.6%)
Saying nice things about them	19 (82.6%)
Touching the child sexually more and more from one time to the next	19 (82.6%)
Saying loving, caring things to the child	16 (69.5%)
Getting the victims sexually excited	15 (65.2%)
Talking more and more about sex	14 (60.8%)
Starting sexual contact as if it were no big deal	14 (60.8%)
Getting the victims very curious about sex	14 (60.8%)
Starting sexual contact when victims were upset or needing attention	9 (39.1%)
Saying how special they are to be doing this with you	4 (17.4%)
Saying that you are going to teach them something	3 (13.0%)
Telling that all their other friends have had sex by now	2 (8.7%)
Wearing less clothing and telling the child to do the same	2 (8.7%)
Saying that you will love them more if they do this with you	2 (8.7%)
Saying that you will spend more time with them	2 (8.7%)

how the particular circumstances of a professional relationship can be sub-
verted. A number of the behaviours described here are echoed in the offence
descriptions of the offenders in the current study.

USE OF THE INTERNET

As a relatively recent phenomenon, use of the internet to access abuse images
of children (child pornography) is still an area with considerable unknowns.
One is the extent of the problem and another the issue of how far accessing
such images is predictive of a likelihood to proceed to other forms of sexual
offending. However, organisations increasingly have to decide on the signifi
cance of inappropriate images viewed by current or potential staff or volunteers. They may also have to make decisions about those who have been
accessing illegal abusive images but are not charged with a criminal offence, as
in the case of Operation Ore in the UK in 2002, when the criminal justice
agencies did not have the logistical capacity to prosecute the number of offenders revealed in their investigation (BBC, 2003). In the context of this report,
therefore, it is appropriate to consider possible risk of abuse from such individuals and their suitability to work in a child care setting.

The increased availability of access to the internet has brought in its wake
the possibility of relatively easy access to images which previously would have
been available only to someone with a significant commitment to obtaining
them by physical, rather than virtual electronic, methods. Middleton, Elliott,
Mandeville-Norden, and Beech (2006) observe that the internet combines
24 hour, 7 day a week access; affordability, with free material of their choice
available to knowledgeable users and anonymity, thus 'increasing the user's
sense of freedom, pace and … willingness to experiment' (p. 589). One, possibly rather startling, realisation is the proportion of the population who, by
accessing these images, do appear to have some level of sexual interest in
children which has not previously been reflected in levels of reporting of
sexual abuse.

In terms of where computers were used for this purpose, a study by Wolak,
Finkelhor, and Mitchell (2005) of 1,713 arrests for relevant offences in the
USA found that 91% did so at home, but 17% had also done so at work, reinforcing the importance of organisational monitoring for inappropriate use of
computer equipment.

Counterintuitive though it may appear, it is not possible to assume a sexual
interest in children on the part of all those who access or possess abusive
images. Wolak *et al.* (2005) suggest that they will include those who are:

- sexually interested in prepubescent children or young adolescents who use
  the images for sexual fantasy and gratification;
- sexually indiscriminate, in that they are seeking new and different stimuli;

- sexually curious, downloading a few images to satisfy that interest;
- interested in profiting financially by the sale of images or establishing pay per access web sites.

Wolak *et al.* (2005) found that 40% of the cases studied involved dual offences of possession of images and sexual assault, brought to light in the course of the same investigation. A further 15% had attempted to commit such offences, identified by soliciting undercover investigators posing as minors. Law-enforcement agencies have reported between 35%–51% of such dual cases when prior convictions were taken into account (Armagh, 2002). However, in the Wolak *et al.* (2005) study, 55% of these dual offenders were detected in investigations which began as allegations of child sexual abuse. When the case originated with an allegation or investigation of child pornography, the figure fell to 16.6%, though the authors consider this to be a conservative estimate.

It is, therefore very difficult to conclusively assess individual sexual interest in children or adolescents, even when there has been use of the internet to view indecent images of children. However, when considering the significance of such behaviours for employment, it would seem that, whatever the motivation, deliberately accessing such images is such a clear violation of accepted norms and expected standards that an individual doing so renders them unsuitable to work with children. In addition, though there is no evidence of a causal link between viewing abusive images and child abuse, it could also be argued that children have the right to be protected from those who might inappropriately regard them as sexual objects, as opposed to acknowledging their legitimate right to an age appropriate sexual identity, and that this in itself is would make them unsuitable to be a worker in this context.

As well as a possible precursor to abuse new technologies and indecent images also pose other risks to children in organisational settings. So for example their image might be captured for onward distribution or images might be used to coerce children into co-operating with abuse. The use of images and hence serve the broader motivation of the emotional and psychological misuse of children.

MOTIVATIONS TO SEXUALLY ABUSE

The question of why someone sexually offends is complex, resulting from a number of factors operating at different levels. In one relatively simple but very accessible model, four stages are suggested as pre-conditions to abuse, with the three factors which comprise the elements of the first pre-condition (those in column 1 of Figure 1.1) described by the author as a framework in which to organise the various theories explaining child sexual abuse. The first concerns the emotional congruence that many child abusers appear to have with children. The second factor is the process whereby an adult would come

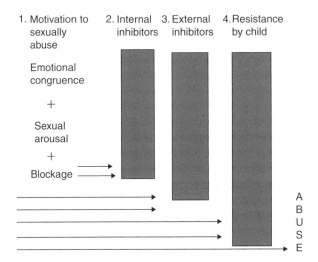

Figure 1.1   Four preconditions model of sexual abuse (Finkelhor, 1984).

to find a child sexually arousing. The third factor addresses the question of why some offenders are 'blocked' in their ability to meet their sexual and emotional needs in appropriate consenting adult relationships. This leads to the precondition whereby the normal inhibitions against having sexual contact with a child are either overcome or not present in those who sexually offend.

The four stage model itself attempts to explain the process by which a sexual offence can come to be committed. Interruption of the process at any stage will prevent the abusive act. The stages are:

MOTIVATION TO ABUSE SEXUALLY

In order for any sexual offence to occur the offender must be motivated to carry out such an act. The motivation is seen as arising from a number of sources which vary according to the individual's experiences and situation and which are addressed in the four factor framework outlined above.

OVERCOMING INTERNAL INHIBITIONS

As is evident from the Freel (2003) and Briere and Runtz (1989) studies, there are a number of individuals who find the prospect of sexual activity with children arousing but who do not offend, presumably because of their internal inhibitions to doing so. The vast majority of sex offenders know that their behaviour is illegal and hence regarded as wrong and in order to offend have had to overcome any such inhibitions. They may do this in a number of ways, such as developing cognitive distortions to justify and excuse their behaviour.

They may also use alcohol or drugs as disinhibitors and then use cognitive distortions to blame the disinhibitors for the offending rather than seeing it as a way of allowing themselves to behave in a way that they already want to. Others may lack these inhibitions altogether.

OVERCOMING EXTERNAL INHIBITIONS

Once any internal inhibitions against carrying out the offence are overcome, an individual must then set up a situation in which the offence can occur and overcome any external obstacles that may arise. The grooming process would be part of this stage, as would seeking employment opportunities which enable access to children.

OVERCOMING THE RESISTANCE OF THE CHILD

The final precondition focuses on the methods the offender employs to over-come any resistance the victim may offer. Grooming of the victim may involve developing a friendship with the child, using bribes of affection and gifts, threats or physical violence. Some offenders may target particular children who are perceived as being vulnerable in some way.

The model has been highly influential, and continues to provide a useful framework within which to consider sexually offending behaviour. Indeed Colton and Vanstone (1998) report that in their study of sexual abuse by men who work with children the four stages in the process were confirmed in all the men's stories. More recent developments offer a more sophisticated approach to the issue and these will be considered below. However, before doing so, it is helpful to briefly consider the implications of the Four Preconditions model for prevention. Aspects of preconditions 1 and 2 may be accessible during a selection and recruitment process, precondition 3 is potentially an issue which can be addressed through organisational situational prevention measures, dis-cussed further below and precondition 4 by organisational empowerment of children about their rights and legitimate expectations of those working with them, This last aspect can only ever be a lesser component of an approach to protecting children and care should be taken to in no way imply that children have the responsibility for their own safety with adults who have a responsibil-ity to care for them.

OTHER MODELS OF KNOWN OFFENDER BEHAVIOUR

Understanding the behaviour of those who sexually abuse children is still a relatively new area of study. Thus models from the 1980s, the four factor model outlined above (Finkelhor, 1984) and the Multi-Factor Model of Deviant Sexuality (Wolf, 1984) which proposed the 'Addiction Cycle' of sexual offending, continued to be influential with practitioners well into the 1990s. There is still no generally accepted model of child sexual abuse (Burn and Brown, 2006) and in view of there being no single causal explanation of sexual offending which has a strong empirical basis, Smallbone and Wortley (2001) suggest that most researchers agree that sexual offending against children is a 'multi-dimensional and multi-determined' phenomenon.

However, more recently, models have been proposed which review existing and more recent data in a continuing attempt to develop understanding of the elements of sexual offending behaviour further. Space precludes detailing them here, but the interested reader is referred to Hanson and Morton-Bourgon's (2004) review of various models based on a meta analysis of 95 studies involving more than 31,000 sex offenders; the multiple pathway model of the sexual offence process proposed by Ward and Hudson (1998) and Ward and Gannon's (2006) 'Comprehensive Good Lives Model of Treatment for Sex Offenders'. Of interest may also be Beech and Ward's (2004) 'The integration of etiology and risk in sexual offenders: A theoretical framework' which thoroughly reviews the most influential models.

THOUGHT PROCESSES AND COGNITIVE DISTORTIONS

One of the issues which many non-specialists find it difficult to reconcile is how an apparently aware and otherwise sensitive professional can sexually abuse a child. Part of the answer may lie in the particular thought processes and cognitive distortions of the individual.

The four preconditions model (Finkelhor, 1984) referred to above includes the need to overcome any internal inhibitors to abuse, one element of which may be 'cognitive distortions' or thinking errors (Maletzky, 1998). Similarly other models consider distorted beliefs to be a contributory factor to the offence process (Ward and Gannon, 2006). Marziano, Ward, Beech, and Pattison (2006) define cognitive distortions as 'fundamental thinking errors that hinder an individual's ability to make realistic formulations and interpretations of the world, others, and him or herself' (p. 97).

Individuals with deviant sexual interest will not be able to commit sexual crimes unless they are willing to hurt others to obtain their goals, feel unable to stop themselves despite any inhibitors or unless they can convince themselves that they are not harming their victims (Hanson and Morton-Bourgon, 2004). Given the qualities sought for those working in 'caring' professions it could be hypothesised that convincing themselves that they are not harming their victims will be the predominant internal process for the majority of professional abusers.

Most people engage in biased or self-deceptive thinking in a number of situations, and usually in ways which are quite innocuous. There is a delicate balance between being motivated to be accurate in our beliefs and the motivation to maintain a positive view of ourselves. The majority manage this balance in a constructive way and acknowledge when thinking needs to be re-examined or conclusions are manifestly not supported by the evidence. However, for child sex offenders, 'the balance is disrupted by deviant motivations that become stronger than the motivation to be accurate ... through the routine activation of normal but biased thinking processes, child molesters gradually construct events in their mind in a way that allows them to protect their self view while bypassing their usual standards of judgement' (Wright and Schneider, 1999, p. 92).

Cognitive distortions can be defined as assumptions, sets of beliefs and self-statements that abusers use to deny, minimise, justify and rationalise their actions which serve to maintain their behaviour. They can thus serve to minimise the seriousness or extent of the offence – 'I didn't really do anything'; move blame away from themselves and so allow a denial of responsibility for their actions – 'I wouldn't have done anything he didn't want to'; view children as holding similar sexual interests or desires as their own – 'Kids enjoy sex with an experienced adult' and misconstrue their victim's behaviour to indicate sexual desire or intent – 'When a child smiles at you it means they want to have sex' (Murphy, 1990).

Biased reasoning includes justifying, minimising and blaming. Possibly because of incredulity that anyone could genuinely hold such beliefs, many people consider offenders' accounts of their own perceptions to be deliberate lies. Whilst this will be the case for some, Wright and Schneider (1999) suggest that, rather than simply lying, these are reflective of general beliefs or assumptions already held by the offender and that they '... actually believe much of their explanation of what occurred or why it occurred despite its inaccuracy' (p. 107).

COGNITIVE DISTORTIONS AND ORGANISATIONAL ABUSERS

There are relatively few studies of the issues of cognitive distortions or emotional functioning which relate specifically to abusers in organisations. Those which do refer predominantly to clerics, predominantly from the catholic church and in one of the few broader study samples, that of Sullivan and Beech (2004) described above, clerics still formed a preponderance of the group. Some degree of caution must, therefore, be exercised in generalising results from these studies to the general population of abusers in organisations. They do, however, offer the most information available about the functioning of those who offend in this way.

From a small sample of 14 Catholic clergy in a residential treatment setting and based on models developed by Thompson, Marolla and Bromley (1998), Saradjian and Nobus (2003) used two broad types of category of distortions: *Disclaimers* and *Accounts*. Disclaimers were prospective interpretations intended to cushion anticipated reaction if the abuse were discovered and

Accounts were retrospective interpretations to explain unanticipated or untoward behaviour. The accounts were further divided into 'justifications that were an admission of responsibility but denial that the action was wrong' and 'excuses – admissions that the act was wrong but a denial of responsibility'. Both clearly served to shift responsibility for the abuse from the offender and enabled them to overcome inhibitions against abusing, minimised their perceptions of the effects of their abuse, reduced their guilt and so maintained the essentially positive self image that most of us need in order to maintain psychological well being.

Saradjian and Nobus (2003) also found that the position of power, trust and high esteem of the clergy proved an important dynamic in facilitating the abuse, in that their distorted belief system became supported and reinforced by selective processing of information derived from their position and the esteem of others. Again this may be a similar process for other organisational offenders, albeit not so pronounced, but relevant to particular positions of power where there is also a pronounced disparity.

FEMALE SEXUAL ABUSERS

One of the most consistent findings in all the research on child abuse offending is that males are overwhelmingly more likely to be perpetrators of child sex abuse than are females. However, given the proportions of women employed or involved in social care and relevant occupations, it is relevant to consider what is established about women known to have abused. Utting (1997) indicates the importance of remaining aware of the possibility of abuse by women and Freel (2003) found 4% of the female public sector child care workers in his sample reported sexual interest in children with 2% indicating at least the possibility of having sex with a child if it was certain no one would find out and there would be no punishment. This is not, therefore, solely a theoretical possibility.

Other than in relation to foster care, where women feature in terms of a range of harmful or abusive behaviours and Nursery and Day Care with its higher reported rates of female sexual abusers, there is relatively little focus on women in the inquiries or literature and the studies which can be identified relate to females who sexually abuse in any setting (Grayston and De Luca, 1999; Matravers, 2005; Robins, 1998). The well publicised case of Vanessa George who sexually abused children in the nursery where she worked is a notable exception (Plymouth SCB, 2010).

Adult female sexual abusers account for only a tiny proportion of recorded sexual offences. Beckett (2005) estimates that adult females account for 5% of sex offending, though there is considerable variation in figures in the literature. Finkelhor (1986) has argued that rates for women who sexually abuse children have been under-estimated in the past, suggesting that the true figure for women who sexually abuse children is 5% for those with girl victims and 20% for boy victims. An analysis of calls to ChildLine (NSPCC, 2009) between April 2008 and March 2009 found that 81% of callers who reported being sexually abused identified the gender of their abuser. Of these 6% of girls and 36% of boys stated that their abuser was female.

Allen, Bear and Knopp (1991) found that the occupational status of female sexual offenders was related to traditional roles occupied by women: 45% were service workers; 14% clerics; 12% labourers; 8% homemakers. Ten percent of the females were from professional occupations, with female offenders three times more likely to have professional occupations that bring them into contact with children compared to male offenders. The female professions included clinical psychology, nursing and nursing supervisors, all of which may have brought the offender into contact with children.

To understand patterns of abuse, a commonly referred to typology is that developed by Speltz, Matthews, and Matthews (1991). This has three types of adult female abuser: Predisposed Offenders, who initially target pre-pubescent children, Teacher-Lover Offenders, who initially target adolescents and view themselves as romantically involved or in love with their victim (the name derived from the view of the women that they are initiating their younger lover into sex), and Male-Coerced Offenders, who were initially coerced into offending by men. This last group are frequently involved in an abusive relationship with the man. There is also a small atypical group which includes those who are non-coerced co-offenders with men, those who are formally mentally ill and those who abuse in the context of ritual.

Reviewing typologies found in the literature, Gannon and Rose (2008) found empirical support for these general typologies, albeit with some suggested refinement within categories. From all the typologies identified they suggest the main categories of female offenders are women who engage with adolescents, usually male; women who offend alongside a co-perpetrating male (sometimes coerced and sometimes not); women who specifically target pre-pubescent children, and women who offend as part of a wider criminal career.

COGNITIVE DISTORTIONS OF FEMALE SEX OFFENDERS

Using the three typologies developed by Speltz et al. (1991), Saradjian (1996) found that those in the Predisposed Offenders category, who initially targeted pre-pubescent children, rated the children's sexual interest as higher than their own and interpreted the children's behaviour as indicating that they wanted sexual contact. Those categorised as Teacher-Lover Offenders, who initially targeted adolescents attributed the sexual desire to the young person, manipulating and coercing the adolescents to act in specific ways and then attributing their compliance as sexual desire. The third category, Male-Coerced Offenders, most commonly interpreted the children's compliance in response to the men's manipulation as sexual desire. For many of the women this perception was also a result of the man 'grooming' their perceptions. Wright and Schneider (1999) suggest similar patterns of cognitive distortions are seen in female offenders as outlined above in relation to males, though other authors are silent on this point.

It will be apparent from these typologies that settings where forming close emotional relationships with children would offer opportunities for this kind of pattern of abuse or indeed for boundaries to become blurred and abusive relationships develop.

CONCLUSIONS

This chapter identifies features of abusers and their behaviour patterns and so illuminates issues which both recruitment and selection processes and development of organisational cultures and norms should take account of. Knowledge of the characteristics of known child abusers may assist in the development of tools for screening, recruitment and monitoring of suitability of staff working with children. In practice, however, child sexual abuse perpetrators are not easy to identify (Sullivan and Beech 2002; Murphy, Rau, and Worley, 1993). As inquiries have shown (e.g. that concerning Frank Beck (Kirkwood, 1993) and Castle Hill School (Brannan *et al.*, 1993a & b) many are intelligent and may be well qualified, present with the responses of a highly competent child care worker and be resourceful in gaining access to children via their employment (Moriarty, 1990). In the case of Vanessa George the Inquiry notes that 'There is no indication from this review that any professional could have reasonably predicted that (she) might be a risk to children. All the evidence currently points to (her) having no sexual interest in children until she made contact with (her co-perpetrator) via the internet' (Plymouth LSCB, 2010, 5.77).

There is no reliable 'profile' describing the characteristics of individuals likely to perpetrate child maltreatment in an organisational or institutional environment. There is no simple preventative or screening measure which can prevent abuse, meaning that current preventative processes are largely limited to vetting for individuals with known problem behaviour (e.g., a conviction).

A values based approach as described in Chapter 7 can add a valuable perspective, with its focus on previous behaviour different to that usually used. In conjunction with existing pre-employment screening process through interview already used by many organisations and systems of staff support, monitoring and evaluation to facilitate the identification and effective management of inappropriate behaviour by staff, particularly in the context of the development of a vigilant organisational culture driven by positive values, can all make a significant contribution to children being safer in organisational relationships.

REFERENCES

Abel, G., Huffman, J., Warberg, B., and Holland. C (1998) Visual reaction time and plethysmography as measures of sexual interest in child molesters. *Sexual Abuse: A Journal of Research and Treatment*, 10(2), 81–95.

Abel, G., Osborn, C., and Twigg, D. (1993) Sexual assault through the life span: Adult offenders with juvenile histories. In H. Barbaree, W. Marshall, and S. Hudson (Eds.), *The Juvenile Sexual Offender* (pp. 104–117). New York: Guilford Press.

Allen, C., Bear, E., and Knopp, F. (Eds.) (1991) *Women and Men Who Sexually Abuse Children: a comparative analysis*, Vermont, Safer Society Press cited in Colquhoun, F. (2004) *Organisational Infiltration: Individual Characteristics and Organisational Cultures*, NSPCC Evaluation Department, unpublished.

Armagh, D., (2002) Virtual child pornography: Criminal conduct or protected speech. *Cardozo Law Review*, 23, 101–117 cited in Wolak, J., Finkelhor, D. and Mitchell, K., (2005) *Child Pornography Possessors Arrested in internet Related Crimes; Findings from the National Juvenile Online Victimization Study*, National Center for Missing and Exploited Children.

Beckett, R., (2005) What are the characteristics of female sex offenders? *NOTA News* 51, 6–7.

BBC (2003) Operation Ore: Can the UK cope? http://news.bbc.co.uk/1/hi/uk/2652465.stm (Accessed 13/9/2010).

Beech, A. R. and Ward, T. (2004). The integration of etiology and risk in sexual offenders: A theoretical framework. *Aggression and Violent Behavior*. 10, 31–63.

Beyer, L., Higgins, D., and Bromfield, L. (2005) *Understanding Organisational Risk Factors for Child Maltreatment: A Review of Literature, National* Child Protection Clearinghouse, Australian Institute of Family Studies.

Brannan, C., Jones, J., and Murch, J. (1993a) *Castle Hill Report: Practice Guide*, Shropshire County Council.

Brannan, C., Jones, J., and Murch, J. (1993b) Lessons from a residential special school enquiry: reflections on the Castle Hill Report, *Child Abuse Review*, 2, 271–275.

Briere, J. and Runtz, M. (1989) University males' sexual interest in children: predicting potential indices of paedophilia in a nonforensic sample. *Child Abuse and Neglect*, 13(1), 11.

Colton, M. and Vanstone, M. (1996) *Betrayal of Trust: Sexual Abuse by Men Who Work with Children*, London: Free Association Books.

Conte, J., Wolf, S. and Smith, T. (1989) What Sexual Offenders tell us about Prevention Strategies, *Child Abuse and Neglect*, 13, pp. 293–301.

Craven, S., Brown, S. and Gilchrist, E, (2006) Sexual Grooming of Children: Review of literature and theoretical considerations. *Journal of Sexual Aggression*, 12(3), 287–299.

Elliott M, Browne K, and Kilcoyne J. (1995) Child sexual abuse prevention: what offenders tell us, *Child Abuse and Neglect*, 19(5), pp. 579–594.

Finkelhor, D. (1984) *Child Sexual Abuse: New theory and research*, Free Press, New York.

Freel, M. (2003) Child sexual abuse and the male monopoly: An empirical exploration of gender and a sexual interest in children. *British Journal of Social Work*. 33, 481–498.

Gallagher, B. (2000) The extent and nature of known cases of institutional child sexual abuse, *British Journal of Social Work*, 30, 795–817.

Gannon, T., Rose, M., and Ward, T. (2008) A descriptive model of the offense process for female sexual offenders. *Sexual Abuse: A Journal of Research and Treatment*, 20(3), 352–374.

Grayston, A. and De Luca, R. (1999) Female perpetrators of child sexual abuse: A review of the clinical and empirical literature. *Aggression and Violent Behavior*, 4(1), 93–106.

Hanson, K. and Morton-Bourgon K. (2004) *Predictors of Sexual Recidivism: An Updated Meta-analysis*. Department of the Solicitor General Canada: Corrections Research Ottawa.

Haywood, T., Kravitz, H., Grossman, L., Wasyliw, O. and Hardy, D. (1996) Psychological aspects of scxual functioning among cleric and noncleric alleged sex offenders. *Child Abuse and Neglect*, 20(6), 527–536.

Hunt, P. (1994) *Report of the Independent Inquiry Into Multiple Abuse in Nursery Classes in Newcastle upon Tyne*. Newcastle upon Tyne, Newcastle upon Tyne County Council.

Kendrick, A. (1997) Safeguarding children living away from home from abuse: A literature review in Kent (1997) *Children's Safeguards Review*, Edinburgh: Social Work Services Inspectorate.

Kirkwood, A. (1993) *The Leicestershire Inquiry 1992. The Report of the Inquiry into Aspects of the Management of Children's Homes in Leicestershire between 1973 and 1986*. Leicester: Leicestershire County Council.

Langevin, R., Curnoe, S. and Bain, J. (2000) A study of clerics who commit sexual offenses: Are they different from other sex offenders? *Child Abuse and Neglect*, 24(4), 535–545.

Leclerc, B., Proulx, J. and McKibben, A. (2005) Modus operandi of sexual offenders working or doing voluntary work with children and adolescents. *Journal of Sexual Aggression*, 11(2), 187–195.

Loftus, J.A. and Camargo, R.J. (1993) Treating the clergy. *Annals of Sex Research*, 6, 287–304. cited in Sullivan, J. and Beech, A. (2004) A comparative study of demographic data relating to intra- and extra-familial child sexual abusers and professional perpetrators, *Journal of Sexual Aggression*, 10(1), 39–50.

Maletzky, B. (1998) Defining our field II: Cycles, chains, and assorted misnomers, *Sexual Abuse: A Journal of Research and Treatment*, 10, 1.

Marziano, V., Ward, T., Beech, A., and Pattison, P. (2006) Identification of five fundamental implicit theories underlying cognitive distortions in child abusers: A preliminary study. *Psychology, Crime and Law*, 12(1), 97–105.

Middleton, D., Elliott, I., Mandeville-Norden, R and Beech, A. (2006) An investigation into the applicability of the ard and Siegert pathways model of child sexual abuse with internet offenders. *Psychology, Crime and Law*, 12(6), 589–603.

Murphy, W. (1990) 'Assessment and modification of cognitive distortions in sex offenders' in W. Marshall, D. Laws and H. Barbaree (Eds.) *Handbook of Sexual Assault* (pp. 331–342) New York, Plenum Press.

NSPCC (2009, November). Children talking to ChildLine about sexual abuse. ChildLine case notes Retrieved January 26, 2011 from http://www.nspcc.org.uk/Inform/publications/casenotes/clcasenotessexualabuse2_wdf64943.pdf.

Plante, T., Manuel, G., and Bryant, C. (1996) Personality and cognitive functioning among hospitalized sexual offending Roman Catholic priests *Pastoral Psychology*, 45(2), 129–139.

Plymouth Safeguarding Children Board, (2010) Case Review Overview Report Executive Summary in respect of Nursery Z, March.

Police Complaints Authority (1993) *Inquiry into the Police Investigation of Complaints of Child and Sexual Abuse in Leicestershire Children's Homes: A Summary.* Police Complaints Authority: London.

Radford, L., Corral, S, Bradley, C, Fisher, H, Bassett, C, and Howat, N. with Collishaw, S. (2011) The Maltreatment and Victimisation of Children in the UK: NSPCC report on a national survey of young peoples', young adults' and caregivers' experiences. London: NSPCC.

Robins, S. (1998) Protecting Our Students: A review to identify and prevent sexual misconduct in Ontario schools. Toronto, Ontario Ministry of the Attorney General, cited in Shakeshaft, C. (2004) *Educator Sexual Misconduct: A Synthesis of Existing Literature*, Washington, D.C.; U.S. Department of Education, Office of the Under Secretary.

Saradjian, J. (1996) *Women who Sexually Abuse Children: From Research to Clinical Practice* Chichester: John Wiley and Sons, Ltd.

Saradjian, A., and Nobus, D. (2003) Cognitive distortions of religious professionals who sexually abuse children, *Journal of Interpersonal Violence*, 18(8), 905–923.

Shakeshaft, C. (2003) Educator sexual abuse. *Hofstra Horizons*, Spring, pp. 10–13.

Shakeshaft, C. (2004) *Educator Sexual Misconduct: A Synthesis of Existing Literature*, Washington, D.C.; U.S. Department of Education, Office of the Under Secretary.

Shakeshaft, C. and Cohan, A. (1995) Sexual abuse of students by school personnel. *Phi Delta Kappan*, 76(7), 513–520.

Smallbone, S. and Wortley, R. (2001) *Child Sexual Abuse: Offender Characteristics and Modus Operandi*, Trends and Issues in Crime and Criminal Justice, No. 193, Australian Institute of Criminology.

Speltz, K., Matthews, J. and Matthews R. (1991) *Female Sexual Offenders: An Exploratory Study*, Vermont; Safer Society Press.

Sullivan, J. and Beech, A. (2002) Professional perpetrators: Sex offenders who use their employment to sexually abuse the children with whom they work. *Child Abuse Review*, 11, 153–167.

Sullivan, J. and Beech, A. (2004) A comparative study of demographic data relating to intra- and extra-familial child sexual abusers and professional perpetrators, *Journal of Sexual Aggression*, 10(1), pp. 39–50.

Sullivan, J., Beech, A., Craig, L., & Gannon, T. (2011) Comparing intra-familial and extra-familial child sexual abusers with professionals who have sexually abused children with whom they work. *International Journal of Offender Therapy and Comparative Criminology*, 55(1) 56–74.

Thompson, J., Marolla, J. and Bromley, D. (1998) Disclaimers and accounts in cases of Catholic priests accused of paedophilia. in A. Shupe (Ed.), *Wolves Within the Fold* (pp. 175–190) New Brunswick, NJ: Rutgers University Press. Cited in Saradjian, A., and Nobus, D. (2003) Cognitive distortions of religious professionals who sexually abuse children, *Journal of Interpersonal Violence*, 18(8), 905–923.

Utting, W. (1997) *People Like Us: The Report of the Review of the Safeguards for Children Living Away from Home*, London, Stationery Office.

Ward, T and Gannon, T. (2006) Rehabilitation, etiology, and self-regulation: The comprehensive good lives model of treatment for sexual offenders, *Aggression and Violent Behavior*, 11(1), 77–94.

Ward, T., and Hudson, S. (1998) The construction and development of theory in the sexual offending area: A meta-theoretical framework. *Sexual Abuse: A Journal of Research and Treatment*, 10, 47–63.

Wolak, J., Finkelhor, D. and Mitchell, K. (2005) *Child Pornography Possessors Arrested in internet Related Crimes; Findings from the National Juvenile Online Victimization Study*, National Center for Missing and Exploited Children.

Wolf, S. (1984) *'A Multifactor Model of Deviant Sexuality'* Paper presented at Third International Conference on Victimology, Lisbon.

Wright R. and Schneider S. (1999) Motivated self-deception in child molesters, *Journal of Child Sexual Abuse*, 8, 89–111.

2 Understanding and Responding to People Who Sexually Abuse Children Whilst Employed In Positions of Trust: An Overview of the Relevant Literature – Part Two: Organisations

Marcus Erooga

CHARACTERISTICS OF 'VULNERABLE ORGANISATIONS' – THE IMPORTANCE OF THE ORGANISATIONAL ENVIRONMENT IN PREVENTING ABUSE

This review now turns from individual characteristics of offenders themselves to issues related to the organisational environment itself in facilitating or preventing abuse.

'Despite the profusion of official inquiries, remarkably little serious attention has been paid to the possible factors associated with abuse of children in residential institutions' (Colton, 2002, p. 34), an observation which seems equally true of abuse by those working with children generally. Thus, whilst there has been exploration of the mechanics of the problem: how the abuse occurred; what the failures to act were, there is relatively little discussion of the underlying issues which allow such situations to arise.

There can be no single factor which will prevent the possibility of children being abused or maltreated by those working with them, but the recurrence of inquiries with similar themes suggests that the organisational context in which the work takes place is an important factor which mediates how likely or possible it is for any such recurrent patterns to occur (Goffman, 1961). As the Department of Health put it 'When a group of people work or live together,

Creating Safer Organisations: Practical Steps to Prevent the Abuse of Children by Those Working with Them, First Edition. Edited by Marcus Erooga.
© 2012 John Wiley & Sons, Ltd. Published 2012 by John Wiley & Sons, Ltd.

a culture evolves: it is something greater than the sum of the behaviour, attitudes and aspirations of the individuals' (Department of Health, 1988, p. 3).

The significance of this is that the organisational environment is a key element in the prevention of abuse. A satisfactory organisational culture has its basis in an organisational commitment to, and defined methods to put into practice and to monitor the effectiveness of, a clearly articulated set of values and desired organisational behaviours with children's welfare and wellbeing at their core.

A number of organisational factors associated with heightened risk to children have been identified. Consideration of those features which lead to high-risk environments is important to guide organisations toward measures which can be implemented to reduce potential risk. This section reviews characteristics of vulnerable organisations, what Hall (2000) refers to as an 'institutional syndrome', and the importance of the organisational environment in minimising potential risk to children.

The literature in this respect tends to focus on institutions where a culture of abusive behaviour has developed (Colton, 2002; Jones, 1994; Colton, Vanstone, and Walby, 2004). However, in trying to offer some explanation of how staff who are supposedly committed to an ethic of care and respect for others in both institutions and organisations become 'corrupted' and abuse their power and their clients, Wardaugh and Wilding (1993) propose a helpful set of factors and other characteristics common to many settings where abuse has occurred can also be identified.

CORRUPTION OF CARE

In his still surprisingly relevant 1961 sociological study of institutions, 'Asylums' Erving Goffman asserts that the 'bad apple' explanation, i.e. that any given situation is explicable in terms of the influence of a particular individual or individuals, is not sufficient, and the corruption of institutional care should be regarded as being produced by factors within the institution.

Wardaugh and Wilding (1993) start from a general assumption based on the argument that the focus of an inquiry into violence should not be on the motives for the violence but on the conditions in which the usual moral inhibitions against violence become weakened (Kelman, 1973).

This perspective seems particularly relevant as the organisational or individual failure to recognise abuse when it is occurring, or to find credible allegations more persuasive, documented repeatedly in inquiries, may be partly attributable to incredulity that those normal moral inhibitions have been so weakened – in effect the difficulty in believing that anyone in a 'caring' role could behave in this way. In the case of Beverley Allitt, the paediatric nurse who murdered children on her ward, the Inquiry comments 'The idea of a nurse taking the lives of children under her charge is almost unthinkable' (Clothier, 1994, 2.1.1); in the case of children's home manager Frank Beck who received seven life sentences for extensive sexual abuse of children in his care, there was a level of disbelief by Leicestershire police that led to a failure to investigate complaints (Police Complaints Authority, 1993). The Judge in the case of Eunice Spry, adoptive parent, childminder, and private and subsequently local authority foster carer who was sentenced to 14 years' imprisonment for 26 offences of abuse of three children commented 'It is difficult for anyone to understand how any human being could have even contemplated what you did, let alone with the regularity and premeditation you employed' (Daily Mail, 2007).

Wardaugh and Wilding (1993) distinguish between this 'ethical corruption' in pursuit of legitimate policy goals and that quite unrelated to policy aims. An example of the former would be the case of the Pindown regime of 'behaviour modification' discipline in children's homes in Staffordshire which, though described by the subsequent inquiry as 'intrinsically unethical, unprofessional and unacceptable' (Levy and Kahan, 1991, p. 167), was designed to bring about generally desired change in young people's behaviour. An example of the latter would be any case of sexual abuse in a professional setting, in that it is unrelated to any organisational policy objectives and, unlike the previous example, not defensible as trying to achieve a legitimate aim in an inappropriate way. Wardaugh and Wilding's hypotheses primarily relate to situations where the means used to attain legitimate policy goals become corrupted, and use examples from the Pindown Inquiry. However, it is also possible to relate these arguments to situations of sexual abuse and examples from other inquiries will be used to illustrate this.

NEUTRALISATION OF NORMAL MORAL CONCERNS

The first proposition is that this 'corruption of care' depends on the neutralisation of normal moral concerns. This suggests that a stage of the process is, effectively, the dehumanisation of the individual '… they (service users) have to come to be regarded as beyond the normal bounds of moral behaviour which governs relations between person and person or carer and client. They have to be seen as less than fully human' (Wardaugh and Wilding, 1993, p. 6). The processes by which individuals join the institution, learn the rules and are expected to subjugate their own preferences to conform, can also serve, in dysfunctional settings, to degrade and humiliate them, reducing them to less than an individual and so become objectified. All of these processes serve to neutralise ordinary moral concerns for their welfare or well being and enable these children to come to be regarded as a means to satisfy the needs of adults.

The purposeful functioning of such a process can be illustrated by reference to Castle Hill School, a privately run residential school where sexual abuse was pervasive, where there was a restrictive regime with fear used to exercise control. An explicit hierarchy was introduced with senior boys, whom the Judge subsequently referred to as the Principal's 'Republican Guard', selected for privileges and given power over others, which then enabled physical and sexual assaults by staff and other boys (Brannan *et al.*, 1993). However, it also possible for a similar, if less pronounced, process to occur in an organisation where service-users come to be regarded as less than people with rights and needs, where they become problems to be resolved or measurable 'units' to be processed.

It is also noteworthy that in their study of sexual abuse by men who work with children, Colton and Vanstone (1998) cite the finding that the majority of perpetrators can conceptualise themselves as powerless and failures as men (Wallis, 1995). Such an inner view may not be apparent to others, but never-theless the potential relationship between the process of becoming powerful through physical or sexual dominance of a child or children and the process described above should not be overlooked.

Hayashino, Wurtele, and Klebe's (1995) found that many men who sexually harm children have elevated levels of social anxiety, fearing social rejection or criticism. An environment where the opportunity to wield power over others is available may, therefore, be particularly attractive to those not otherwise aware of their propensity for abuse. Colton and Vanstone (1998) suggest that needs related to self worth and reassurance may also be factors in sexually abusive behaviour in organisational settings.

Some authors (Pringle, 1992; Colton, 2002) have considered the gendered nature of the incidence of maltreatment, with the great majority of such abuse committed by men, and have drawn attention to the lack of attention to gender issues when addressing issues of prevention. Certainly a feature of a number of inquiries is evidence of a negative, male dominated, culture in residential settings where there has been physical and sexual abuse, from Kincora, to Castle Hill to the Leicestershire Children's homes, the Pindown regime to Bryn Estyn where

> 'There was a pervasive culture ... of immature and damaging attitudes to sexuality ... and it is not surprising that some of the admitted bullying amongst boys had sexual overtones' (Waterhouse, 2000, p. 85).

Colton and Vanstone (1998) suggest that in such workplaces imbalances of power between staff are also not addressed, with sexism and sexual harassment often ignored. In an environment where other power imbalances are overlooked, it is suggested, there is a greater likelihood of imbalance of power between adults and children, including abuse, to also not be addressed. To this one might add the potential for racism, with a black member of staff describing graphic examples of racist abuse by Beck, who was able to create an environment which allowed him to abuse children in a number of homes (Kirkwood, 1993).

FAILURES OF MANAGEMENT

Management failures underlie the corruption of care, referring to a compre-hensive failure in a range of responsibilities by management at every level (Wardaugh and Wilding, 1993). Without clear aims and objectives for the organisation, secondary aims become predominant. The efficient operation of the organisation becomes the key concern, at the expense of consideration of the legitimate needs and interests of the individual. Care and rehabilitation become subordinate to priorities of order and control. In the case of the Pindown regime, used for six years, physical and emotional abuse became the norm throughout the County, known about and supported by managers, with its perceived effectiveness leading it to be considered a model for other homes. Similarly, in the Leicestershire cases, Frank Beck was supported and encouraged by senior management in developing (what transpired to be an abusive) regime of 'regression therapy' (Kirkwood, 1993) with the incoming senior manager acknowledging that weak organisational management pertained at the time (Waller, 1997).

Without the clarity of organisational aims and objectives, and the framework of good practice which they reinforce, '... too much depends on the attitudes and judgments of fallible individuals' (Wardaugh and Wilding 1993, p. 18). Colton (2002) also suggests that without effective management and accountability structures, staff can become a law unto themselves and in this situation an individual organisational culture develops. Examples of this are apparent in a number of the inquiries into institutional abuse, such as Bryn Estyn Children's Homes where between 1973 and 1984 boys are known to have been sexually abused, where there was the creation of an elite group of boys, widely 'groomed' by privileges, with an inappropriate sexualised culture in addition to the abuse, for example, pornographic videos being shown to boys by staff (Waterhouse, 2000) or Castle Hill School with multiple physical and sexual abuse of, and by, pupils.

Another conspicuous aspect of management failure is the failure to respond to concerns. 'The damning reality is that it has taken media exposure of these large institutions not only to reveal that widespread abuse is incubated inside but also to force the hierarchies of such organisations to admit to it and to deal with the abusers they have been ignoring and sometimes hiding' (Doran and Brannan, 1996, p. 159). Such failure is not pathological but likely to be a feature of organisational pressure and functioning, a dysfunctional culture that places an emphasis on apparently effective functioning with a minimum of disruption '... few questions will be asked about exactly what is being done, so long as the lid is successfully kept on the system' (Wardaugh and Wilding, 1993, p. 16).

This may also be a defensive response designed to 'protect' the organisation or individual careers.

'Management may wittingly or unwittingly obstruct the investigation because it is reluctant to have failures or weaknesses exposed or is unable to acknowledge the possibility of harmful misconduct by its employees' (Utting, 1997, pp. 182–3).

The Inquiry into sexual abuse of residents, including the making of indecent images, by the Officer in Charge of Leeways Children's Home in Lewisham (Lawson, 1985) indicated that for some six years the immediate managers were aware of unacceptable behaviour with sexual implications by the officer in charge but did not act on those concerns. It concluded that 'at almost every point at which collectively or individually the people involved had to choose between making the welfare of the child the first consideration, and some conflicting loyalty or priority, they chose the latter' (cited in Warner, 1992)

Beyer *et al.* (2005) cite an Australian example from researchers Davidson and McNamara (1999) which illustrates this process starkly. Based on interviews conducted in the 1990s they reported disclosure of abuse by victims and staff in a Sydney psychiatric institution. Disclosures were '… met with inaction, further victimisation and threats of retribution. Frequent and direct attempts were made to silence and punish staff who attempted to take action about an incident of sexual abuse. Whistleblower staff were ridiculed, reprimanded, discredited, encouraged to resign or were sacked, their expertise called into question, threatened with loss of promotion, with transfer, less favourable work hours, assigned the worst rosters and refused leave at times they wished to take it, given the silent treatment and some began to feel fearful in the workplace' (p. 45).

Publicised whistleblowing policies and procedures, when they are followed, are one element for ensuring appropriate responses to issues of concern and for communicating to service-users and staff the organisational commitment to openness and addressing difficult issues when necessary. The Huston Inquiry (Social Services Inspectorate, 1994) recommended that agencies providing services to children or vulnerable adults should ensure that a culture of openness and trust is fostered within the organisation, in which staff can share any concerns about the conduct of colleagues and be assured that these will be received in a sensitive manner. Staff should also be encouraged, through formal and informal channels of communication, to question, express concerns or pass on significant information to management regarding the protection of children or vulnerable adults.

'CLOSED' ORGANISATIONS

The 'corruption of care', it is suggested, is more likely to occur in enclosed, inward-looking organisations. Organisations managed along hierarchical lines can become so highly controlled that it is not possible to challenge their practices. The abuser in this type of organisation is more commonly an authority figure in the institution and protected, albeit unwittingly, by the hierarchical systems in place (Beyer *et al.*, 2005). Common elements of such organisations can be identified: criticism and complaint are easily stifled; new ideas are discouraged and rigid and conservative routines and patterns of practice encouraged; group norms become so ingrained that to challenge them can be enormously personally and professionally threatening; an absence of any external moral or professional challenge to established practice; patterns of practice have increasingly low standards and aspirations become those of control, order and the absence of problems. The distance from this to becoming a 'corrupted system' is relatively small. This will be compounded when external regulation is also lacking. Beyer *et al.* (2005) found that staff in Australian children's homes where abuse had been a feature were predominantly not held accountable for their actions because inspections by child welfare authorities were infrequent and ineffective.

MODELS OF AUTHORITY

Many of the features proposed by Wardaugh and Wilding are echoed in the administrative styles associated with institutional sexual abuse identified by Rindfleisch (1984), aspects of which are reflected in the inquiries referred to above: an autocratic Officer in Charge, protected by a strong political and administrative network, with participation in shared decision-making by staff and residents discouraged, so giving both a sense of helplessness and power-lessness. The difficulty of managing residents is emphasised, with implicit or overt permission to control at any cost, and so ultimately to abuse; a theoretical and ideological model is introduced which tends to 'distance, dehumanise and devalue relationships with residents'. Other approaches are discouraged or devalued, to increase the status of the preferred method; an 'oppressor mental-ity' that reflects, encourages or tolerates hostility towards females, children or minorities exists or is encouraged (Rindfleisch, 1984), a situation described in the Inquiry into the use of the 'Pindown' regime (Levy and Kahan, 1991).

Within such an environment it becomes more possible for a motivated individual to abuse. Doran and Brannan (1996) suggest there are two principal archetypes of institutional abusers. The first is the 'charismatic, articulate, well networked "caring professional" who is usually a part of the leadership of the institution' (p. 158) a description which fits the descriptions of a number of the abusers described in the Waterhouse Inquiry (2000) into abuse of children in care in North Wales; Frank Beck, the subject of the Kirkwood Inquiry (1993) into abuse in Leicestershire and Ralph Morris, the Principal at Castle Hill School, a man apparently academically well qualified, respected within the local community who had recruited a board of governors of eminent people whom he had convinced to support his apparently legitimate enterprise (Brannan *et al.*, 1993). As well as enabling the conditions for the abuse to occur, another function of such a personal image is the added obstacle it presents to disclosure. Children being subjected to such abuse are likely to understand that when making allegations against such a figure they may struggle to be found credible. Where others outside the institution are also involved, as in the case of Kincora Boys' Hostel (Hughes, 1986), which was found to be the centre of a 'paedophile ring', the barriers to disclosure must appear almost insurmountable.

The second archetype is the '… isolated but dutiful staff member who is perhaps over helpful to colleagues and children, and frequently does things outside normal duties' (Doran and Brannan, 1996, p. 158). It is clear that neither fits the popular stereotype of an abuser and as in the case of paediatric nurse Beverley Allitt, the Inquiry said of her behaviour at work, '… the overwhelming burden of the evidence was that she did indeed appear to be like everybody else'. (Clothier, 1994, para. 5.7.2). Similarly, a study of files held by the Department of Health (Rowlands, 1995), found that while some abusers were authoritarian or charismatic, others were judged to be quiet, unassuming or inadequate, lending support to the argument that there is no 'typical' profile.

Jones (1994) uses Weberian constructs of 'traditional' and 'charismatic' authority to analyse power relationships, drawing on the example of Castle Hill School. Traditional authority is based on inherited or ascribed status, charismatic authority based on demonstration of apparent qualities. Thus, for example, Frank Beck in Leicestershire, with no relevant qualification or demonstrably adequate knowledge base, was regarded as a skilled therapist capable of developing and supported in introducing a treatment model of regression therapy, which was in fact '… threatening, violent and humiliating' (Kirkwood, 1993, p. 56).

A key argument for Jones is that for vulnerable children in such a setting the combination of traditional and charismatic authority in an adult carer may be especially powerful. These children, often with negative experiences of authority elsewhere, may find the 'invitation' to be associated with, and 'follow', such a leader, what Jones describes as becoming 'his disciple' (p. 72) an opportunity to gain a sense of self-esteem and power for themselves, something lacking in other areas of their lives, leading to the development of a pervasive culture as described above at Castle Hill School.

CHARACTERISTICS OF SEXUAL ABUSE IN SPECIFIC ORGANISATIONAL SETTINGS

This section provides specific examples from the literature about abuse in particular organisational settings. Included are settings such as education, nursery and daycare, chosen for inclusion here as they provide some learning about settings represented in the current study. Further discussion of these and other settings can be found in the literature review mentioned above (Erooga, 2009).

EDUCATION

In most societies school is considered a normal part of a child's development, consequently between the ages of five and sixteen children spend a significant proportion of their time at school. Being in the same institution with the same staff for a number of years creates the potential for ongoing abuse. Additionally, the regard in which most educational institutions and those who work within them are held, can also be risk factors (Wolfe *et al.*, 2003).

Alleged abusers

As with other abuse in these settings, there is no single feature which makes an individual an easily identifiable danger to children.

In terms of gender, in a Department for Children, Schools and Families (DCSF) survey 62% of allegations were made against men and 31% against women, with gender not recorded in 7% of allegations (Lawrie, 2006). Shakeshaft and Cohan (1995) found that in 96% of reported sexual abuse cases by teachers, the abuser was male and 76% of victims female. For female abusers, 86% of victims were female. However, a Harris poll for the American Association of University Women (2001) found approximately 40% of female abusers and 40% of their victims to be male. Whilst, therefore, official figures reflect male abuse of females, confidential self-report is more likely to indicate higher proportions of female abusers and male victims.

The barriers to reporting related to gender are common across settings. For males abused by a woman the likely credibility of an allegation may be perceived as lower because of the broad societal perception that, for a male any sexual contact with a female would be welcome. For males abused by a male, fear of a homophobic response may be a significant inhibitor to reporting.

The consensus from the research appears to indicate that those who sexually abuse students are often among the most competent and popular staff (Bithell, 1991). Indeed, a number of education workers known to have sexually abused children had been awarded prizes for outstanding teaching (Shakeshaft and Cohan, 1995). 'The majority of educator exploiters are highly respected by their colleagues, supervisors and parents. Perhaps most important, they often are adored by their students. Educators, parents and students find it difficult to believe their favourite teacher could molest a youngster' (Shoop, 2004, p. 19).

Shakeshaft (2004) suggests that this is more common amongst those who abuse young children and that the teaching relationship is both a key factor in enabling the abuse and serves to confound colleagues and officials leading to allegations being discounted, a feature of the Castle Hill School case described above.

In so far as these staff are more likely to be more experienced, analysis of the DCSF data is relevant, with staff with under two years or over 16 years' service most likely to have allegations made against them (Lawrie, 2006). Clearly the latter group may be those referred to variously by Bithell, Shakeshaft and Cohen and Shoop above.

Patterns of abuse

'Sexual abusers use many strategies to entrap students. They lie to them, isolate them, make them feel complicit, and force them to have sexual contact. Often teachers target vulnerable or marginal students who feel especially gratified by attention and whom the teachers know will be disbelieved if they report abuse' (Shakeshaft, 2004 p. 10).

Although not every instance of educator sexual misconduct includes a 'grooming' phase, Robins (1998) describes a process very similar to that in other forms of sexual abuse, though one which exploits the particular features of an education setting. Here an abuser selects a student, gives them attention and rewards, provides support and understanding, whilst slowly increasing the amount of touch or other sexual behaviour. The purpose of this process to test the extent of the child's difficulty in disclosing, to desensitise them through progressive sexual behaviours, to provide non-sexual experiences they value and won't want to lose, to learn information that will discredit the child, and to gain approval from parents. Robins suggests that more widespread understanding of grooming patterns would aid prevention and detection of such abuse.

The methods of maintaining secrecy and silence reported are again similar to that of sexual abuse in other settings but adapted to the particular features of an education setting. Shakeshaft (2004) suggests that almost always there is intimidation and threats of various sorts exploiting the power structure 'if you tell, I'll fail you'; using relative credibility 'if you tell, no one will believe you', or manipulating the child's affections 'if you tell, I'll get in trouble'.

Shakeshaft (2004) comments 'Abuse is allowed to continue because even when children report abuse, they are not believed. Because of the power differential, the reputation difference between the educator and the child, or the mindset that children are untruthful, many reports by children are ignored or given minimal attention' (p. 41), a description strikingly similar to that outlined in the Child Sexual Abuse Accommodation Syndrome by Summit (1983) two decades earlier. It might be concluded that whilst the painful process of recognising that carers can sexually abuse has progressed such that there is more likelihood of disclosures being responded to, there is still a level of denial in relation to workers.

The power that the awareness of such a dynamic can have should not be underestimated. Shakeshaft and Cohan (1995) cite a case of a class where the teacher would call boys up to his desk at the front of the room and, one at a time, while discussing homework, would touch each boy's penis. Whilst all the children knew what was happening and talked about it amongst themselves, the teacher repeated this behaviour for 15 years before one student finally reported it to an adult who would act on the information.

NURSERY AND DAY CARE

The substantive information in the UK is from the Hunt Inquiry into the sexual abuse of children in nursery classes by 20 year old student on placement, Jason Dabbs and the recent Little Ted's Nursery case. The potential for abuse in such a setting is possibly indicated by the Hunt report's description of '... a history of abuse in which the sheer normality and vibrant, busy activity of the nursery classroom provided both the opportunity and means of concealment' (Hunt, 1994, para. 2.6.27). The Inquiry concluded that nothing in Dabbs' past life gave an indication of a propensity to abuse and he was regarded as a model student. Indeed, a particular strength was described as 'an ability to relate ... to individual children with sympathy and understanding' (6.4.5)

The fact that a student could commit such offences raises the issue of student selection for courses which include contact with children, for example whilst on placement or teaching practice. The Hunt Inquiry was clear that '... the supervision of a student whilst on placement in a nursery class cannot of itself be regarded as an absolute safeguard against crimes of this type' (4.3.7). Indeed, as is self evidently the case in a setting like a nursery, where contact with children is usually very public and visible, it would seem even more relevant to other settings, not least social care.

A more recent example is the sexual abuse of children in nursery (Plymouth SCB, 2010) where Vanessa George, a mother of two was a nursery worker. She was jailed in December 2009 for an indeterminate period for sexually abusing children in her care and exchanging images that she took of the abuse with two other people, one of them another woman (Plymouth Safeguarding Children Board, 2010). She used a mobile phone to take pictures of herself abusing children at Little Ted's Nursery in Plymouth and exchanged more than 7,000 texts, photographs and calls with her two co-defendants over a sixth-month period (The Times, 2009). The initial contact with one of her co-defendants, Colin Blanchard, was made on a Facebook page called 'Are You Interested?' and was followed by a request for her to send pictures of children with whom she worked. She responded initially by sending pictures of herself changing babies' nappies, but these later included images of real, or simulated, penetration of children with objects.

The Serious Case Review convened following her conviction found no evidence of a sexual interest in children prior to the internet relationship with Colin Blanchard, 'and it is therefore unlikely that a sexual interest in children would have been apparent prior to (VG) "meeting" him' (Plymouth Safeguarding Children Board, 2010, 5.1). It was considered, however, that she was an emotionally vulnerable woman who used the opportunity presented by her employment for her own ends.

Again the issue of the lack of privacy required for the offences to take place is instructive. Children's nappies were changed in the toilet area which could be seen from the area of a main room in the nursery. The toilet door was reported to be usually propped open and there were four cubicles in a row, one with a full sized door, and three others with a half door. Most staff changed nappies on the main nappy changing area easily visible to other staff. Mrs George, however, started to use the cubicle with the full door, saying she could not bend down due to her (physical) size. Although the door was open her body blocked the line of vision from the nursery to the child. It was here that abusive acts occurred and the photographs were taken. Without this evidence many would consider that a greater degree of isolation would be required for such acts to take place but clearly not.

In the North American literature, day care settings have been a particular focus for some authors and one where female perpetrators of sexual abuse are more evident. One key study is that by Finkelhor, Williams and Burns (1988). This was a review of the incidence over a three year period of 'substantiated' sexual abuse in day care facilities, derived from official sources. Cases included were those which involved at least one child under age six years. Whilst the intention was to include all reported incidence across the USA, unsurprisingly given the scale of the enterprise, the sample was ultimately incomplete. The study identified 270 centres with 1,639 victims (484 male, 296 female and 859 not specified) and 382 perpetrators (222 male, 147 female and 13 not specified). It was estimated that 25% of allegations were substantiated and when the figures were extrapolated to make a national estimate, it suggested that in 500–550 centres some 2,500 children would have been sexually victimised over three years.

Twenty-five per cent of the abusers were owners /directors, of whom 50% acted alone. Relatively few appear to have established the institution in order to abuse. 30% of abusers were teachers/child care professionals, of whom 66% abused in conjunction with another and 15% were non-professional child care staff. Disproportionately represented were non-child care staff, who committed 20% of cases in centres where they were employed and who were often unscreened because of their role. Particular characteristics of these offenders were that they were typically male, acted alone, had not been screened and were quite possibly not employed by the day care facility but by another provider or agency.

Another noticeable phenomenon observed in the study was abuse of children by people not working in, or attached to, the day care centre, but by others whom staff allowed to have access to the children. Any process which focused on staff member's propensity for abuse would certainly not address such a possibility. This would suggest that an important area for selection for roles with responsibility for children's safety is to ensure a sufficient focus on an individual's commitment to protect children from others who might present a risk to them.

In terms of gender of abuser, 36% (96/270) of cases involved female perpetrators, with a total of 147 female perpetrators out of 358. 90% were employees and unlikely to be detected by a criminal records nor had any prior known deviant behaviour. A key difference also identified in more general literature on female offenders is that 73% acted with other abusers, whilst only 19% of the men did this. There is frequently a minimisation of abuse by females in the media and it is instructive, therefore, to note that amongst the female abusers there was a higher frequency of more serious (invasive) abuse and use of threats as well as actual force.

MOTIVATIONS TO ABUSE

In terms of motives, Finkelhor *et al.* (1988) suggest that much sexual abuse in these settings does not grow out of a specific conscious and pre-existing sexual preference for children of this age. Rather, they suggest much of the abuse is opportunistic, by which they mean that the abuse has a more general and diffuse motivation than specific sexual attraction and that the key factor was not the particular sexual attraction but rather the availability and vulnerability of the children. Thus, it is suggested, they probably would not have abused such young children, and possibly not abused at all, were they in not in such close and constant interaction with young children. This is a provocative hypothesis but, given the credibility of the lead researcher in the field of sexual abuse, one which merits careful consideration. Certainly one implication is that screening for offences, or for sexual interest in children, is not likely to be effective for such potential abusers. It may be that a selection process which reviews attitudes to children, individual motivation to work with them, or in their interests, and so partly focuses on potential inhibitors to acting on any emergent sexual interest in children, may be more indicative.

Certainly these authors conclude that '… most abusers cannot be identified on the basis of prior sex-abuse records, and even where there are records they are ambiguous in their meaning' (i.e. relevance to risk to children) (Finkelhor *et al.*, 1988, p. 65).

SCREENING FOR A PRE-DISPOSITION TO ABUSE?

A long standing stereotype of sex offenders is that of '… a sophisticated and well organised, predatory individual' (Jenkins, 1990) with its implications of intentionality in the process of finding settings where vulnerable children may be accessed. The concern that offenders will target occupations or activities which will provide access to children is a long standing one and therefore a focus of interest in this research. Whilst it may appear self evident, the issue of what it is that needs to be 'selected out' is not necessarily clear cut.

Child sexual offenders are widely agreed in the literature to be heterogeneous, that is there is considerable variation in the ways in which they select and groom children, in their sexual and other related behaviours and their means of avoiding detection (Boer, Wilson, Gauthier, and Hart, 1987). Characteristics of offenders are similarly varied in terms of age, ethnicity, offending background, level of sexual interest in children and relationship with their victims. (Smallbone and Wortley 2001). There is, therefore, no single test or screening process which can identify an individual with the propensity to sexually harm a child.

DEVELOPING PREVENTATIVE STRATEGIES

OFFENDER MOTIVATIONS AND SITUATIONAL PREVENTION

'Although it is important that risk factors for children, adults and organisations are identified, it is equally important to draw on the knowledge about the features that make organisations safer for children.' (Beyer *et al.*, 2005, p. 106)

From this chapter and the preceding one it is clear that there is no 'typical' profile of an offender in this context. Previous research which included psychological testing, as discussed above, has identified some common factors, though as noted, this tended to be with relatively skewed samples. Overall, whilst the stereotypes of professional offenders are helpful in that they guide attention towards areas of potential risk, caution should be exercised in the false security that is likely to be derived from thinking that there is a typical profile.

By contrast to the commonly held view in organisations that CRB and related organisational screening methods will adequately protect children, whilst they are clearly necessary it is apparent from the number of previously non-convicted offenders referred to here and in the research, they are not sufficient. An approach which explores applicants' values and underlying motivation more thoroughly, like Value Based Interviews, as described in Chapter Seven, has a contribution to make there are no currently available screening measures which would both be acceptable for general use and sufficiently accurate to identify propensity for sexual abuse of children.

It seems clear therefore that the optimal combination of approaches which will maximise protection of children from harm by staff and volunteers is a thorough and consistently implemented recruitment and selection process and an organisation with clear values, expected behaviours which consciously integrate a situational prevention approach into practice.

The popular understanding of 'paedophiles' is that they are a homogenous group, seeking out opportunities to sexually assault children and prepared to lie and deceive in order to do so (NSPCC, 2009) The literature indicates that this is an over simplistic picture and that as with most human behaviour the reality is more nuanced.

The important contribution of situational prevention measures are considered further in Chapter Eight.

REFERENCES

American Association of University Women (2001) *Hostile Hallways*, Washington, D.C.: AAUW Educational Foundation.

Beyer, L., Higgins, D. and Bromfield, L. (2005) *Understanding Organisational Risk Factors for Child Maltreatment: A Review of Literature, National* Child Protection Clearinghouse, Australian Institute of Family Studies.

Bithell, S. (1991) *Educator Sexual Abuse: A guide for prevention in the schools.* Boise, ID: Tudor House Publishing Company. cited in Virginia Child Protection Newsletter (2006) *Sexual Abuse by Educators and School Staff*, Issue 76, Spring.

Boer, D.P., Wilson, R.J., Gauthier, C.M, & Hart, S.D. (1997). Assessing risk for sexual violence: Guidelines for clinical practice. In C.D. Webster & M.A. Jackson (Eds.), *Impulsivity: Theory, Assessment and Treatment* (pp. 326–342). New York: Guilford Press.

Brannan, C., Jones, J., and Murch, J. (1993) *Castle Hill Report: Practice Guide*, Shropshire County Council.

Clothier C. (1994) *The Allitt Inquiry. Independent Inquiry Relating to Deaths and Injuries on the Children's Ward at Grantham and Kesteven General Hospital during the period February to April 1991*. HMSO, London.

Colton, M (2002) Factors associated with abuse in residential child care institutions. *Children and Society*, 16(1), 33–44.

Colton, M. and Vanstone, M. (1998) Sexual abuse by men who work with children: an exploratory study. *British Journal of Social Work*, 28(4), 511–523.

Colton, M., Vanstone, M., and Walby, C. (2002) Victimization, care and justice: reflections on the experiences of victims/survivors involved in large-scale investigations of child sexual abuse in residential institutions. *British Journal of Social Work*. 32, 541–551.

Daily Mail (2007) Foster mother jailed for 'horrifying' cruelty and sadism, 19th April, www.dailymail.co.uk/pages/live/articles/news/news.html (accessed 29 May 2007).

Department of Health and Social Security (1988) *'Protection of Children: disclosure of criminal background of those with access to children'*. Circular HC (88) 9 2/3/88.

Doran, C. and Brannan, C. (1996), 'Institutional Abuse', in P. C. Bibby (ed.), *Organised Abuse: The Current Debate*, pp. 155–166, Ashgate Publishing, London.

Davidson, J. and McNamara, L. (1999), 'Systems that silence: Lifting the lid on psychiatric institutional sexual abuse', in J. Breckenridge and L. Laing (Eds.), *Challenging Silence: Innovative responses to sexual and domestic violence*, Allen and Unwin, Sydney.

Erooga, M. (2009) *Towards Safer Organisations: Adults who pose a risk to children in the workplace and implications for recruitment and selection*, NSPCC, London.

Finkelhor, D., Williams, L. and Burns, N. (1988) *Nursery Crimes: A study of sexual abuse in daycare*, Newbury Park: Sage.

Goffman, E (1961) *Asylums: Essays on the social situation of mental patients and other inmates*, London, Pelican.

Hall, M (2000) After Waterhouse: vicarious liability and the tort of institutional abuse. *Journal of Social Welfare and Family Law*, 22(2) 159–173.

Hayashino, D., Wurtele, S. and Klebe, K. (1995) Child molesters: an examination of cognitive factors. *Journal of Interpersonal Violence*, 10(1), 106–116.

Hunt, P (1994) *Report of the Independent Inquiry into Multiple Abuse in Nursery Classes in Newcastle upon Tyne*. Newcastle upon Tyne, Newcastle upon Tyne County Council.

Hughes, W. (1986) *Report of the Committee of Inquiry into Children's Homes and Hostels* (Kincora Inquiry) Belfast, Her Majesty's Stationery Office (HMSO).

Jenkins A (1990) *Invitations to Responsibility: the therapeutic engagement of men who are violent and abusive* Adelaide: Dulwich Centre Publications.

Jones, J. (1994) Toward an understanding of power relationships in institutional abuse', *Early Child Development and Care*, 100, 69–76.

Kelman, H. (1973) Violence without moral restraint: reflections on the dehumanisation of victims and victimisers, *Journal of Social Issues*, 29.

Kirkwood, A. (1993) *The Leicestershire Inquiry 1992. The Report of the Inquiry into Aspects of the Management of Children's Homes in Leicestershire between 1973 and 1986*. Leicester: Leicestershire County Council.

Lawrie, B (2006) Allegations against education staff: is age a risk factor? *Protecting Children Update*, July.

Lawson, E. (1985) *The Leeways Inquiry Report*, London Borough of Lewisham.

Levy, A. and Kahan, B. (1991) *The Pindown Experience and the Protection of Children: The Report of the Staffordshire Child Care Inquiry*, Stafford: Staffordshire County Council.

NSPCC (2009) Statement about vetting and barring, 13 September.

Plymouth Safeguarding Children Board (2010) *Case Review Overview Report Executive Summary in respect of Nursery Z*, March.

Police Complaints Authority (1993) *Inquiry into the Police Investigation of Complaints of Child and Sexual Abuse in Leicestershire Children's Homes*. London, Police Complaints Authority.

Pringle, K (1992) Child sexual abuse perpetrated by welfare personnel and the problem of men. *Critical Social Policy*, 12(3), 16.

Rindfleisch N. (1984) *Factors which influence the severity of adverse events in residential facilities*. Paper presented at the International Congress on Child Abuse and Neglect, Montreal, Canada, September 18–19.

Robins, S. (1998) Protecting our students: A review to identify and prevent sexual misconduct in Ontario schools. Toronto, Ontario Ministry of the Attorney General.

Rowlands, (1995) Personal communication cited in Gallagher, B. (1999) The abuse of children in public care. *Child Abuse Review*, 8, 357–365.

Shakeshaft, C. (2004) *Educator Sexual Misconduct: A Synthesis of Existing Literature*, Washington, D.C.; U.S. Department of Education, Office of the Under Secretary.

Shakeshaft, C. and Cohan, A. (1995) Sexual abuse of students by school personnel. *Phi Delta Kappan*, 76(7), 513–520.

Shoop, R. (2004) *Sexual Exploitation in Schools: How to spot it and stop it*. Thousand Oaks, CA: Corwin Press. Cited in Virginia Child Protection Newsletter (2006) *Sexual Abuse by Educators and School Staff*, Issue 76, Spring.

Smallbone, S. and Wortley, R. (2001) *Child Sexual Abuse: Offender Characteristics and Modus Operandi*, Trends and Issues in Crime and Criminal Justice, No. 193, Australian Institute of Criminology.

Social Services Inspectorate (1994) *'An Abuse of Trust', The Report of the Social Services Inspectorate Investigation into the case of Martin Huston, January 1994*, Belfast, Social Services Inspectorate.

Summit, R., (1983) The child sexual abuse accommodation syndrome, *Child Abuse and Neglect*, 7, 177–193.

The Times, 11 June 2009, Little Ted's nursery worker Vanessa George charged with child abuse, *www.timesonline.co.uk/tol/news/uk/crome/article6471327.ece* (retrieved 15 December 2009).

Utting, W. (1997) People Like Us: The Report of the Review of the Safeguards for Children Living Away from Home, London, Stationery Office.

Waller, B. (1997) *From the Front Line – A Local Authority Perspective*, in Child Sexual Abuse: Myth and Reality – proceedings of a conference (ed.) S. Hayman, London: ISTD.

Wallis, K. (1995) 'Perspectives on Offenders' in F. Briggs, (ed) *From Victim to Offender: How Child Sexual Abuse Victims Become Offenders*, Sydney, Allen and Unwin.

Wardaugh, J. and Wilding, P. (1993) Towards an explanation of the corruption of social care, *Critical Social Policy*, 13(37), 4–31.

Warner, N. (1992) *'Choosing with Care'* The Report of the Committee of Inquiry into the Selection, Development and Management of Staff in Children's Homes, London, HMSO.

Waterhouse, R. (2000) *'Lost in Care' Report of the Tribunal of Inquiry into the abuse of children in care in the former county council areas of Gwynedd and Clwyd since 1974,* 'House of Commons', London, The Stationery Office.

Wolfe, D., Jaffe, P., Jette, J. and Poisson, S. (2003) The impact of child abuse in community institutions and organizations: Advancing professional and scientific understanding, *Clinical Psychology: Science and Practice*, 10, 2.

3 Policy and Legislation – Changing Responses to an Emerging Problem

Kerry Cleary and Marcus Erooga

The purpose of legislation and regulation in safeguarding the vulnerable is to enable the State to set minimum standards of expected behaviour and prescribe sanctions where behaviour contravenes those standards. It is not intended, nor can it hope, to provide a comprehensive framework for ensuring the safety of vulnerable people in organisations. Much of what we have learnt from the research is that culture, attitudes and practice have a significant role to play in the establishment of a true safeguarding culture (Erooga, 2009), much of which can be neither prescribed in legislation or regulation nor effectively monitored.

This chapter reviews the development of measures designed to prevent inappropriate people from working with children, and the principles which underlie those approaches. Although the chapter focuses primarily on arrangements in England and Wales, there are parallels with developments in Scotland and Northern Ireland and the Scottish approach to the current legislation in particular will be considered below. Rapid policy and legislative change means the information on current legislation on vetting and barring is subject to change. Current information can be found on the Home Office website (www.homeoffice.gov.uk/crime) or other specialist resources. The chapter then considers the strengths and shortcomings of the various legislative frameworks and concludes with an examination of the role regulation and legislation has in supporting the development of safeguarding cultures within organisations.

Creating Safer Organisations: Practical Steps to Prevent the Abuse of Children by Those Working with Them, First Edition. Edited by Marcus Erooga.
© 2012 John Wiley & Sons, Ltd. Published 2012 by John Wiley & Sons, Ltd.

GENERAL ORGANISATIONAL LEGAL RESPONSIBILITIES

Organisations have broad based legal responsibilities for protecting and safeguarding children. The United Nations Convention on the Rights of the Child (UNCRC), of which the UK is a signatory, provides some of the wider policy context and a framework for signatories to develop policy in the best interests of the child. Article 19 of the UNCRC obliges States to protect children from all forms of maltreatment perpetrated by parents or *others responsible for their care* (our italics). The Convention is clear that every child has the right to be safe from harm and that organisations entrusted with the care of children, or that regularly come into contact with children, are required to create and provide safe environments for them. Ensuring that individuals who work with children are appropriate to do so is encompassed within this (Institute of Child Protection Studies, 2005).

Other relevant legislation includes the Human Rights Act 1998 which sets out principles regarding protection of individuals by State organisations or those working for such organisations. The Health and Safety at Work Act 1974 gives employees a duty to take care of themselves and anyone else that may be affected by their actions or failings. In addition the Act gives employers a 'duty of care' toward paid and unpaid employees. This requires the provision of a safe working environment and guidance about safe working practices. Providing clear expectations and guidance about expected standards of behaviour and safe practice is therefore a responsibility for organisations. All this points towards various responsibilities for the safety and well being of children in contact with organisations.

Consideration of individual implementation of the measures outlined below should therefore be viewed in light of these responsibilities.

CHILD CARE FOCUSSED POLICY AND LEGISLATION

Gallagher (2000) suggests that policy and legislative responses to concerns about abuse or maltreatment of children by those working with them can be divided into two broad categories: those with a focus on child care practice and those that attempt to control abusers.

CHILD CARE PRACTICE

Although the first inquiry into the maltreatment of children in public care was in 1945 (Monkton, 1945) Sullivan and Beech (2002) date the beginning of efforts to address the issue of institutional abuse with the 1986 Home

Office Circular (Home Office, 1986) subsequently revised in the 1993 Home Office Circular (Home Office, 1993a). This produced guidelines covering local authority staff, teachers, social workers, child minders and foster parents. A Department of Health & Social Services (DHSS) circular, which addressed National Health Service workers' contact with children, followed two years later in 1988 (DHSS, 1988).

The Children Act 1989 brought the first major legislative response to institutional abuse and provided the impetus for a series of attempts to regulate and standardise practice within residential and day care facilities (Gallagher, 2000), including guidance for action if staff in a children's home suspected abuse by a colleague (Thomas, 2005). The Act, whose primary thrust was the concept of the State working in partnership with parents and carers, strengthened safeguards for children living away from home both generally and specifically, with existing regulations revised and new ones introduced to cover both the placement of children in public care and the conditions in which they lived.

Guidelines for workers in voluntary agencies, however, were not produced until the 1993 Home Office Code of Practice *Safe from Harm* (Home Office, 1993b). This made recommendations in respect of managing organisations in order to protect children; managing paid staff and volunteers in order to protect children; choosing the right paid staff and volunteers in order to protect children; dealing with abuse that has been disclosed or discovered; and training.

Following the publication of *People Like Us: Safeguards for Children Living Away from Home* (Utting, 1997) the UK Government introduced *Quality Protects*: a major three-year programme designed to transform the management and delivery of social services for children in England (Department of Health, 1998a). In 2001 the General Social Care Council (GSCC) was established with a remit to set standards for social care and regulate the activity of all those using the title 'social worker'. In 2012 this body will be amalgamated with the Health Professions Council. In Scotland the equivalent is the Scottish Social Services Council (SSSC) established under 2001 legislation. The Care Council for Wales (CCW) was established under 2000 legislation and the Northern Social Care Council (NISSC) established in 2001.

The Children Act 2004, through the Stay Safe outcome of the Every Child Matters Change for Children Programme, gives organisations and individuals a duty to safeguard and promote the wellbeing of children. In addition, *Working Together to Safeguard Children* (HM Government, 2009) in England; *National Guidance for Child Protection in Scotland*, (The Scottish Government, 2010); *Safeguarding Children: Working Together Under the Children Act, 2004* (Welsh Assembly Government, 2006) and *Co-operating to safeguard children* (DHSSPS, 2003) gives all agencies responsibilities for having effective recruitment and human resources procedures, including checking all new staff and volunteers to ensure they are safe to work with children and young people.

MEASURES TO CONTROL ABUSERS

Measures to control abusers fall into three categories:

- Offences specifically created to further protect from abuse those children in especially vulnerable or dependent positions, such as the Abuse of Trust legislation.
- Mandatory measures for employers and specified individuals; and discretionary measures for employers (Thomas, 2005). Mandatory measures are legal prohibitions on certain people working with children and both the individual and employer commit an offence if such employment takes place.
- Discretionary measures are those steps potential employers may take to obtain relevant information when considering a potential member of staff or volunteer, and include Criminal Records Bureau (CRB) checks.

The following are some of the key measures implemented over time to control identified abusers. As clarified below, not all these measures remain in place.

DEPARTMENT FOR CHILDREN, SCHOOLS AND FAMILIES LIST 99

First established under the Home Office Consultancy Service in 1955, what subsequently developed into List 99 was maintained by the Department for Children, Schools and Families (DCSF), previously the Department for Education and Skills (DfES) and the Department for Education and Employment (DfEE). This was a confidential list of people whom the Secretary of State for Education had directed may not be employed by local education authorities (LEAs), schools (including independent schools) or further education (FE) institutions as a teacher or in work involving regular contact with children under 18 years of age. List 99 also included details of people the Secretary of State had directed could only be employed subject to specific conditions.

LEAs, schools, FE institutions and other employers had to make reports to the DCSF if they had either ceased to use a person's services on grounds of misconduct or unsuitability to work with children, or if someone had left in circumstances where the employer might have ceased to use their services on one of those grounds.

Following further amendments to List 99 in 2006 those convicted of one of a number of sexual offences against a child under 16 years of age were automatically deemed unsuitable to work with children and included on List 99. Those subject to a disqualification order and those permanently included on the Protection of Children Act (PoCA) List were also included on List 99 automatically (NSPCC, 2006).

PROTECTION OF CHILDREN ACT (PoCA) LIST

Established under the Children Act 1999, the PoCA list gave the relevant
Secretary of State power to keep a list of people unsuitable to work with children in childcare positions. Child care organisations in the regulated sector were
required to make a report to the Secretary of State in specified circumstances,
principally if they dismissed a person for misconduct that harmed a child or put
a child at risk of harm, or if a person resigned in circumstances where s/he might
have been dismissed for that reason. Other organisations that employ childcare
workers could also make reports in those circumstances, but did not have to. In
1996 there were some 7,000 names on the PoCA list (Thomas, 2005).

Childcare organisations were required to check the PoCA list (and List 99)
before employing someone in a childcare position. Other bodies such as children's uniformed and voluntary organisations could check the Lists and make
referrals but were under no statutory obligation to do so.

The PoCA list also incorporated the Department of Health Consultancy
Service Index, which covered people working in health settings who had regular unsupervised access to children, and social workers who worked with children. Names were placed on the Index of those who had been prosecuted for
an offence against a child or where there had been specified circumstances that
give rise to concern about their suitability to work with children.

In Northern Ireland the Protection of children and Vulnerable Adults
(Northern Ireland) Order 2003 created the equivalent lists, the Disqualification from Working with Children (DWC) and Disqualification from working with vulnerable adults (DWVA) lists. In Scotland The Protection of
Children (Scotland) Act 2003 created a list of those barred from working with
children but they did not have an equivalent list for vulnerable adults.

From October 2009 List 99 and the PoCA List and the Northern Ireland
equivalent have been replaced by the Children's Barred List established under
the Safeguarding Vulnerable Groups Act 2006 (SVGA); the names of those
listed are being transferred incrementally to this new list, which is now held by
the Independent Safeguarding Authority (ISA). In February 2011 the Scottish
Government introduced the Protecting Vulnerable Groups (PVG) Scheme
managed by Disclosure Scotland replacing the existing barring list.

DISQUALIFICATION ORDERS AND REGULATED POSITIONS (REPLACED BY THE SAFEGUARDING VULNERABLE GROUPS ACT, 2006)

Under the provisions of the Criminal Justice and Courts Services Act 2000 if
a person had committed certain sexual or violent offences that resulted in a
custodial sentence of more than 12 months, they almost always received a

disqualification order, which barred them from working in a number of specified regulated positions. If they sought work in any of these settings, in a paid or voluntary capacity, they were committing an offence. Disqualification Orders have now been replaced by the automatic barring provisions within the SVGA.

SEX OFFENDER REGISTER NOTIFICATION ARRANGEMENTS

Sex Offender notification arrangements (often referred to as the Sex Offenders Register) were first established in 1997. These provide for recording of details of those convicted or cautioned for certain sexual offences, and place automatic notification requirements on these individuals. These notification requirements are intended to ensure that the police are informed of the whereabouts of offenders in the community. They do not bar offenders from certain types of employment or from being alone with children although in appropriate cases such conditions may be applied at time of sentence. In addition, where a specific risk can be demonstrated the police can apply to the courts for the imposition of a number of civil orders such as a Sexual Offences Prevention Order (SOPO) that can be used to restrict an offender's specific activities or movements.

CRIMINAL RECORDS CHECKS

In 1986, a process to allow police records to be checked by relevant employers was established to allow agencies to investigate whether an individual had criminal convictions for offences against children. Subsequent inquiries into the abuse of children by professionals have raised questions about the accuracy of police checks and the consistency of agencies in using the system (Sullivan and Beech, 2002). The Utting Report (1998) expressed 'serious concerns about the manner in which police checks were handled' and noted that insufficient consideration was given to references. This echoed some of the concerns of the Warner Report (1992), which found that ten per cent of heads of children's homes and one third of care workers took up their posts before references were received.

The Police Act 1997 allowed the development of the Criminal Records Bureau (CRB) in England, which came into being in 2001. The Criminal Records Bureau is an executive agency of the Home Office administered by a private company, thus relieving the police of the duty of conducting criminal record checks. It carries out relevant checks, now called 'disclosures', in England and Wales. Implementation of the Part V of the Police Act in Northern Ireland allowed government to establish AccessNI for managing the disclosure process there whilst in Scotland, Disclosure Scotland was established to perform these duties. Beyer et al. (2005) suggest that no vetting processes can be considered thorough without a database that enables a check of all relevant information. The intended value of the central Criminal Records Bureau is that it minimises overlaps, duplications and inconsistencies and the inherent 'snapshot' approach of previous screening searches, and relieves the police of the responsibility of deciding what information should be released (Bichard, 2004).

SHORTCOMINGS OF THESE ARRANGEMENTS

There were a number of inadequacies in these arrangements. Partly because of their disparate evolution, the lists were uncoordinated and had different purposes, so people could be included on one list but not on others, e.g. an individual could be placed on the Sex Offenders Register as the result of a conviction but, until 2006, not included on List 99. Ministers and officials, rather than experts with specific knowledge of child protection and risk management, made decisions about inclusion on the lists. Grounds for inclusion on the lists were largely restricted to dismissal for misconduct that led to harm or risk of harm, thus not including soft data and intelligence about significant concerns (NSPCC, 2007). It was less than clear whether barring in one part of the UK was enforceable in another jurisdiction.

As a consequence of these concerns, and primarily as a result of the murders in Soham of Jessica Chapman and Holly Wells and the Bichard Inquiry, new arrangements were brought into law with the Safeguarding Vulnerable Groups Act 2006. The Protection of Vulnerable Groups (Scotland) Act 2007 and The Safeguarding Vulnerable Groups (Northern Ireland) Order 2007 which all gave effect to Recommendation 19 of the Bichard Inquiry report (2004): 'New arrangements should be introduced requiring those who wish to work with children, or vulnerable adults, to be registered. This register – perhaps supported by a card or licence – would confirm that there is no known reason why an individual should not work with these client groups'.

THE SAFEGUARDING VULNERABLE GROUPS ACT, 2006 (ENGLAND, WALES AND NORTHERN IRELAND)

The Safeguarding Vulnerable Groups Act 2006 introduced a new vetting and barring scheme (the VBS) designed to prevent those deemed unsuitable to work with children and vulnerable adults from gaining access to them through their work. The VBS replaces the existing List 99, Protection of Children Act (1999) List (PoCA), Protection of Vulnerable Adults scheme (PoVA) and Disqualification Orders (and equivalent lists in NI). It does not cover Scotland.

The full implementation of the Act was due in 2010 when individuals would be required to begin to register with the scheme. Although, as discussed below the scheme was scrapped prior to implementation, the components of the scheme are outlined below to give the reader an indication of what an adequate protective scheme was considered to comprise at that time:

- A single barring list for those barred from working with children and vulnerable adults by bringing together the lists outlined above and an Adults' Barred List for settings with vulnerable adults.
- The creation of the Independent Safeguarding Authority (ISA), an executive non-departmental public body sponsored by the Home Office, comprising a small expert board of public appointees and 200–250 employees.
- A wider range of posts and roles falling within the definition of 'regulated activity' and requiring employers to carry out an enhanced disclosure check to ensure that new entrants to the workforce are members of the continuous monitoring element of the VBS. The Act did not distinguish who is required to be checked with the vetting and barring scheme on the basis of whether they are in a paid or voluntary position. Instead, it provided that certain activities in relation to vulnerable groups were 'regulated' or 'controlled'. Regulations would make it mandatory to check an individual working in both controlled and regulated activities.
- The capacity for parents to check whether an employee working with their children under privately made family arrangements (e.g. a nanny) had applied to be a member with the new scheme, is not barred as a result of that vetting, and to ask for any disclosable information known about them.
- The original decision (on application to the scheme) not to bar an individual would be continuously updated on receipt of new information, such as convictions or referrals from employers. Employers would be notified, where they had registered an interest, if the status of their employee changed.

However, following the election of May 2010 and a change of government to one with a different philosophy about the role of the State, the scheme was put on hold pending a full review. In fact two separate reviews, the internal and cross departmental review of vetting and barring and a parallel review of the criminal records regime by the Government's Independent Advisor on Criminality Information Management, Sunita Mason.

On 11th February 2011 Deputy Prime Minister Nick Clegg announced the findings of the reviews into the vetting and barring scheme[1] and the criminal records checking regime, 'A Common Sense Approach'.[2] The proposal was that both regimes would be scaled back to 'common sense levels' (www.home-office.co.uk). Mr Clegg announced:

'The (Protection of) Freedoms Bill[3] will protect millions of people from state intrusion in their private lives and mark a return to common sense government.

[1] http://www.homeoffice.gov.uk/publications/crime/vbs-report.
[2] http://www.homeoffice.gov.uk/publications/crime/criminal-records-review-phase1/.
[3] The legislation under which the changes would be implemented.

It delivers on our commitment to restore hard-won British liberties with sweeping reforms that will end the unnecessary scrutiny of law-abiding individuals.

We inherited a messy criminal records regime that developed piecemeal and defied common sense. Our reviews concluded that the systems were not proportionate and needed to be less bureaucratic. They will now be scaled back to sensible levels whilst at the same time protecting vulnerable people'.

At the time of writing the proposed changes to the Vetting and Barring Scheme and criminal records regime are contained in the Protection of Freedoms Bill making its passage through Parliament. The final edition of the Bill is expected in Spring 2012. One aim of the Bill is to reform and simplify the existing system. Whilst the overall direction of the Bill and the proposals to maintain key protective provisions in the Safeguarding Vulnerable Groups Act 2006, and the aim of simplifying the arrangements has received general support, a number of concerns remain about the detail of the proposed arrangements. For example in relation to the definition of 'regulated activity', the fact that barred individuals can work with children and young people in non-regulated activity without employers being alerted to the risk they pose, and the practical issues that need to be resolved in order to ensure that checks are portable.

Current information about the arrangements in place and proposed changes can be found at www.homeoffice.gov.uk/crime. However, the key recommendations from the vetting and barring review which the Government accepted are:

a) A State body should continue to provide a barring function to help employers protect those at risk from people who seek to do them harm via work or volunteering roles.
b) The Criminal Records Bureau (CRB) and Independent Safeguarding Authority (ISA) should be merged and a single agency created to provide a barring and criminal records disclosure service.
c) The new barring regime should cover only those who may have regular or close contact with vulnerable groups (i.e. reducing he criteria for eligibility).
d) Barring should continue to apply to both paid and unpaid roles.
e) There should be automatic barring for serious offences that clearly indicate risk.
f) Registration should be scrapped – there should be no requirement for people to register with the scheme and no ongoing monitoring.
h) Criminal records disclosures should continue to be available to employers and voluntary bodies but become portable through continuous updating (to prevent the need for a new check when a new or changed employment occurs).
i) Current arrangements for referrals to the barring body (currently the ISA) by employers and certain regulatory bodies should remain where individuals have demonstrated a risk of harm to children or vulnerable adults.

l) Services relating to criminal records disclosure and barring provisions should be self-financing by raising the cost of the criminal records disclosure fee to cover the costs incurred.

m) The new system will retain two offences – it will continue to be an offence for a barred person to work with vulnerable groups in regulated activity roles. It will also be an offence for an employer or voluntary organisation knowingly to employ a barred person in a regulated activity role.

n) Finally, the Government should raise awareness of safeguarding issues and should widely promote the part everyone has to play in ensuring proper safeguarding amongst employers, volunteer organisations, families and the wider community.

THE PROTECTION OF VULNERABLE GROUPS (SCOTLAND) ACT 2007

The Scottish Government decided not to halt the implementation of their PVG Act and in February 2011 the new Protecting Vulnerable Groups (PVG) scheme was introduced in Scotland. The scheme is managed by Disclosure Scotland, which, through their Protection Unit, will make decisions on behalf of Scottish ministers about who should be barred from working with children and vulnerable adults. Membership of the new PVG scheme is not compulsory for people in 'regulated positions' but enhanced criminal records checks are no longer available to people in 'regulated positions' and people who work with children and vulnerable adults are encouraged to join the scheme.

The offences related to the scheme are the same as those currently in operation in England, Scotland and Northern Ireland in that a barred individual commits an offence if they apply for or undertake work in a regulated position, and an organisation commits an offence if they knowingly employ a barred individual in a regulated position. Organisations must also refer individuals to the scheme if they dismiss or would have dismissed an individual from a regulated position because they have harmed a child.

The new PVG scheme has put in place many of then features intended for the Vetting and Barring scheme, which are now under review in England, Wales and Northern Ireland. These include:

- Continuous updating of an individuals record once they are a member of the scheme and notification of organisations who register an interest in the individual of any changes to the barred status of that individual.
- Barring decisions being taken by the Protection Unit of Disclosure Scotland and not by ministers. This continues to be a function of the ISA.
- Streamlined disclosures for individuals once they are scheme members meaning that organisations can carry out a much cheaper and quicker PVG scheme record update when employing an individual who is already a

scheme member, unless this indicates there is new information or information
they should consider when they can still request a full PVG scheme record.
- Personal employers (e.g. parents employing personal tutors for their children) can request individuals are registered with the scheme and can ask to
see a PVG scheme membership statement if the individual is already a
scheme member.
- The scheme will be phased in over 4 years with new staff and those changing
roles the first to be able to register followed by existing staff.

Further information is available at www.infoscotland.com/pvgscheme.

STRENGTHS AND LIMITATIONS
OF LEGISLATION AND REGULATION

There are a number of relative strengths and weaknesses in the legislative and
regulatory frameworks currently in place:

STRENGTHS OF THE CURRENT ARRANGEMENTS

Research undertaken by MORI for the Criminal Records Bureau (Ipsos Mori,
2008) of a sample of 3,671 members of the public in England and Wales shows
that in 2008 around 18,000 unsuitable people were prevented from working
with children or vulnerable adults as a direct result of a CRB check. Between
2003 and 2008 they calculate this figure to be around 98,000 unsuitable people.
Such a legislative process therefore has a key role in preventing those individuals who do have a relevant criminal history from being able to move about
different organisations securing positions with children.

Although the evidence from the MORI survey shows that 19,000 people in
2008 applied for posts for which their convictions rendered them unsuitable, it
is not possible to measure how many people were deterred from applying
because of the criminal records checking regime.

The survey also found that 75% of respondents agreed that CRB checks
were likely to act as a deterrent to unsuitable people, though it is questionable
what value this finding has, based as it is on 'common-sense' assumptions.
However, the US-based Center for Sex Offender Management (2000) has
observed that the public's perspective on social issues establishes the 'boundaries of political permission' (Yankelovich, 1991), these being the limits or borders within which policy will be supported actively or acquiesced to by the
public.

In a democracy, therefore, political leadership is ultimately accountable to
the will of the people. Regardless of the subject area, those who make policy
outside these boundaries of permission may have them repudiated by the
public, members of whom may advocate replacing it with a radically different

approach. In such cases, public opinion leads to a changed political landscape and new 'boundaries of permission' are established.

The significance of this in the current context is that public perception of measures has an important influence in what is expected and what is ultimately enacted. Indeed it could be argued that it is public perceptions of the ISA, rather than how the scheme would operate in reality, which caused it to exceed the 'boundaries of political permission' as it was perceived as being too intrusive into the lives of ordinary citizens. Although there is little evidence that this was true, and charities and other organisations that work with children warned against any 'rash' dilution of the scheme at the expense of the safety of children (The Guardian, 5th June 2010), it was the view held by some highly vocal and influential public figures including children's author Phillip Pullman.

The existence of legislation and regulation such as criminal records checks appears to also give the public positive assurances that steps are being taken to make organisations a safer place for children, as organisations who may not have done so voluntarily are compelled to invest time in activities such as criminal records checking. Again the MORI survey showed that 70% of respondents agreed that CRB was making a positive different to the protection of children and vulnerable adults.

The establishment of the CRB, and equivalent systems in Scotland and Northern Ireland, has increased public awareness and interest in child abuse and the mechanisms by which children can be better safeguarded in organisations. The MORI survey showed that 33% of people could name the CRB as the organisation that carries out checks on applicants for work with children and vulnerable adults, and awareness has increased significantly from 2005 when it was 1 in 5.

This is important as it mirrors increased public awareness, possibly fuelled through press reporting of cases of abuse of children by professionals over recent years. This has lowered the threshold for believing this is an issue relevant to them and that it is possible that it could occur in their church or youth group and hence the need for vigilance in carrying out thorough checks.

Also encouragingly 91% of respondents to the MORI survey demonstrated strong acceptance of the criminal records checking process and its necessity, stating it would not put them off applying to work with children. This is significant, as much of the rationale for the review of ISA in 2010 centred on the argument that ISA registration was a disproportionate response to the problem of child abuse in organisations and was not widely publicly supported or accepted. Evidence from the MORI survey, and from many voluntary and statutory organisations, is that the ISA would have been a welcome additional safeguard which was a proportionate response to a real risk, and would provide greater clarity than the current criminal records checking system in terms of who should be registered, so removing ambiguity. The government response to the protestations of a small minority of highly vocal public figures, including broadcasters and authors could itself be regarded as disproportionate, undermining the creation of a much clearer wide reaching and potentially effective vetting process. It is also of interest that the Scottish Government has implemented many of the features of the proposed Vetting and Barring scheme in the PVG scheme in Scotland and while they have worked on the definition of 'regulated position' to be clear on who it applies to and have not made it compulsory, the reality is for the majority of individuals and organisation it will become a minimum standard which the apply to working in such posts.

A key strength of the Safeguarding Vulnerable Groups Act 2006 has been its ability to standardise the process for assessment of suitability and the criteria against which individuals could be barred from working with children. Under the previous system the criteria applied by List 99, PoCA and for Disqualification Orders were diverse and decisions were also made by different departments and individuals. The new single barring lists for children and vulnerable adults and the decision making power of the ISA, and the PVG scheme in Scotland are an important step forward in standardising the decisions around suitability and in ensuring experts are making such decisions on the basis of risk assessment without undue influence by political agendas from government.

LIMITATIONS OF CURRENT LEGISLATIVE FRAMEWORKS

Much of the current legislation and regulation is targeted at the statutory rather than the voluntary and private sectors. The Protection of Children Act, 1999 provided a useful precursor to the ISA barring scheme with the introduction of the PoCA list but it was only mandatory for public sector organisations to comply with the legislation, with other organisations having a *right* to check and refer to the list, but not a *duty*. This created a lack of clarity for organisations in the voluntary sector in particular and also led to differing standards of organisational safeguarding between the statutory and voluntary sector. The Safeguarding Vulnerable Groups Act 2006 and equivalents addressed this issue by broadening the duty and coverage of the legislation to all sectors working with children.

The legislation is also difficult to enforce outside of the statutory sector. In organisations such as schools, which are inspected by bodies such as OFSTED, there are mechanisms in place to ensure that, for example, all relevant staff are CRB checked and that decisions about suitability have been made. In voluntary and other non regulated organisations it is difficult to monitor compliance with legislation and a weakness in the SVG Act is that while organisations had a duty to refer unsuitable people to the barring scheme, there is no way to ensure that every unsuitable individual is referred to the scheme.

Similarly the CRB in its early years established a team which was to have a remit to regularly visit and inspect organisations that used the CRB service and potentially withdraw their registration if they were found to be using it inappropriately. However, as the scale of the number of organisations carrying out checks has increased this task has proved a difficult one and is now carried out on an exceptions basis where issues emerge over time.

A further key issue with legislating to prevent those who are unsuitable to work with children is that it can only identify those who have been found to be acting inappropriately to a degree that meets the required threshold for barring, an issue explored further in Chapter 9. It is therefore inevitably limited in terms of the number of people who can be identified and therefore prevented from working with children. Since 2003 many organisations have put the criminal records checking process at the heart of organisational safeguarding and regard it as the minimum, and regrettably often the maximum, standard in ensuring unsuitable individuals do not join their organisation. They trust that the information provided to them has been assessed by people better qualified than them to judge its relevance and therefore put great weight on this part of the process. The weakness in such an extensive and well managed criminal records checking regime, such as exists in the UK, is that organisations may consequently not invest sufficient energy in other potentially effective recruitment safeguards such as in depth interviewing and interrogation of references, and also in the other aspects of safeguarding culture as discussed elsewhere in this book.

The current criminal records checking systems and barring systems are only accurate at the time the check is made and generally not repeated once someone has joined the organisation. One of the key strengths of the proposed vetting and barring scheme to be administered by the ISA was that the information about barring was continually updated so if new information came to light employers would be automatically notified. This is in place in the new PVG scheme in Scotland providing a valuable additional safeguard for employers.

A continual weakness in the development of legislation and regulation in this area is the tension between the complex nature of the legislation required and the relative simplicity and transparency needed for it be accessible for organisations of all sizes and levels of sophistication. Legislation in this area is also used by lay audiences such as voluntary and private organisations and individuals, and in the case of the ISA by parents and carers. Nearly a decade after its establishment the legislation supporting the criminal records checking regime continues to confuse organisations.

A key challenge for the ISA and the government was how to explain a hugely complex piece of legislation to organisations is and individuals who need to use it and understand it. This tension was evident in the development of the SVGA where repeated consultations demonstrated that the legislation was too complex and had too many areas of ambiguity and more clarity and simplicity was required which conflicted with the government's desire not to be disproportionately prescriptive within the legislation. Legislation could, therefore, have a far greater impact on organisational safeguarding if it was easier to understand and therefore more effectively used.

Above all it is imperative that it is recognised that legislation and regulation is necessary but not sufficient. Many of the key features of safer organisations, including regular supervision, clear and relevant induction and training and effective whistle blowing policies can be mandated in sectors which are covered by regulation but not in the vast number of unregulated organisations who work with children. Organisations therefore need to adopt a safeguarding mindset which goes beyond legislation and regulation, seeing it as the minimum standard of what is prescribed or measured, and should develop all the features of a safeguarding culture because it is the right and demonstrably effective thing to do to safeguard children in their organisation.

WHAT DO DEVELOPMENTS IN LEGISLATION AND REGULATION INDICATE ABOUT DESIRABLE CULTURES FOR ORGANISATIONAL SAFEGUARDING BY GOVERNMENT ORGANISATIONS AND INDIVIDUALS?

Yankelovich's concept of 'boundaries of political permission' (Yankelovich, 1991), the limits or borders within which policy will be supported actively or acquiesced to by the public, was described above. The Safeguarding Vulnerable Groups Act was developed as a response to the Bichard Enquiry into the process failures that failed to prevent the Soham murders and Bichard's recommendation that the current criminal record checking and information sharing systems were insufficient to protect children and vulnerable adults.

The public outcry and high profile nature of the murders and the recommendations made by Bichard then provided the direction for government policy around assessing the suitability of individuals to work with children for the next 6 years. The public and media response about the perceived disproportionate nature of the proposed vetting and barring scheme was again high profile and led to the government asking Sir Roger Singleton to carry out a review of the scheme, Drawing the Line, A report on the Governments Vetting and Barring Scheme (December 2009). This led to a number of amendments being made which did not fundamentally alter the principles of the scheme, which was that it should have wide coverage across all sectors, that it made barring decisions based on a range of information and that it was continually updated.

In 2010 the same complaints that led to the Singleton review, were used by the new government to indicate that the scheme, had little public support and was disproportionate as a response to the scale of the problem, halting the planned launch of the new vetting and barring scheme in 2010 and leading to a fundamental review of the scheme in 2011, which at the time of writing has yet to reach a conclusion. The key point about the process which has taken place with the SVG Act over the last few years is that although attitudes and public opinion, often generated by high profile cases of abuse, have a key role to place in driving the creation of legislation and regulation in this area, the ideology, policy position and priorities of the government of the day has an even more powerful impact on the way in which legislation is designed and implemented.

A MODEL

This simple model (Figure 3.1) shows how attitudes, perception and understanding from the public often informed by information made available through the media can have a major impact on the policy position of government, but how that information fits with the government's own agendas will determine what form the legislation or regulation takes which in turn has an effect on attitudes and understanding around safeguarding.

Again using the example of the SVG Act and the ISA, the scheme that was due to be launched in 2010 would have sent strong messages to organisations about the need to have the basic safeguards in place and that they were equally at risk of employing someone unsuitable as were larger, statutory organisations. Under the proposed scaling back of the vetting and barring scheme it is likely that the coverage of the scheme will be greatly reduced from the original scheme and may not even cover the voluntary sector. This is likely to support attitudes about safeguarding requirements in other sectors being less robust than statutory sector and for less committed organisations may well mean the standard of safeguarding will continue to be concerningly low.

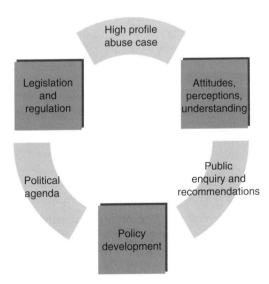

Figure 3.1 How attitudes, perception and understanding from the public can have a major impact on the policy position of government.

HOW SHOULD LEGISLATION AND REGULATION SUPPORT THE DEVELOPMENT OF SAFER ORGANISATIONAL CULTURES?

Much of the legislation and regulation that has been developed over the past 20 years has been reactive in nature, developed following enquiries into abuse of children in care homes (Warner 1992, and Utting (1997) or schools (Bichard (2004). Some proactive work has then resulted in terms of the production of guidance for schools (DCSF, 2009) but the primary impctus for the creation of the legislation has been as a reaction to a specific incidence of abuse in an organisational setting. Having said that, prior to the Bichard Enquiry some voluntary organisations had been campaigning the government to broaden the legislation around criminal record checking and PoCA listings to include those who work with children in other settings as a statutory requirement. However, the timing of the Huntley case and the public outcry that followed made such changes more of a priority for the government.

This chapter has focused on regulation and legislation, but as has already been stated, this is a small part of the jigsaw that makes up a true safeguarding culture. Despite lobbying by a range of organisations at the time of the inception of the CRB and then the ISA, the government has continued to be resistant to giving such bodies a broader remit for advising organisations on situational prevention strategies that ultimately would make a far more significant impact on the safeguarding of children in organisations. Organisations such as the Children's Workforce Development Council (CWDC) have produced guidance and training on safer recruitment and organisational safeguarding but this remains optional for non-regulated childcare organisations to use and not as widely known as it perhaps needs to be. With the political will, if government publicly supported such situational prevention strategies and made funding available for organisations such as CWDC or ISA to increase awareness of their importance and to provide supporting advice and training, it could have a far greater impact on organisational safeguarding than legislation alone.

Three key points should be taken from this discussion of the strengths and limitations of legislation and regulation:

* Legislation and regulation are important minimum safeguards
* Legislation and regulation can change as a result of a change government or other external factors, but does not necessarily reflect the albeit developing evidence about risk to children in terms of safeguarding
* Given the limitation of current legislative and regulatory frameworks and processes it is imperative that organisations regard basic standards as just that, a basic minimum and strive to create a safeguarding culture.

The following chapters provide information about ways in which organisations can create a safer organisational culture.

REFERENCES

Beyer, L., Higgins, D. and Bromfield, L. (2005) *Understanding Organisational Risk Factors for Child Maltreatment: A Review of Literature, National* Child Protection Clearinghouse, Australian Institute of Family Studies.

Bichard, M. (2004), *The Bichard Inquiry Report – An independent inquiry arising from the Soham murders.* House of Commons: London, The Stationery Office.

Center for Sex Offender Management (2000). *Public Opinion and the Criminal Justice System: Building Support for Sex Offender Management Programs*, April. Silver Spring, MD: CSOM.

CRB – Ipsos Mori Customer Service Research. www.crb.homeoffice.gov.uk/resource_library/business-publications.

Department for Children, Schools and Families (2009) *Guidance on Managing Staff Employment in Schools*, HMSO.

Department of Health and Social Security (1988) *Protection of Children: disclosure of criminal background of those with access to children.* Circular HC (88) 9 2/3/88.

Erooga, M. (2009) *Towards Safer Organisations: Adults who pose a risk to children in the workplace and implications for recruitment and selection*, NSPCC, London.

Gallagher, B. (2000) The extent and nature of known cases of institutional child sexual abuse. *British Journal of Social Work*, 30, 795–817.

HM Government (2010) *Working Together to Safeguard Children*, London, TSO.

Home Office (1993a) 'Protection of Children: disclosure of criminal background of those with access to children'. Circular HOC 47/93.

Home Office (1993b) *Safe from Harm: A code of practice for safeguarding the welfare of children in voluntary organisations in England and Wales*, London, Home Office.

Home Office (1986) 'Protection of children: disclosure of criminal background of those with access to children'. Circular HOC (86) 44.

Home Office website www.homeoffice.gov.uk/crime.

Institute of Child Protection Studies (2005) *Screening of People Working with Children and Young People: Issues Paper*, Australian Catholic University.

Marshall, W., Hamilton, K and Fernandez, Y. (2001) Empathy deficits and cognitive distortions in child molesters. *Sexual Abuse: A Journal of Research and Treatment*, 13(2), 123–131.

Mason, S. (2011) *A Common Sense Approach, A review of the criminal records regime in England and Wales*, London, Home Office.

Monkton, W. (1945) *Report of Sir Walter Monkton on the Circumstances which Led to the Boarding Out of Dennis and Terence O'Neill at Bank Farm, Minsterly and the Steps Taken to Supervise their Welfare*, London, HMSO, Cmnd. 6636.

NSPCC (2006) *An NSPCC Factsheet on How Sex Offenders are Prevented from Working with Children*, NSPCC Policy Department, unpublished.

NSPCC (2007) *Thematic Report of the Inspection of Equality and Diversity in the NSPCC*, NSPCC Inspection Unit, unpublished.

Sullivan, J. and Beech, A. (2002) Professional perpetrators: Sex offenders who use their employment to sexually abuse the children with whom they work. *Child Abuse Review*, 11, 153–167.

Thomas, T. (2005) *Sex Crime: Sex offending and society*, Devon, Willan Publishing.

Utting, W. (1997) *People Like Us: The report of the review of the safeguards for children living away from home*, London, The Stationery Office.

Warner, N. (1992) '*Choosing with Care*' The Report of the Committee of Inquiry into the Selection, Development and Management of Staff in Children's Homes, HMSO: London.

Yankelovich, D. (1991). *Coming to Public Judgment*. Syracuse, NY, Syracuse University Press.

4 Sexual Abuse of Children By People In Organisations: What Offenders Can Teach Us About Protection

Marcus Erooga, Debra Allnock
and Paula Telford

INTRODUCTION

Whilst there are a number of research studies undertaken with 'professional perpetrators', as outlined in Chapter One, these primarily focus on their psychological functioning, with only one (Colton and Vanstone, 1996) using a narrative from offenders themselves about their behaviour. The research study described in this chapter builds on this small evidence base by conducting in-depth interviews with 26 people convicted of sexual offences against children. The focus of the study is on those who have committed these offences within an organisational setting. Nineteen of the total 26 the 'core' sample, comprising participants who strictly fitted the research criteria. A further seven interviews were conducted with individuals who fell outside of the research criteria, as it was thought that some complementary learning could be drawn from their experience. This chapter reports only on the 19 participants in the core sample, but interested readers can find information on the non-core sample in the larger report published by the NSPCC (Erooga *et al.*, 2012). Rather than focusing on the characteristics of the offenders themselves the primary aim of the study was to identify organisational risk factors and the ways in which offenders become part of organisations, in order to propose good practice in recruitment and in work settings with children and young people.

Creating Safer Organisations: Practical Steps to Prevent the Abuse of Children by Those Working with Them, First Edition. Edited by Marcus Erooga.

Key research questions were:

- What is the relationship between abuse in the context of positions of trust and the setting in which the abuse is committed?
- Were there characteristics of an organisation which informed any choice they made about gaining access to them?
- What would be the characteristics of organisations, or measures taken by organisations, which would deter offenders from choosing to access that organisation?
- How did they groom their victims, in particular were there context specific methods of securing compliance and ongoing non disclosure of offending?

METHODOLOGY

This study was qualitative, involving in-depth interviews alongside some data collection from participants' case records. The unique focus of the study was on the characteristics of organisations, and the processes in place to protect children, described from the perspective of the offender.

Participants within the core group were either prisoners whose recruitment was facilitated by Her Majesty's Prison Service or offenders in the community identified by Probation Areas whose involvement was facilitated by the National Offender Management Service (NOMS). The primary group targeted for the study were those who had undertaken the Sex Offender Treatment Programme (SOTP), a framework for the integrated assessment and treatment of sex offenders in prison and the community (Mann and Thornton, 1998). Although not all of the participants had taken part in this programme, it was seen as desirable as those who had were likely to have a greater awareness of their motivations and behaviours than non-treated offenders.

Further, some participants' offences occurred historically. Historical offences, for the purpose of this research, are defined as offences which occurred prior to the introduction of current screening policies, primarily through the Criminal Records Bureau. Finally, it was regarded as desirable to include female participants as far as possible. Although perpetrators of sexual abuse and violence are most often male, there has been increasing attention paid to females who abuse and for this reason female participants were included as far as possible. Limited success was achieved in this respect with the inclusion of only three female offenders. Key contacts in both agencies facilitated the recruitment process by identifying participants who fitted the research criteria.

Ethical approval for the study was obtained from the NSPCC Research Ethics Committee and permission to undertake the research was then obtained from HM Prison Service and the National Offender Management Service. Participant agreement to take part in the study was obtained by designated contacts in the Prison and Probation services, who also gained consent for the researchers to review participants' case records prior to interview. The researchers undertook a more formal consent process at the start of the interview.

During the consent process, participants were advised that the researchers were ethically obliged to report any information disclosed relating to crimes against children not previously known to relevant agencies or which indicated that a child might be at current risk of harm. Additionally, participant disclosure of any risk to themselves or others or (where relevant) to breach prison security would require this to be reported to the appropriate authorities.

Following the interviews a thematic analysis was undertaken in order to identify common patterns and themes. NVivo8, a qualitative software programme, was used to manage the interview and case file information and to analyse the data. Presenting the data thematically also serves to reduce the likelihood of participants being identified within publications.

Although a representative sample was not an objective of this study it is still necessary to emphasise that the results should be interpreted with caution. Those that chose to participate do not represent a wider group of offenders and findings related to their characteristics may not be more widely generalisable.

THE SAMPLE

The core sample for this study included 19 participants, two of whom were female. All the participants in this group were White British. At the time of data collection, seven participants were in custody and 12 were in the community under the supervision of the National Probation Service. Table 4.1 illustrates the diverse organisational positions held by participants.

Table 4.1   Core sample: positions held at the time of offending.

	Education	Care workers	Voluntary posts	Other
Core sample n = 19	Boarding school = 2* Primary = 1 Secondary = 1 Special needs = 1 Support assistant in EBD school = 1 Education Welfare Officer = 1	Residential social work manager = 1 care worker = 1 LA Foster Carer = 1	Cub scout leader = 1 Volunteer in national tourist attraction = 1 National Choirs Director = 1 Sea cadet = 1 Army cadet = 1 Sports coach = 1	Self-employed broadcast journalist and trainer = 1 Director of Naturist Club = 1 Stables Manager/ Farrier = 1

*One of the teachers was also a priest.

Not all of the offences were recent. Nine core participants' offences were 'historical', committed prior to current child protection and screening policies, including Criminal Records Bureau checks. Despite these offences taking place outside of the current child protection context, there are organisational commonalities between the historical offences and those committed more recently.

The average age of the core sample at the time of their offence/s was 37 years, with the youngest offender aged 25 and the oldest 66. Their mean ages at time of conviction was higher at 51.15 years, indicating that conviction often occurred on average 14.15 years after the offence. Delayed arrest and convictions were usually associated with disclosure by victims many years after the abuse occurred.

Seven (37%) of the core sample were married at the time of their offence, with four of these divorcing as a result. A further six (31%) of the core sample were single (both unmarried and without a partner) at the time of offence. Of these, four reported that they had never had adult sexual relationships. Two had been in previous relationships but were single at the time of offence. Five (26%) reported they had been in an unmarried relationship at the time of offence. One (5%) was divorced and otherwise single. Nine (47%) of the core participants have biological children; one has step children.

Participants had diverse educational qualifications. Fifteen (79%) finished secondary school; six of these have a university degree; and seven have teaching qualifications. Four core participants (21%) left school without any qualifications.

Six (32%) of the core sample reported that they had been victims of sexual abuse when they were children; four of these experienced sexual abuse by people in positions of trust including a scout leader, a headmaster, a music teacher, and by teachers at a boarding school. The remaining two had been abused by family members. There were two participants whose records indicated they had experienced abuse in childhood but the nature and extent of this was unclear. Eleven participants' case records indicated there was no known abuse in their childhood.

None of the core sample had previous criminal convictions of any sort (sexual or non-sexual offending), except one whose conviction was for indecent exposure before the age of 16 and some 30 years previously. Organisations that employed the offenders in this sample would not therefore have screened them out on the basis of a criminal records check. It is not surprising that perpetrators with more recent offences did not have a history of conviction for sexual offences as recent policy and legislative changes have made it more difficult to obtain employment with a conviction for these types of offences.

All of those core participants who *could* have been subject to a CRB check were checked: nine had been appropriately CRB checked in an organisation where it would be expected. Six core participants offended in an organisation prior to the existence of CRB procedures.

Table 4.2   Abuse type by core participants perpetrating abuse type.

Abuse type	Number of core participants
Contact abuse with penetration	6
Contact abuse without penetration	6
Contact abuse with and without penetration	4
Contact abuse with and without penetration and non-contact abuse (use of images)	1
Non-contact abuse (recording images of children)	2

Sixteen (84%) of the core sample received custodial sentences which ranged from six months to life imprisonment with an average custodial sentence of 6.6. years. The remaining three participants received Community Orders which were between two and three years. All were subject to Sex Offender Registration and most had specific orders and disqualifications as conditions of their sentence. The length of time participants were subject to Sex Offender Registration requirements ranged from a minimum of five years to life.

Some participants were also subject to Sex Offences Prevention Orders (SOPOs) with varying conditions. SOPOs are for a minimum of five years, but some participants in this study were subject to indefinite orders. The majority of these SOPOs specified that the participant should not work with or live with children and young people under the age of 18. One participant had a further condition that he was barred from using computers at home or as part of his work. Disqualification Orders were also a part of a majority of participants' conditions.

The type of abuse committed against children in the core sample varied, as shown in Table 4.2 below. Six (31%) of participants perpetrated contact sexual abuse with penetration; 6 (31%) committed contact sexual abuse without penetration (e.g. masturbation); 4 (21%) abused children both through contact and non-contact offences; 1 (5%) participant perpetrated contact and non-contact abuse using images; and 2 (10%) used recording equipment to video children who were unaware of this.

All of the participants exclusively abused one gender, and the majority abused boys (74%). None of the offences involved multiple perpetrators. Twenty-three per cent of the sample abused pre-pubescent children (the youngest was six). The fewest number of victims abused as part of these offences was one; the highest number was 13, with an average number of victims being 2.8. However, the total number of victims can be considered as much higher than this, as one conviction involved over 150 images of pre-pubescent children.

Participants were asked only about their index offences; for ethical reasons, they were not asked about offences for which they had not been convicted. It is, possible, therefore, that participants had abused other children but did not disclose the detail. This was known to be the case with at least one participant.

Some characteristics of the sample are comparable with samples in other research, while some characteristics are distinctly different. For example, this sample roughly compares with Sullivan and Beech's (2004) sample (excluding clerical staff) in respect of history of childhood abuse. The current sample differs however from other studies (Finkelhor *et al.*, 1988; Gallagher, 1999; White, 1995) in that there were no cases of multiple perpetrators. Further, Sullivan and Beech's (2004) sample showed more varied sexual interests, abusing boys and girls, where this sample exclusively abused one gender.

The sample in this study highlights the diversity of those who commit sexual offences in organisational positions of trust. It is clear that there is no single 'profile' of a professional perpetrator. None of the characteristics described above, therefore, can fully predict who will be most likely to abuse a child in a professional setting.

FINDINGS

The findings presented here reflect the primary themes which emerged from the interviews. The focus of this section will be on organisational characteristics and processes described by participants in relation to the organisational settings in which they committed their sexual offences. These are referred to as 'organisational facilitating factors', as they describe aspects of the organisation which reflect complacent processes in respect of child protection. This section will also more briefly describe individual characteristics of the offenders, such as their grooming techniques within the organisations, here referred to as 'individual facilitating factors'.

ORGANISATIONAL FACILITATING FACTORS

Organisational facilitating factors include the process of recruitment, which includes recruitment procedures such as applications, interviews, Criminal Records Bureau checks and references. A further important organisational factor which emerged concerned organisational culture.

RECRUITMENT AND SCREENING

The literature review chapters outline the importance of a thorough, procedure driven, recruitment practice with clear criteria and screening processes used consistently in order to select high quality candidates and minimise the likelihood of risk to children from employees. Participants were asked to describe recruitment processes including the application, interview, references and CRB checks (where these were relevant, e.g. historical cases would not have had CRBs completed). In this study, participants generally described recruitment and screening processes which were not particularly robust or consistent, despite more recent offences occurring in the context of more rigorous child protection regulations.

Participants described a range of ways they came into employment. Some had applied directly, whilst others had been invited to apply. None indicated they applied for the job with the intention of accessing children to abuse. Although all participants indicated they had been through some form of recruitment process, some were unable to comment on specifics because the offences occurred so long in the past. One such participant was able to recall the job application and his response reflected how fallible he regarded screening processes: 'In them days, if you filled in your job application and you got to that question "Have you ever been convicted of a criminal offence?" I always put "No" because 5 out of 10 wouldn't check. Of the rest that did, 9 out of 10 the other 5 would just sack you'.

Recent offenders, however, did not describe screening processes which were noticeably more rigorous. One participant described being less than honest at interview.

In response to the researcher's question '… you're a man applying to work with primary school children … one of the reasons there's a national shortage is because there's always a question mark … was that explored at all with you?' he responded: 'I think there was a short interview … it was a case of … I didn't have to lie, I just had to … be lenient with the truth I suppose … but there were plenty of correct and valid reasons why I wanted to do it'.

Screening processes in historical cases were generally described as informal and largely focused on basic competence and personal 'fit'. Later screening processes were more thorough in some respects but were often focused on technical knowledge and ability to do the task rather than on aptitude and attitude to work with a vulnerable population. The overall impression was that there was an assumption that possible risk to children by staff was not an issue that needed to be considered. It appears therefore that there has been limited improvement in selection processes across the time scale represented by this sample.

Once in post, participants with more recent offences reported appropriate CRB checks had been carried out. Of the 19 core participants, seven (37%) had previously been employed or volunteered in settings where they had contact with children. Of these in only one case were concerns identified but not formally acted on, as far as this research exercise was able to ascertain. In two cases however, participants had taken up their posts before CRB checks had been completed, and one had taken up their post before references had been received by the employing organisation, echoing Warner's (1992) finding that 10% of Heads of Children's Homes and a third of care workers took up their posts before references were received.

Where CRB checks were not undertaken, there were a variety of reasons for this: that it was prior to the CRB process being available; that the offender was outside a regulated system, for example a private tutor; or the volunteer based organisations regarded them as too onerous. As one participant said: 'No, no. Really, to go down the CRB check route, you would have to check every single member, and this would have created an awful problem for the (volunteer organisation)'.

One of the issues of interest was whether offenders deliberately 'misdirected' employers to referees who were most likely to give an unduly positive impression. For the majority the choice of referees was uncontentious and straightforward, often because there were no significant issues to be avoided. In one case it was notable that two organisations had significant concerns not reflected in references, thus for example one gave a reference but declined to comment on the individuals 'honesty and integrity'. He subsequently gained employment via an agency, which then gave a good reference based on performance. No further checks were made by the new employer.

This case indicates the importance both of seeking information from a number of historical sources but also access to appropriate HR advice to understand the significance of any information which is out of the ordinary – for example omissions in references or 'agreed references', both often indicators of unvoiced concerns.

Participants were asked what sort of overall messages they were given during the recruitment process about the organisation, particularly with regard to children and expectations of how they were to be treated. Almost none recalled specific mention of children in this way, and there was little variation in this aspect between those interviewed some years ago and those more recently. Only in a few cases did participants mention child protection procedures, which were typically described as 'being in a book' and rarely disseminated amongst staff as an important feature of work.

One participant commented on how over-protective organisations can be counter-productive: 'Because the perception is, you can't do anything, and you're letting the kids down, because you know you can't even give the kid that's upset a hug. You can't do this, and given that undertone, that actually leaves it quite easy. There are all these messages about what you can and can't do and so many of them seem to be overly, overbearing and self-destructive. I suppose it dilutes the core message of what's really trying to be achieved to some extent ... and then you're actually getting very blurred lines rather than definite lines and where you've got blurred lines, you can do what you like can't you pretty much. Not what you like, but it's easy to get away with blurring lines'.

ORGANISATIONAL CULTURE

Rather like 'good practice' it is easy to assume that organisational values will be understood by those working within it, particularly when the organisation is one which has a public service or welfare remit. None of the participants described an organisational culture which was directly focussed on the welfare of children and young people.

At least two participants described environments in which management of children and young people was the central priority. For example: 'Because the clients were difficult, they could be violent or aggressive, if you've got 8 or 10 of them, and there's only 2 of you … one's dealing with one of the boys over there, and the other one's dealing with the other one there … in another room….its impossible, you know … there were times that happened, quite a lot.' The interviewer went on to ask 'Did you get a sense that there was a lot of concern bout the welfare of the young people?' to which the participant replied: 'There was concern … probably not enough though … It was very blasé I think in a way.'

Organisational messages and rules were commonly described as lacking clarity and consistency, and even non-existent. When participants with both historical and recent offences were asked about induction and whether child protection procedures had been explained to them the response was typically that they had not received either.

Expectations of staff and their relationships with children and young people were rarely explicit, as one participant put it: 'I think it was just understood that … it was expected that you knew'. Some participants described an absolute lack of guidance, as reflected in an interview with a participant with a recent offence. When asked about the existence of specific rules about being on alone with children they replied that there were no rules or guidnace about good or safe prcatice.

By contrast, where such issues were attended to the likelihood of abuse was reduced. One participant abused a number of children prior to working in an Assessment Centre and did so subsequently as an Education Social Worker but maintained that he had not abused when working in a residential setting (and had no allegations of doing so). He described a positive child-centred organisational culture in the residential setting: 'I think they just had good staff and good rotas; there was always lots of people about … I just can't imagine looking back at it that you would ever have asked if you could (take kids out) – it wouldn't have been part of the norm … it just wasn't in that environment … that was a good environment in terms of … child protection, yeah absolutely. … you know it's all the same things – there's boundaries, professionalism …'

It was notable that in the case of both female participants they felt unable to speak about concerns they had about precipitating events in their work setting. When asked whether there was someone in the school to talk to about diffcultes or concerns the participant replied: 'No 'cos they all just seemed to think it was the norm (physical restraint of the children in a very male orientated environment), everybody seemed to think that, that was it, I think a lot of them had been there a long time and it was just their way of dealing with it.'

Some organisations had well developed processes, with one participant describing very clear guidance about contact between adults and children which was adhered to, whilst another explained that on occasion it was difficult to follow through even if the ethos was understood: 'One of the things that had been spoken about in this school, was if you reprimanded a child or were talking to a child, make sure there's a door open, and quite right and I think that's a good thing, it's good practical advice … But that situation was always gonna happen, how do you not do that? A kid came to me "Sir can I speak to you at the end please", and you know "I want you to know I might get a bit teary from time to time, mum's got cancer". They don't want to say that in front of loads of people …'

In others regulations were considered too onerous to be followed. In this case of a voluntary organisation the offender was a member of the Board and it would seem to have been in his interest that this view was taken. 'Had anyone, in the experience you had there, expressed any concerns about there being no rules or procedures or messages about children and children's welfare? Yes it had been mentioned at Society and Board level on a number of occasions. But it was decided that because it was so unclear and unwieldy and impossible to introduce, not to do anything.'

Often overlooked as a significant factor, this would seem to suggest that as well as the contribution to risk of individual factors, the culture of the organisation also has a significant part to play in risk minimisation.

Organisational culture also manifested itself through the behaviour of participants' colleagues. Participants' were asked to describe any issues related to colleagues, for example, whether they felt their colleagues were aware of their behaviour with children, what their colleagues thought of them, colleagues' responses to requests for support at the time of the abuse; and colleagues' continued support post conviction.

There were a number of participants who fitted Doran and Brannon's (1996) description of an 'isolated over committed and dutiful' member of staff but it was clear in some cases that those qualities had more meaning in a context where other colleagues were willing to let children fend for themselves. One offender, a priest and teacher described vividly such a situation in the boarding and day school where he taught: 'If they'd (colleagues) shown more interest. They were all getting on with their own lives and were doing their own things, doing their, whatever work they do, marking or going out. It was to me the boarders came … I was terribly stretched myself, but I would never turn them away and they (colleagues) used to say "my, oh why don't you send them upstairs?". But if they came to me and I used to say to my colleagues, "well they must want something different, they must get fed up with where they are for a few minutes". I would never, ever, turn them away, never'.

A number of participants, particularly in schools and children's homes described colleagues' negative views of the children and young people. Wardaugh and Wilding (1993) describe certain populations, including children in social care as being held in less regard than others in society. Colton *et al.* (2002) similarly argue that 'looked after children are a population most likely to comprise a group widely stigmatised as the 'underclass' with an essential ambivalence in society between sympathy for the victims of child abuse generally and the threat to social order represented by 'troubled and troublesome youth' (p. 549).

In this research there were a number of occasions where these attitudes were a feature. A man who had been both a manager and a practitioner in a children's home described how it was easier for him and for colleagues to dismiss disclosures from the boys in their care because of the prevailing attitudes towards them. In the case of both women working in teaching settings their victims were generally viewed as disruptive and troublesome. In some cases it was notable that participants thought that despite being in organisations which have a duty of care toward children colleagues expressed more concern about the professional's vulnerability than that of the children.

This participant was perceived by a female colleague as putting himself at risk, '... and I always remember her saying to me, she says "one of them girls has a crush on you and be careful" and she did, she used to follow me round you know and If I went in the changing rooms she'd come round you know ... and I made sure I never went anywhere without somebody else if she were about.'

Some participants expressed incredulity that no one was concerned about their behaviour, or if they did that they did not intervene, acknowledging the fact that they were giving off likely signals of problematic behaviour towards children: *Do you think any of your colleagues had any sort of inkling about what was happening at any point, was anyone suspicious?*
I'm sure ... no, nobody said anything. I think they did use the words X's favourites, but I'm sure they were suspicious because they'd be silly if they weren't ... Well I think if I put myself in that situation, you know I think I would have brought in all sorts of regulations that this type of thing shouldn't be able to happen'.

Other participants acknowledged their position prevented colleagues from questioning them: 'I have often thought why didn't the other people within the organisation and I have asked them "why didn't you say anything to me about the control?" and they said "Well we have known you so long and respected you so much we didn't think, we thought you just having a bad time because of what was going on with you wife and you know and your divorce and we were just trying to support you" and I was "you should have just slapped me round the face"'

It would appear from reviewing participants' depositions that in at least three instances colleagues had had concerns about participants' behaviour but this did not come to light until after the abuse was disclosed.

INDIVIDUAL FACILITATING FACTORS

Where facilitating factors concern the offender, the study focused on the perspective they took on their offending, grooming and selection processes, the characteristics of their job at the time of the offences and aspects of organisational isolation they might have experienced. While a number of the study's findings are also relevant to adults who abuse and are not in organisational positions of trust there were results that seem to be specific to this population.

SELECTION AND GROOMING

Themes around 'grooming' children, families and colleagues emerged as one of the primary individual factors which facilitated abuse. Grooming has been defined by Craven *et al.* (2006) as: 'A process by which a person prepares a child, significant adults and the environment for the abuse of this child. Specific goals include gaining access to the child, gaining the child's compliance and maintaining the child's secrecy to avoid disclosure. This process serves to strengthen the offender's abusive pattern, as it may be used as a means of justifying or denying their actions' (p. 297).

Eighty-four per cent of this study's core sample identified vulnerability in their victims, and 79% manipulated this vulnerability in order to abuse. This has also been found in other studies such as Conte *et al.* (1989) and Elliott *et al.* (1995). One participant described this vividly: 'Yeah, right, that one, she … she started coming to cadets and then, she'd got a lot of problems at home which she started to tell us about … her mother was an alcoholic, her step father was quite a violent man from what she said … not to her, but to her mother … they weren't very supportive of her and it ended up, because me and my partner only lived just down the road, it ended up, most of the time, we would pick her up on the way to cadets. … God knows how, but it even got to the point where she was asking us will you adopt us?'

Perceived emotional vulnerability was also a factor for one teacher who was also a priest, providing pastoral care for boarders whose parents lived abroad: 'When they got fed up or depressed or down hearted they would come to me, to my room on the floor above … I might be thrown together with a boy or two boys one evening maybe … it's a situation where I'm trying to weigh up where you're suddenly thrown into perhaps a one to one, usually one to one, where something could easily happen'.

Developing special relationships with children and young people was key to some offender's management of abuse. This dynamic was observed in 68% of the core participants interviews and has also been reflected in other studies (Elliott *et al.*, 1995). In these cases, relationships were either defined by the participants as special or the participant perceived that the child or young person saw *them* as special. One teacher in this study described it thus: 'Yes I did try to make them feel special to enhance their abilities, to make them feel they were very capable of performing well'. In another case of a school sports teacher, victim depositions indicated that more than one boy described feeling they had a special relationship with him. The Education Welfare Officer described above had a sophisticated approach towards developing these special relationships: 'I used to go camping quite a lot, 'cos like I could take a group of boys camping. There'd be one special boy in that group that would be my number one ... and everyone understood that he was my number one ... but probably didn't understand more than that.'

Nurturing common interests with children and young people was noted by 7 core participants (37%), for example: 'He loved coming up with me on the railway. There were other times, especially in 2006, he'd done four days worth of school work experience and he'd done that with the trains ... He was looking towards perhaps joining the railways when he left school and at that time, he'd come up midweek.' A teacher in a boarding school used one young boy's love of football to build a rapport with him on the way to abusing.

Taking children away on trips was another grooming method described. In the current sample none of the participants described using trips as opportunities to abuse, but rather to develop closer relationships with children: 'I'd known her for some years I suppose ... I suppose we became more friends rather than just instructor, cadet when we took them (away), 'cause we were together for a fortnight, she was one of the older ones and would rather sit and talk to us rather than talk to the younger kids that were there, you know, who were a bit babyish ...'

Emotional congruence with children inevitably facilitated the grooming and maintenance of abuse, and was a factor in a number of the offences for the participants, as with this Children's Home Worker: 'Well, it's funny that it's come to mind now but I used to spend hours talking to these kids. One of the mistakes that I made, and it would never happen again, is that I kind of cut off adults and only moving among children and I've always said that for me was one of the big mistakes. I was, at 35 I was a very immature man moving in a very immature atmosphere with some really primitive, I can say that, very primitive stresses and well basically that was the underlying thing.'

It has long been established that in grooming children for sexual contact some offenders use pornography or sexually explicit dialogue as a facilitator to legitimise the sexual acts and to gain compliance in sexual activity (Conte et al., 1989; Kaufman et al., 1998), and as such, this issue was of interest in this study.

Two participants reported using magazines of photographic indecent images of children in the period prior to the availability of the internet. One also reported using video games and video of sexually explicit activity immediately preceding the offences.

Two others had accessed images but had not shared these with their victims, citing sexual inquisitiveness or confusion as their reason for doing so. Both denied any sexual interest in children or an overtly sexual motivation to their offending.

Only four participants reported, or had mention in the case files, of text messaging (texts). In three cases this was either part of the process of grooming or of developing a more intimate relationship, in the context of breaching other boundaries of appropriate behaviour. In all cases this seemed to be part of a pattern of presenting themselves as quasi peers to their victim, with texts being the way in which most of the young person's peer group communicated frequently.

In the fourth case the texts were themselves the vehicle for the offences, in that as a member of the teaching staff she initially exchanged a photograph of a family pet (at the young person's request) but once this contact was established it led to an exchange of sexually explicit text messages with the 14 year old male pupil.

CHARACTERISTICS OF THE JOB WHICH FACILITATED ABUSE

There were a number of ways in which particular characteristics of offender's jobs played a part in enabling the abuse. For two participants, geographical and emotional isolation may have contributed to their opportunity to abuse.

Two female participants, both working in educational settings, cited both physical and emotional isolation as having contributed to their abusive behaviour, reflecting Doran and Brannon's (1996) notion of the '... isolated but dutiful staff member who is perhaps over helpful to colleagues and children, and frequently does things outside the normal duties' (p. 158). One described it in this way: 'To me I think the main factor in my offending was the sense of isolation I had in that school ... although it was a very big school with a huge number of students and staff, I did feel quite isolated I think. Partly because of how the department was and how people didn't seem to interact ... and also ... physically it was sort of on the corner of the site. She continued: But any issues that arose ... I didn't know who to speak to about them, I didn't feel I could talk to my head of department because he wasn't effective in addressing anything ...'. This same participant confided in her female colleague that she was having sex with a male pupil, to which her colleague advised her not to disclose this as she wouldn't be believed.

The second of the women, a teaching support assistant also in a special needs setting who had offended against an adolescent boy by sending text messages spoke of the cumulative effects of being personally stressed and working in a male environment in which seeking support was not encouraged:

'I think I was so, so low at the time and it was a bit of attention I think. And that's how I got into that., I'd just had a cancer scare and I was ... I didn't communicate with my husband as I should have done but now we do communicate so much better'. She went on to say that the male dominated environment was not one in which she could have looked for support and that, in her view, had she been able to it might not have sought closeness through the abusive behaviour.

A further characteristic of participant's jobs which appear to have played a part in abuse is the pastoral or disciplinarian responsibilities to children. This was evident in four cases. The Education Welfare Officer described it in this way: 'He (child) also had a temper, throw things about and that. So often instead of sending him to a teacher they would send him to me. I'm pretty sure that was how I first met him.'

MAINTENANCE OF ABUSE

Wolfe *et al.* (2003) highlighted the issue of children's perceptions of the abuser's relative power over them as a significant reason why children might find it difficult if not impossible to prevent, stop or disclose the abuse. While that disparity of power between child and adult was often identified in this study as a reason for the child being unable to tell there were a range of other factors which the participant's perceived to prevent disclosure.

Eight participants perceived that children did not disclose abuse for the following reasons: because they simply asked the child not to tell; they were aware that disclosure was prevented in order to protect family members; and they acknowledged that their status in the organisation or the community prevented disclosure, for example: 'There would be no question of them telling on me ... they were in a position where they saw me as their friend, their best friend and it would have been *unimaginable for them to complain and they never did.*'

Grooming children's families was a particular method of ensuring children did not disclose abuse. In at least four cases, trusting relationships developed between the participants and children's family members and were seen as significant in inhibiting victims' disclosure. Finally, some participants' believed that there was a reciprocal 'relationship' with the child and as such did not feel there was anything to be concerned about regarding possible disclosure: 'No I didn't [think he might mention it (to his girlfriend]. And we spoke about what the consequences were for both of us if this was involved [people getting to know], and you know his words, "well no one is gonna know."'

MOTIVATIONS

A longstanding stereotype of sex offenders is that of '... a sophisticated and well organised, predatory individual' (Jenkins, 1990) with its implications of intentionality in the process of finding settings where vulnerable children may be accessed.

In the current research none of the sample acknowledged potential sexual access to children as a motivating factor in their choice of profession or volunteering. Ten core participants (53%) reported that they had no awareness of a sexual interest in children prior to the offences. Two (11%) reported that they became aware of their interest in children in adulthood. Four (21%) reported that they were under 11 years when they became aware of sexual interest in younger children. A further three (16%) reported that they were aware of a sexual interest in children, but it was unclear when this awareness developed (see Table 4.3).

Table 4.3 Awareness of sexual interest in children by when awareness developed.

	Awareness before taking job where offence took place	
	Yes	No
No awareness reported	0	10
Awareness emerged in adulthood	2	0
Awareness emerged in pre-pubescent stage	4	0
Awareness reported but unclear when this developed	4	0

Eighteen participants told us they had no intention or motivation to abuse any children in their employment, while one participant admitted he was unsure if this was the case. Instead, they described a whole range of other reasons for being in the job/organisation they were in when they offended. For example, some said they did not seek out the job but were invited to apply, while others were transferred by their employers into a new role which involved children.

However, as can be seen from the table, regardless of reported intentions, all of those who were aware of a sexual interest in children had known this *prior* to taking employment in those organisations where their offences took place.

Being able to acknowledge such a motivation, with intentionality bringing with it implications of culpability which go even further than the commission of the offences themselves may be more challenging for some offenders. It may be that to acknowledge such an intention would be to contradict their self image of 'someone who made a mistake' or arouse anxiety about a negative response from the researchers at interview. For these reasons amongst others there is no reliable indicator of what the actual situation may have been and responses from participants should be viewed in that context.

One man who acknowledged he had abused children regularly in every setting he had worked in was nonetheless adamant that sexual attraction to children was not a factor in his motivation: 'I can honestly say, I mean, you must understand when I say, that I actually destroyed myself thinking about what I'd done, not just to these boys, but to all those others who were involved in this betrayal of trust, but I can honestly say, I can, my conscience is quite clear that I did not go on the staff … to get the opportunity for molesting …'

It may be significant that this interviewee had not yet participated in a treatment programme.

One participant recognised that there was a discrepancy between his knowing his predisposition to abuse and his choice of work setting being unrelated, acknowledging that this was a possible motivation: 'Do you think that was in your consciousness when you applied for the job or do you think it was part of your motivation for applying for the job to get access to be able to abuse the boys or … No I don't think that was in my conscious thoughts, whether it was subconscious or not I just do not know.'

Another was able to identify that his distorted thinking allowed him to convince himself that he was not going to abuse, despite this seeming not credible to an objective observer: 'I did have a CD (cognitive distortion) ... a massive CD, really effective CD, that I'm okay, you know ... and I could be okay.'

Findings from this sample are in contrast to Sullivan and Beech's (2008) study, where 15% of their professional perpetrator sample took the job solely in order to abuse children 41.5% said they took the job partly to abuse children; 19.5% said they were unsure if abuse was a motivation; and 25% said they did not intend to abuse children.

DISCUSSION

When considering suitability, competence, skill and aptitude are all important components of someone fit to take the responsibilities of working with children, or working in an environment where they may be present. Conversely an unwillingness or inability to follow procedure, an inflated view of therapeutic competence or an unreflective or mechanistic approach to practice can all, in very different ways, contribute to a failure to meet standards of care which children are entitled to expect in a relationship with a worker. Whilst, therefore, the focus of this study has been on more obvious characteristics, these others should not be overlooked in considering optimal selection methods.

Whilst the primary focus of concern in this context tends to be on those who abuse or actively harm children, there is a spectrum of concerns and behaviours which may make an individual inappropriate to work with children, ranging from those who actively present a risk to those adults who are not a risk but nevertheless are otherwise unsuitable.

The category of those who present a risk is extremely broad. It includes individuals who deliberately and knowingly seek posts in order to gain access to children and, as this research has shown, those without a previous history of abusive behaviour who react sexually to the availability and vulnerability of the children with an inappropriate and sexualised response. There are others with belief systems which justify unacceptable behaviour, as with a proportion of those foster carers who use physical violence toward children in their care, and those who collude with inappropriate uses of discipline or repressive regimes through 'fitting in' to a dysfunctional organisational culture.

Stark et al. (1997) suggest the best way to avoid harm to children is to avoid dangerous practice, rather than attempt to screen out allegedly dangerous people. The discussion above has indicated the importance of clearly articulated values in organisations and the impact these can have on organisational culture and day to day practice. An integrated approach to value based recruitment and selection, management and practice, with a clear ethos of acting in the best interests of children would seem to offer an effective way of responding to the challenge of ensuring that children receive the respectful and above all safe service that every organisation aspires to provide.

A key message from the findings is that the screening procedures which were in place in all cases were not sufficient to prevent the employment of people inappropriate to work with children. In all organisations where a CRB check was required (e.g. organisations which are externally regulated via child protection procedures), there were no relevant offences which screened out potential abusers, nor were screening procedures such as interviews or references which were able to eliminate the risk of employing someone with the potential to abuse a child. These findings highlight the necessity of strengthening organisational activities which can reduce the likelihood of abuse taking place. This is not to suggest that situational prevention will provide the 'silver bullet' which will stop abuse taking place in professional settings. Indeed, situational prevention techniques should be used in conjunction with thorough screening procedures. However, participants in this study described organisational processes which were relaxed and complacent and in a few cases, careless.

There were a number of participants who had worked or volunteered for organisations which were not part of any wider external child protection system (e.g. a naturist club and a national tourist attraction), and CRB checks were not required. These participants described organisations which had low levels of concern for the well being of the children who came into contact with them. This finding suggests that it is not only organisations with direct mandates to work with children who should be concerned about strengthening screening and situational prevention measures, but also those outside the child protection system yet whose work involves significant involvement of children.

Grooming patterns identified in this study are not unique and have previously been described in terms of a broader population of sex offenders, i.e. not just professional perpetrators (Elliot et al., 1995). The current study however has been able to explore these processes in depth with professional perpetrators in order to identify how an offender's position of trust specifically enables abuse to occur. The interviews revealed the ways in which offenders develop knowledge about children and their perceived vulnerabilities, and how they were able to use this knowledge to identify children to abuse, to groom them and then abuse them. These grooming patterns were evident in both historical cases as well as current offences, suggesting that, despite decades of policy development around child protection, individuals with a propensity to abuse children have not altered their methods of grooming.

There was evidence, for example, in both historical and 'current' offences that offenders used status to manipulate secrecy from the victim. Knowledge about disclosure patterns (Allnock, 2010) underscores the difficulties that children have in telling someone about abuse, particularly where the abuser is known to the child and has a particular status. In light of this, organisations should find ways to strengthen messages about their concern for children, develop a culture of openness between staff and management so that staff who hold any concerns can report them without consequence to themselves, and should also be strengthening staff supervision so that developing relationships between staff and children can be openly examined.

Isolation of staff (either geographical or emotional) was identified as a factor which facilitated abuse for some of the participants. This isolation, particularly coupled with responsibility for children perceived to be vulnerable or who have particular needs, can produce a level of stress for those with a duty of care. Isolation potentially creates situations where there are no reference points for staff and may contribute to a sense of powerlessness among staff which in fact, for some of our participants, led to a crossing of boundaries. If organisations find ways of reducing situations where staff feel isolated, possibly by way of improved supervision this may help to highlight the development of inappropriate relationships and also reinforce organisational messages about the importance of the welfare of children. A further function of positive supervisory relationships is the potential for providing a feedback processes whereby inappropriate organisational cultures which have been, or may be, developing, can be identified and so become a priority for action.

The findings also highlighted that there may well have been suspicion shared by the offender's colleagues. It is impossible to know for sure why colleagues did not report the participant to management, yet it can be reasonably assumed that at least some held suspicions which were relayed to the participant. Beyer *et al.* (2005) raised concerns, in particular for organisations with overly hierarchical systems where there is no procedure in place for making complaints. An organisational culture with strong messages about the respect of children, no matter their backgrounds and circumstances, should be developed. There should also be an openness and clear path for staff to raise concerns about colleagues.

SITUATIONAL CRIME PREVENTION AS A RESPONSE

'*Understanding environmental factors external to the individual and which influence behaviour is the cornerstone of much of the current crime prevention work. Situational crime prevention is based on the premise that all behaviour is the result of interactions between the actor, the characteristics of the actor and the circumstances in which an act is performed*' (Beyer *et al.*, 2005, p. 13).

Beyer *et al.* (2005) explain that situational crime prevention, in which organisational factors are used to reduce opportunities for abuse, can be grouped into several overall objectives known to have an influence on offending behaviour. Promisingly, particularly in this context, they also report that evaluations of situational prevention projects have not shown significant displacement of offences (Clarke 1997; Sherman 1990) thus the effect of protecting children in one organisation would not be to divert offenders to other, less rigorous, settings.

This research supports the potential efficacy of using situational prevention approaches, discussed further in Chapter Eight.

CONCLUSION AND RECOMMENDATIONS

'Although it is important that risk factors for children, adults and organisations are identified, it is equally important to draw on the knowledge about the features that make organisations safer for children' (Beyer *et al.*, 2005, p. 106).

There are some clear themes in this research which challenge the widely held view that there typical 'paedophiles' seeking out opportunities to sexually assault children and prepared to lie and deceive in order to do so. Undoubtedly there are some individuals whose primary sexual interest is children and who will indeed lie and deceive in order to sexually abuse, but for a significant proportion in this sample, and arguably more generally in this population, the reality is more nuanced. The findings support the notion that there is no way of clearly identifying those who may be unsuitable to work with children; therefore whilst screening is undoubtedly necessary it cannot be sufficient to effectively protect children.

It will be apparent that those who offend in organisational positions of trust are not always actively seeking to abuse children; some abuse children because the combination of opportunity and personal potentiators occur simultaneously. A reasonable hypothesis therefore is that situational prevention measures, as outlined above, in conjunction with appropriate screening and selection processes form the foundation of a basic, adequate environment for an appropriate and safe setting for work with children and young people. Organisations which do not have a formal 'duty of care' to children, yet still engage with them regularly (e.g. tourist attractions, etc.) should also be actively implementing situational prevention measures.

This research has highlighted important organisational contexts for protecting children from the perspective of those who have offended against children in employment or volunteer settings. A primary limitation of the study is the small number of women included and further research would be warranted to better understand differences in offending patterns between genders. It may also be that different offending patterns may interact with different organisational issues for men and women. As so much of the current research identified the difficulties which organisations seem to have in developing and following adequate procedures, an area of further investigation which would complement and amplify the findings in this report would be with organisations directly about their culture, policies and practice. Specifically where research could be undertaken with organisations that had specific issues about abuse or inappropriate relationships between staff and children or young people, the focus would then be on what it was that led them to believe that their procedures at the time were adequate, what they now understand to have been the shortcomings and what their learning is about organisational perception of risk and safety which could usefully be disseminated.

The single most important message from this research is that a wider focus than deterring or preventing 'paedophiles' is required for organisations to appropriately safeguard children. As well as providing appropriate 'barriers' by way of selection and screening processes it is also necessary to manage organisational processes so that the possibility of inappropriate or abusive behaviour developing or occurring is minimised.

REFERENCES

Allnock, D. (2010). *Children and Young People Disclosing Abuse: A research briefing*. London: NSPCC.

Beyer, L., Higgins, D. and Bromfield, L. (2005) *Understanding Organisational Risk Factors for Child Maltreatment: A Review of Literature*, National Child Protection Clearinghouse, Australian Institute of Family Studies.

Clarke, R. V. (1997), *Situational Crime Prevention: Successful case studies*, 2nd ed., Harrow and Heston, Albany, New York.

Colton, M. and Vanstone, M. (1996) *Betrayal of Trust: Sexual abuse by men who work with children*, London: Free Association Books.

Colton, M., Vanstone, M and Walby, C. (2002) Victimisation, care and justice: Reflections on the experiences of victims/survivors involved in large-scale investigations of child sexual abuse in residential institutions. *British Journal of Social Work*, 32, 541–551.

Conte, J., Wolf, S. and Smith, T. (1989) What sexual offenders tell us about prevention strategies. *Child Abuse and Neglect*, 13, 293–301.

Craven, S., Brown, S. and Gilchrist, E, (2006) Sexual grooming of children: Review of literature and theoretical considerations, *Journal of Sexual Aggression*, 12(3), 287–299.

Doran, C. and Brannan, C. (1996) 'Institutional Abuse', in P. C. Bibby (ed.), *Organised Abuse: The current debate*, pp. 155–166, Ashgate Publishing, London.

Elliot, M., Browne, K., and Kilcoyne, J. (1995) Child sexual abuse prevention: what offenders tell us. *Child Abuse and Neglect*, 19(5), 579–594.

Erooga, M., Allnock, D., and Telford, P. (2012) *Creating Safer Organisations: Using the perspectives of convicted sex offenders to inform organisational safeguarding of children*, London, NSPCC.

Finkelhor, D., Williams, L. and Burns, N. (1988) *Nursery Crimes: A study of sexual abuse in daycare*, Newbury Park: Sage.

Gallagher, B. (1999) The abuse of children in public care, *Child Abuse Review*, 8, 357–365.

Jenkins, P (1990) *Intimate Enemies: Moral Panics in Contemporary Great Britain: Social problems and social issues*, Guernsey; The Book Repository.

Kaufman, K., J. Holmberg, K. Orts, F. McGrady, A. Rotzien and E. Daleiden (1998) Factors influencing sexual offenders' modus operandi: An examination of victim-offender relatedness and age. *Child Maltreatment* 3(4), 349–361.

Mann, R. E., and Thornton, D. (1998) The evolution of a multisite sexual offender program. In W. L. Marshall, Y. M. Fernandez, S. M. Hudson, and T. Ward (Eds.)., *Sourcebook of Treatment Programs for Sexual Offenders* (pp. 47–57). New York: Plenum.

Sherman, L. (1990) Police crackdowns: Initial and residual deterrence, in N. Morris (ed.), *Crime and Justice: A review of research Vol. 12* (pp. 1–48), University of Chicago Press, Chicago.

Stark C., Paterson B., Henderson T., Kidd B., and Godwin M. (1997) *Counting the dead. Nursing Times*, 93, 34–37.

Sullivan, J. and Beech, A. (2004) A comparative study of demographic data relating to intra- and extra-familial child sexual abusers and professional perpetrators, *Journal of Sexual Aggression*, 10(1), 39–50.

Wardaugh, J. and Wilding, P. (1993) Towards an explanation of the corruption of social care. *Critical Social Policy*, 13(37), 4–31.

Wardaugh, J. and Wilding, P. (1993) Towards an explanation of the corruption of social care. *Critical Social Policy*, 13(37), 4–31.

Warner, N. (1992) *'Choosing with Care'* The Report of the Committee of Inquiry into the Selection, Development and Management of Staff in Children's Homes, HMSO: London.

White, I. (1995) Report of the Management of Child Care in the London Borough of Islington, London Borough of Islington, cited in Corby, B., Doig, A., and Roberts, V. (2001) *Public Inquiries Into Abuse of Children In Residential Care*. London, Jessica Kingsley.

Wolfe, D., Jaffe, P., Jette, J., and Poisson, S. (2003) The impact of Child Abuse in Community Institutions and Organizations: Advancing Professional and Scientific Understanding. *Clinical Psychology: Science and Practice*, 10, 2.

5 Manipulation Styles of Abusers Who Work With Children

Joe Sullivan and Ethel Quayle

INTRODUCTION

In recent years the press has reported numerous scandals and inquiries into child sexual abuse perpetrated by professionals who work with children. Such abusive practices have not only focussed on the individuals who have committed the abuse but also the organisations who have failed in their child protection duties. The Roman Catholic Church is still facing accusations that Vatican officials advised Ireland's Catholic bishops in 1997 not to report priests suspected of child abuse to the police (BBC News, 19 January, 2011). Much of the contemporary research, along with government and local authority initiatives, have focused on improving the policies and procedures within the institutions and organisations where the abuse has taken place. For example, a Serious Case Review was undertaken in Buckinghamshire after the conviction of the Head of Care of six offences of abuse against four boys aged between 11 and 14 (Held, 2009). While these developments are necessary, more needs to be known about the perpetrators to determine whether the implementation of child protection measures would be effective. In addition, better understanding this abuser group could lead to more effective identification of potentially dangerous persons seeking to work with children.

This chapter outlines the key findings of a research study into professionals who used their work as a cover for targeting, sexually manipulating and abusing the children with whom they worked. The findings of two previously published preliminary studies (Sullivan and Beech 2004; Sullivan, Beech, Craig, and Gannon, 2010) are initially discussed followed by the results of a substantive qualitative study (Sullivan, 2009). The aim of this chapter is to describe what

Creating Safer Organisations: Practical Steps to Prevent the Abuse of Children by Those Working with Them, First Edition. Edited by Marcus Erooga.
© 2012 John Wiley & Sons, Ltd. Published 2012 by John Wiley & Sons, Ltd.

this group of people tell us about the ways that they manipulate the children and adults within their organisation to enable them to commit sexual abuse. These 'manipulative styles' may be important indicators of problematic behaviour by professionals and enable us to reflect more clearly on people who work with children and the rare, but significant, harms that can follow from violating professional boundaries.

DEMOGRAPHIC PROFILE AND OFFENDING PATTERNS OF PROFESSIONAL PERPETRATORS

In the first part of the research project an original study group of 41 professional perpetrators was identified from within a specialist residential assessment and treatment centre for child sexual abusers (Sullivan and Beech, 2004). People attending the treatment centre had usually been convicted of serious sex offences and therefore may not be a representative sample. Their demographic characteristics and abusing patterns were explored and these were compared with 264 intra and extra-familial child sexual abusers. As had been the case in other research (Langevin *et al.*, 2000), it was found that unlike the control groups the professional perpetrators were more likely to sexually abuse male children. However, these professional perpetrators would also seem to represent a significant risk to female children, as 44% did also report a sexual interest in them. It would also appear from this research that like other child sexual abusers a significant proportion of professional perpetrators are aware of their sexual interest in younger children by the time they reach adulthood.

Importantly, the majority of these offenders acknowledged that they chose their work to gain access to children for the purpose of committing abuse. Of the study group 92.5% said they were aware of their sexual interest in children before joining the profession in which they subsequently abused children and 57% indicated that gaining access to children to sexually abuse was either a primary or partial motivation for working with children. The study also found that there were some commonalities in the ways professional perpetrators groomed, or prepared, children for abuse. For example, a significant majority (78%) disclosed that they arranged to meet children outside work in order to facilitate abuse. This seems to support the position that a better understanding of the behaviour of professional perpetrators is likely to lead to more effective child protection procedures.

PSYCHOMETRIC COMPARISONS WITH INTRA- AND EXTRA-FAMILIAL CHILD ABUSERS

In a second preliminary study the psychometric profiles of 31 professional perpetrators were compared with other child abusers to establish whether there were aspects of their personalities that could be identified through psychometric measures (Sullivan *et al.*, 2010). On the whole it was not possible to distinguish the professional perpetrator group clearly from the control groups using the selected measures. It is unclear whether the measures were not sufficiently sensitive to demonstrate differences, or whether they were 'fit for purpose' in terms of what they were trying to measure (Gannon, Keown, and Rose, 2009). The need for more and better targeted instruments was identified as an issue for future research in this area.

RATIONALE FOR A QUALITATIVE METHODOLOGY

With the psychometric analysis of professional perpetrators offering limited insights it was decided to seek a richer body of data by using a qualitative methodology to explore participants' experiences. Qualitative research methodologies offer the opportunity to examine how participants make sense of events within their own context and so assist in the development of causal explanations (Maxwell, 1996). The aim was to explore and understand the meanings which professional perpetrators attributed to their experiences. Sixteen of the original study group were selected and engaged in a semi-structured interview exploring the processes involved in developing a pattern of sexually abusive behaviour towards children. It is important to note that the people who participated in these interviews had often been successful in their careers, and not seen by other staff within their organisations as 'monsters'. To help us understand how they engaged with children in order to offend, it might be useful to initially consider that factors that influenced their motivation to offend.

MOTIVATION TO SEXUALLY OFFEND

The first part of the interviews focussed on the participants' perception of the factors which combined to shape their sexually abusive behaviour towards children. Their accounts were dominated by what Ward and Hudson (1998) called 'distal factors'; historical and developmental experiences seemed critical to understanding how someone becomes a child abuser. The analysis of the interviews suggested that the participants believed that these early life experiences had a formative effect on their sexual arousal, thinking, beliefs and behaviour. Participants identified five key factors as influencing their future behaviour. The most common of these was early sexual experiences, which participants typically said normalised sexual behaviour and influenced their view of self, others, sex and the world, irrespective of whether the events were perceived as abusive. This is similar to the findings from other research that suggests that that early experience may influence developmental trajectories and offending pathways (e.g. Collins and Woollons, 2008). Other significant life events described by participants included experiences within their families which were emotionally or physically damaging and other experiences outside the family such as restrictive regimes, peer isolation or bullying.

While it is not possible to discuss this in any detail, it did appear that these early life events help form core beliefs about the world and their place in it, which could be called *life theories*, which are similar to the implicit theories described by Ward and Keenan (1999) These *life theories* influence three key areas of development: their sexual interests and arousal; perceptions and beliefs; and their behaviour, all inter-relating, informing and being informed by subsequent events. Among the more interesting results of this study was the importance which professional perpetrators placed on the need to feel a sense of power or control over others.

However, the participants in this study also suggested that there were blocks to their ability to commit offences against children, which included general concerns about the legality or morality of what they wanted to do, or how this ran contrary to their religious beliefs. There were also more specific blocks such as the damaging features of the abuse for the child or potentially danger- ous consequences for themselves. However, these blocks were overcome and participants engaged in a lot of offence supportive thinking to enable the com- mission of an offence. Such distortions in thinking patterns are clearly related to the life theories held by these offenders and pervaded the whole offence process (see Gannon, Ward and Collie, 2007 for a review of related literature). The distortions identified included *challenging* the perception that their behaviour was wrong and justifying their sexual contact with children as *enti- tlement*. In addition, participants described minimising the abuse by the 'com- partmentalisation' of the abuse and defining it as a small part of them or denial through the suggestion they were *abdicating responsibility* for their actions. Other distortions included defending their behaviour as causing a measure of *acceptable harm* or excusing the abuse by telling themselves *children are sexual anyway*.

Of interest is that professional perpetrators generally described a level of complexity to their thinking which, while observable in other child abusers, appears to be more common in this group. This may be explained by the fact that they were likely to have been surrounded by child protection messages in their workplaces which they had managed to discount. This may have implica- tions for treatment, but more importantly for the context of this book, may mean that procedures and messages in organisations need to be clearly sig- nalled and stringently reinforced. In part it may be possible to 'discount' child protection messages because of the high levels of sexual arousal to children, supported by fantasies of control and supremacy and resulting in masturba- tion. Such fantasies resonated with their own early experiences and became part of the process of victim selection, grooming activity and abuse.

VICTIM SELECTION, GROOMING AND ABUSE

This next section will focus on participants' accounts of their selection of victims and the grooming techniques employed before, during and after the abuse. The cohort identified three factors that primarily influenced their selection of a potential victim, namely *vulnerability, availability* and *attractiveness*. The fact that only a few gave much consideration to the attractiveness of the child, compared to the unanimous acknowledgement of vulnerability as the key element in victim selection, suggests that participants were most concerned with succeeding in sexually abusing a child and avoiding detection rather than pursuing their 'ideal' child. This may prove to be different for other groups of child abusers. There were differences in how they evaluated the vulnerability of a child and it would seem that this was, in part, influenced by the *life theory* and the manipulation style each individual developed. Maybe it is not surprising that the availability of the victim was also highlighted by participants as an important factor in determining the selection of victims. While the work of many professional abusers brings them into close contact with children, this does not always imply availability. Many child protection policies within organisations seek to limit the opportunities that individuals might have to spend time alone with a child, or to communicate with a child outside of the organisational setting. However, it is apparent that with these men such strategies were not in themselves sufficient to prevent abuse.

Although children were targeted within the workplace, the study group most often sexually abused children in neutral locations and/or their own homes as opposed to the professional environment. While this finding serves to support current child protective policies which prohibit contact outside the professional context between professionals and the children with whom they work, it does suggest that policy adherence needs to be both monitored and reinforced. Of concern, typically, professional perpetrators who had children of their own used them as a cover for the sexual abuse of other children.

Grooming activity by the offender focused on two groups of people: the victim and others who might protect the child or hinder the abuse in some way. Grooming functioned in three discrete ways. The first related to *manipulating perception*, of the child or other adults, as central to achieving their goal; *creating opportunities* to be sexual with children; and *preventing suspicion, discovery or disclosure* of the abuse. Perhaps because of the context in which they were offending, professional perpetrators generally appeared to be more intricate and in some cases almost convoluted in their planning and execution of sexually manipulative behaviour than other sexual offenders. The manipulation, or grooming techniques, used by professional perpetrators varied considerably depending upon their perception of their strengths and qualities and how these would be perceived by others. The context within which they were abusing was also found to be important and professional perpetrators often modified and adapted their grooming behaviour depending upon the environment. In addition, the degree to which the behaviour was instinctive or premeditated appeared to differ within the cohort. While both were in existence, it seemed likely, from the accounts given, that the more sophisticated and complex manipulations were deliberate and calculated.

MANIPULATION STYLES

Within this sample, professional perpetrators employed a number of different ploys to groom the children in their care. In examining these ploys it was possible to see a range of different manipulation styles that were used to achieve their goals with targeted children and other people who might seek to protect them. The way in which a manipulation or grooming ploy was delivered was found to be as important as the ploy itself. Manipulation styles could not be identified as being associated with any specific motivation to offend, although future research could explore the degree to which distortions and abuse supportive cognitions are predictive of a manipulation style. If any such predictive capability were established it could in turn be used to improve the selection and monitoring of those who choose to work with children.

Research with police interviews has shown that offenders will typically attempt to influence how people interpret their behaviour, generating potentially self-serving testimonies (Benneworth, 2009; Lippert, Cross, Jones, and Walsh, 2010). This is a self-protection mechanism and is often described as denial (Harkins, Beech, and Goodwill, 2010). At interview, understanding the manipulation styles employed by the subject offers an understanding of their behavioural patterns which can be useful at several levels. First it provides the interviewer with insight into the likely experience of the child victim and may explain why they are behaving in a particular manner. Second, it may also provide access to the offender's motivation and the component elements of their fantasy world. As important, however, is the insight which understanding the manipulation styles of a subject offers the interviewers into how they are likely to be manipulated by the subject in interview. This is because people tend to default to their preferred manipulation styles. Hence there is a predictive element to understanding manipulation styles which can help interviewers decide on the approach to any given subject which is most likely to work.

This research identified five primary manipulation styles, each with a variety of methods of delivery:

- Integrity Manipulation Style
- Intimidating Manipulation Style
- Suffering Manipulation Style
- Liberal Manipulation Style
- Blocking Manipulation Style

INTEGRITY MANIPULATION STYLE

The most common Manipulation Style described involved participants presenting themselves as a person of integrity who was beyond suspicion. It seemed that the objective was to gain the trust and confidence of victims and others and often involved presenting themselves as altruistic, magnanimous and kind. Participants spoke of ensuring others witnessed them engaged in good works in the hope it would be broadly communicated and thus become an accepted part of their public persona. Those who used this style often invoked the support of other adults in order to bolster their image and to support them in the denial of any inappropriate behaviour.

It is perhaps not surprising that all of the participants reported using this *Integrity Manipulation* style, as the associated characteristics are often common and desirable amongst professionals who work with children. There were many examples of participants presenting themselves as good people; however, Alan described an interesting variation. He admitted to parents of intended victims that he had previously been convicted of sexually abusing children. He then followed up with assurances that he did not pose a risk to their children and persuaded them to trust him, saying:

> 'I'd even admit to the parents that I'd been convicted of a sexual offence but convince them that I was different now having learned [to control my behaviour] from prison, probation and treatment [programmes].'

INTIMIDATING MANIPULATION STYLE

The intimidation manipulation style was presented by participants in three different forms. Each approached the process of intimidation in diverse ways and were categorised as:

- Aggressive
- Insidious Controlling
- Overt Controlling

Aggressive

Aggressiveness as an *Intimidating Manipulation Style* was more commonly used with victims rather than potentially protective others. Some participants described the direct use of threats to prevent detection of the abuse. Bob was the most consistent in his use of threats with his victims. The majority of his victims were infants who were not yet able to speak, although he did continue to abuse children over a number of years as in the case of the three-year-old girl and a five-year-old boy he was babysitting for in the description below:

> 'I told her to lay [sic] on the bed, which she did reluctantly, then she called for her brother, who came in, he flew at me from the doorway with fists flying. He said

"Leave my sister alone, leave my sister alone!" I managed to grab his hands and shouted at him to get back to his room or he would be next. I remember him looking at his sister and his sister looking at him, the exchange of eyes, there was no exchange of words, but the eyes said it all, 'I'm sorry I can't help you'. So he went back to his room. I shut the door and I continued to abuse his sister.'

When asked how he felt about seeing the look of resignation in the eyes of the children Bob said he found it highly arousing, as he believed he had *'won'*. He estimated he had sexually abused between 80 and 100 children in the context of his nursery care and babysitting work, with offences ranging from touching genitals to penetration.

Insidious controlling

The term *Insidious Controlling* was used to categorise the behaviours of those participants who appeared to approach life as though it were a game of strategy, second-guessing the moves of others, devising and performing tactics to lure them into the most advantageous mindset or position. In most cases, this style involved presenting the world with one image of themselves (most often the *Integrity Projection*), while also creating a cognitive dissonance by conveying an underlying nastiness that could not be challenged easily. The efforts Chris put into creating and maintaining a confidence trick, which ultimately trapped his victims into believing they were responsible for the sexual activity, generated much arousal for him. Chris stated:

'An awful lot of that is what gave me the buzz, that I had control, the manipulation over that particular person. Even days before, I knew exactly every move that boy was going to do. I could drool over the excitement of what was going to happen and I'm not sure if it was only to do with sex. I think an awful lot of it was the power and manipulation I would have. He thought I was helping him but I knew everything that was going to happen in that session!'

The process of discussing potential sexual contact with a child victim appeared to be used by Chris to normalise the behaviour and to make the victim feel a part of the process.

Overt controlling

Those who appeared to use what will be referred to as the *Overt Manipulation* style were directive and explicit in their controlling of victims and others. Often this style seemed to be built upon the portrayal of a superiority which in many cases was intrinsically linked to the power differential between the professional service provider and the service users. The *Overt Manipulation* style seemed to work most effectively where others felt they had something to lose or that the professional was perceived as a higher authority. Having encouraged his son to invite school friends to their home, Alan presented as a stern authoritarian to the children to ensure they behaved in the manner he wished. In this case, Alan rewarded compliance with his authority to reinforce the message that he was in control.

SUFFERING MANIPULATION STYLE

Many participants spoke of presenting themselves as undervalued martyrs who often needed sympathy, support and help from others. The *Suffering Manipulation Style* often involved the participant presenting themselves as the injured party. When using this manipulation with intended victims the participants would often present themselves as troubled by their weakness yet unable to resist temptation. Some participants indicated that they volunteered to undertake extra tasks and then drew attention to the fact they were overworked. David attempted to gain sympathy from the victim and highlighted the fact that he was held in high esteem because he worked so hard, thereby encouraging the victim to think that they would not be believed, stating:

> 'In most cases I would "share" aspects of my life with them by telling them how busy I was, overworked, misunderstood, lonely. … I would go on to tell them that without their friendship, understanding, support, etc I would not do what I did for everyone.'

LIBERAL MANIPULATION STYLE

Most of the study participants presented themselves as broad-minded and liberal in their attitudes generally and to sex in particular. Eric disguised his sexual abuse of children as homosexuality and encouraged children he abused to explore their sexuality. Having prompted a child to kiss him he would then use the boy's inquisitiveness as a justification for the further sexualisation of the encounter. Eric spoke of showing his victim homosexual pornography and sex aids as a way of intriguing him and further sexualising the relationship, describing the process as follows:

> 'I started with sexually arousing touches and by showing [victim's name] some porn pictures. I also took him to a sex sauna when we were on holidays. I used a vibrator on him a few times. The abuse would involve kissing him sexually on the mouth and masturbating him, both oral and manual masturbation with him over three years. Later it progressed to acts of buggery on him on two or three occasions.'

Other participants described being liberal in their interpretation of organisation rules or, in the case of the Faith community leaders, church doctrine when they felt this would communicate an impression which was helpful for them.

BLOCKING MANIPULATION STYLE

The *Blocking Manipulation Style* was presented by participants in three different forms. Each approached the process of intimidation in diverse ways and were categorised as:

- Obstructing
- Jesting
- Confounding

Obstructing

Examples of participants attempting to shut out any significant interactions with those perceived as likely to impede or present as a threat were categorised as the *Obstructing within the Blocking Manipulation Style* manipulation style. Participants who used this manipulation often excluded themselves from adult relationships or presented as private, distant or at times aloof. Others ignored the responses of those they were seeking to manipulate and carried on as though there was no issue. Frank explained how he prevented the disclosure of the abuse by using silence. Acting as though everything was normal and making no reference to the abusive behaviour as it was being perpetrated was a powerful way of silencing the victim. He stated:

> 'I invited the lad to sit on my lap. I touched his penis while he was on my lap, nothing was said. It was all done in silence.'

Jesting

Participants who encouraged others to view them as fun and risqué while minimising the perceived seriousness of their behaviour were categorised as using the *Jesting* manipulation style. This manipulation style was most commonly used to introduce or normalise a sexual content in conversations/activities. Gary would use sexual jokes as part of a gradual process of sexualisation with boys he was intending to sexually abuse, describing his strategy as follows:

> 'My next step would be to introduce sexualised humour to see if they laughed and gauge their level of responsiveness and check out how vulnerable they were.'

David spoke of using sexual innuendo to manipulate others as well as the victims. This manipulation style was also used to encourage children and adults to view the participant as fun to be with.

Confounding

Another common approach to the manipulation of children and others described by participants was to create confusion around their behaviour or intentions. In what will be referred to as the *Confounding*, participants used ambiguous behaviour and words to distract, deflect and confuse. Howard spoke of how he engaged one of his victims in protracted debates about homosexuality; occasionally weaving into the discussions issues which he wanted the boy to pick up on. This ultimately left the victim confused. Howard also used several different and often contradictory *Manipulation Styles* to generate confusion for his victims. By using at times a *Liberal Manipulation S*tyle on one issue and a dogmatic *Intimidation Manipulation S*tyle on others he created an uncertainty for them about where he stood on any given issue.

CONCLUSIONS

Demonising child abusers makes us less effective in child protection (Finkelhor, 2003). Better understanding the offender and the nature of the risk they pose are essential steps towards more effective safeguarding of children. Despite the fact that professionals who sexually abuse children within the context of their work are drawn from a narrow range of the child molester population they still represent a highly heterogeneous group whose motivations for sexually offending are varied and whose manipulations are diverse.

Typically, they are aware of their sexual interest in children before they join the organisation within which they will abuse. They use the automatic and unquestioned status and authority afforded them by their professional role to facilitate the sexual abuse of children. In addition, Faith communities need to be aware of the extent to which clergy child sex abusers can use the spiritual dimension of their work to further facilitate the sexual abuse of children. The public behaviour of child abusers is often indistinguishable from that of non-abusive colleagues. In addition, recognising that abusers' manipulations can manifest in a variety of forms may go some way to explain why it is so difficult to identify the behaviour of a potentially abusive employee. Further exploration of *Manipulation Styles* could offer greater clarity and improve our understanding of child abuser behaviour.

The enhanced understanding of professional perpetrators offered by this study raises several implications for employers and institutions involved with children. The findings affirm the importance of child protection policies which restrict the contact between employees and the children with whom they work. As contact with children outside the work environment was the primary technique used by participants in the study for facilitating the sexual abuse of children clear contractual boundaries are required. These conditions of service need to be broad enough to cover all forms of communication including text, email and social networking websites. They also need to be regularly reviewed and adapted to encompass emerging areas of vulnerability. This aspect of policies and procedures is likely to present a considerable challenge for agencies and institutions that traditionally rely on the goodwill and volunteering from staff to undertake additional tasks. A strong 'culture of safety' and ethos of accountability within an organisation does protect children. As many of the participants spoke of undermining these policies to create the opportunity to sexually abuse children it is important that all staff and service users recognise the need for such policies and understand how inappropriate behaviour can be questioned. It is important that employees and service users accept that assuming anyone could represent a risk to children does not mean that organisations do not value and respect people. Whistle-blowing remains a fraught and unpopular course of action and participants cited examples of how they used the adversarial nature of the disciplinary procedures to personalise the issue, marginalise the accuser and encourage others to take sides.

Police checks do provide a minimum standard in the evaluation of the risk posed by a potential employee. However, as none of the study participants had previous convictions prior to joining the organisations within which they worked and subsequently sexually abused children such checks are limited in the assurances they offer. The ongoing supervision and monitoring of staff should include an evaluation of the degree to which the staff member's behaviour conforms to and supports the culture of safety. Some specialist law enforcement agencies in North America have chosen to use the polygraph as an independent evaluation of risk within their selection and evaluation procedures for staff. The deployment of such an intrusive technique is unlikely to become part of the mainstream selection procedures for those wishing to work with children in the UK due to the human rights and resource implications. Consequently, selection procedures will need to build upon the existing approaches available to employers. No single procedure is likely to offer a conclusive guarantee that someone is either safe or unsafe to work with children. The use of value and belief-based interviews, however, is supported by the findings of this study and can be used to complement the psychometric evaluations currently available.

The degree to which participants used their status as a professional working with children to gain access to children in other child-focused settings raises concerns about the automatic assumption of suitability traditionally afforded to them. Voluntary organisations will need to satisfy themselves that each candidate is suitable irrespective of previous qualifications, status or experience.

Further research will be required to determine if a more sophisticated set of psychometric measures or methodologies for analysing the personalities of potentially dangerous adults can be created to enhance current child protection procedures. An emerging trend from the recent police investigations into internet-facilitated sexual abuse of children has shown significant numbers of professionals, who work with children, offending in this way. Future research should explore this type of sexual offending by professional perpetrators as it will be important to understand the potential risk posed by those who collect indecent images of children who also work with children.

In conclusion, this chapter has focused on a small yet significant group of professionals who have used their positions of authority to gain access to children in order to sexually molest them. It is important to keep perspective on the issue of risk and recognise that the vast majority of professionals work-ing with children are dedicated and devoted individuals. By better understand-ing professionals who sexually abuse the children with whom they work a more effective and realistic response to the risk they present can be forged.

MULTI DISCIPLINARY ISSUES

Currently there would appear to be a lack a consistency within and between agencies responsible for assessing and managing risk in cases of child sexual exploitation. One possible explanation for this lies in the language used by professionals to describe the issues they need to focus on within specific cases. The language of health professionals, police, and probation will reflect the con-text and focus of their disciplines, leading to confusion and even contradiction between professionals and agencies which can blur the safeguarding agenda. Were professionals in this area to adopt a more consistent language and focus for the assessment of those accused of sexual crimes against children the task of protecting children would become less complex.

FUTURE DIRECTIONS

More exploration of those who sexually abuse children within the course of their work is required to better understand the factors which might distinguish them from professions who do not pose a risk to children. The use of different and perhaps more specifically targeted psychometric measures may have shown more clearly identifiable differences between the professional perpetra-tors and other child sex abusers. It is hoped that this study will offer insights which will assist future research in developing and/or selecting psychometric instruments which target relevant aspects of professional perpetrators' person-alities. This could lead to early identification of unsuitable candidates applying for posts giving them access to children.

Analysis of the responses of participants suggests they used their inherent strengths and abilities in choosing their manipulation styles, although this asso-ciation will need further research to establish the level of consistency among this group of child abusers and a broader spectrum of abusers. This study iden-tified the potential link between *Life Theories* acquired and the manipulation style subsequently developed by participants. The parameters of this study did not allow for a more elaborate exploration of this possible association. This is an area which will need further research in order to establish whether a rela-tionship actually exists between the two factors. If this was found to be the case it might suggest areas which future psychometric evaluation could target in seeking to identify potentially dangerous applicants for work with children.

In the context of other future research there may be a benefit in creating a more comprehensive list of the grooming behaviours used by professional perpetrators. These manipulations may be helpful in shaping future employee selection procedures and organisational child protection policies.

REFERENCES

BBC News 19 January (2011). *Vatican Officials Told Irish Not to Report Child Abuse.* Available online at http://www.bbc.co.uk/news/world-europe-12222612.

Benneworth, K. (2009) Police interviews with suspected pedophiles: a discourse analysis. *Discourse Society*, 20, 555–569.

Bolton, G. (2005). *Reflective Practice*. London, Sage.

Collins, M. and Woollons, R. (2008) Childhood sexual experience and adult offending: an exploratory comparison of three criminal groups. *Child Abuse Review*, 17, 2, 119–132.

Finkelhor, D. (2003). The legacy of clergy abuse scandal. *Child Abuse and Neglect*, 27, 1225–1229.

Gannon, T.A., Keown, K. and Rose, M.R. (2009) An Examination of Current Psychometric Assessments of Child Molesters' Offense-Supportive Beliefs Using Ward's Implicit Theories. *Int J Offender Ther Comp Criminol* 53, 316–333.

Gannon, T.A., Ward, T. and Collie, R. (2007) Cognitive distortions in child molesters: theoretical and research developments over the past two decades. *Aggression and Violent Behavior* 12(4): 402–416.

Harkins, L., Beech, A.R. and Goodwill, A.M. (2010) Examining the influence of denial, motivation, and risk on sexual recidivism. *Sexual Abuse: A Journal of Research and Treatment*, 22(1), 78–94.

Held, J. (2009) *A Serious Case Review of Child Sexual Abuse at Stony Dean School, Buckinghamshire: executive summary report: a chapter 8 report for: Buckinghamshire Safeguarding Children's Board and Buckinghamshire County Council.* London: Verita.

Langevin, R. Curnoe, S., and Bain, J. (2000). A study of clerics who commit sexual offenses: Are they different from other sex offenders. *Child Abuse and Neglect*, 4, 535–545.

Lippert, T., Cross, T.P., Jones, L., and Walsh, W. (2010) Suspect confession of child sexual abuse to investigators. *Child Maltreatment*, 15(2), 161–170.

Maxwell, J.A. (1996). *Qualitative Research Design: An interactive approach.* London: Sage.

Sullivan, J and Beech, A. (2004) A comparative study of demographic data relating to intra and extra-familial child sexual abusers and professional perpetrators. *Journal of Sexual Aggression.* 1, 39–50.

Sullivan, J., Beech, A. R., Craig, L., and Gannon, T. (2010) Comparing intra-familial and extra-familial child sexual abusers with professionals who have sexually abused children with whom they work. *International Journal of Offender Therapy and Comparative Criminology*, 1–19.

Ward, T., Hudson, S.M., Johnson, L. and Marshall, W.L. (1997). Cognitive distortions in sex offenders: An integrative review. *Clinical Psychology Review*, 17, 479–507.

Ward, T. and Hudson, S. M. (1998). The construction and development of theory in the sexual offending area: A meta-theoretical framework. *Sexual Abuse: A Journal of Research and Treatment*, 10, 47–63.

6 Organisational Issues and New Technologies

Ethel Quayle

AN EVOLVING ISSUE

The word 'cyberspace' was coined by the science fiction author William Gibson in 1984 in his attempt to find a name to describe a vision of a global computer network, linking all people, machines and sources of information in the world, and through which one could move or 'navigate' as through a virtual space (Gibson, 1984). The reality of what cyberspace has become opens up infinite new possibilities and with the right equipment, technical knowledge and inclination it is possible to go on a global shopping spree with someone else's credit card, break into a bank's security system, plan a demonstration in another country and hack into the Pentagon–all on the same day (Jewkes and Sharpe, 2002).

For most people the internet has grown during the last decade from a curiosity used by relatively few to an essential element of everyday life. In March 2010 the BBC reported that almost four in five people around the world believe that access to the internet is a fundamental right, with countries such as Finland and Estonia already having declared that access is a human right for their citizens (BBC News, 2010). Internet usage statistics for June 2010 indicated that nearly 60% of all Europeans and 77% of North Americans had access to the internet, a growth in Europe of 352% since 2000 (Internet World Stats, 2010).

Regrettably it has also become apparent that technology-mediated crime includes activities that target children in abusive and exploitative ways. It is perhaps not surprising that the World Report on Violence against Children (Pinheiro, 2006) identified cyberspace as one of the many social spaces which children occupy frequently and where they are both vulnerable and require

Creating Safer Organisations: Practical Steps to Prevent the Abuse of Children by Those Working with Them, First Edition. Edited by Marcus Erooga.
© 2012 John Wiley & Sons, Ltd. Published 2012 by John Wiley & Sons, Ltd.

protection. One conclusion of the UK Government commissioned Byron Review into 'Children and New Technologies', was that 'In relation to the internet we need a shared culture of responsibility with families, industry, government and others in the public and third sectors all playing their part to reduce the availability of potentially harmful material, restrict access to it by children and to increase children's resilience' (Byron, 2008, p. 2).

This chapter considers some of the situations in which technology may be used in ways which are harmful to children in organisational settings It begins by looking at examples that made the news in 2009 and 2010 and where these fit in our thinking about harms against children before considering specifically the production and sharing of abusive images, commonly referred to as 'child pornography'. The chapter further considers the characteristics of people who offend and the organisational contexts that offer opportunity for such offences to take place. It concludes with consideration of what can be done to create safer organisations in relation to these new technologies.

TECHNOLOGY IN THE WORKPLACE

For many of us technology use has become so routine that it blurs the boundaries between different aspects of our lives, such as work and social activity, and it is now difficult to imagine a world without technology-mediated communication. These fuzzy boundaries create considerable challenges for organisations with an increasing concern about 'cyberloafing' (Blanchard and Henle, 2008) – the use of the internet at work for personal reasons rather than solely for work-related tasks. This might include sending emails to family and friends, reading the online news, shopping or checking for inexpensive holidays. Weatherbee (2010) has suggested that as these technologies grow in capability, speed and connectivity so misuse in organisational settings develops in ever more novel ways and a wide range of behaviours evolve in tandem with enabling technology. Few would have thought that the use of SMS and Twitter would have become so all-pervasive, with sites such as 'Tweetminster' (http://tweetminster.co.uk/) encouraging us to 'Keep track and interact with the people, the conversations and the issues that are shaping current affairs right now....'

It also seems that the permeability of these boundaries means that behaviours learned or practiced in one domain can be expected to cross over into the other, posing an escalating challenge to the prevention and management of cyberdeviant behaviours in organisations (Weatherbee, 2010). This becomes more challenging because the geographical and physical boundaries that might have traditionally 'contained' some behaviours have largely disappeared. Abusive practices with origins in the workplace can now easily be maintained outside of that context. For example, a member of school staff who makes inappropriate sexual comments to a pupil and followed these with texts to a mobile phone, comments posted on a social networking site and so on. It might also be the case that the reverse may be true with increasing concern over the content of sites such as RateMyTeacher.com.

Technology affords opportunities for all those in organisations to engage not only in behaviour which is problematic in terms of child protection but which also challenge the respect and dignity of those who are employed. The potential for such behaviour should not be underestimated. In 2010 the *Guardian* newspaper reported that a female teacher had found out that an ex-student had created a group for people to join if they thought she was 'still a virgin' (guardian.co.uk, 2010). In another case 650 Facebook users joined a group called 'Ban Andrea Charman from Teaching Anywhere', and ultimately hounded the headmistress from her post after primary school pupils were told of a plan to slaughter a school lamb as part of a farming project (*Sunday Times*, 2010). Steps taken to prevent the technology-mediated abuse of children by those who work with them may also provide a safer workplace for employees.

Some of these technology related problems can be illustrated with reference to a recent UK case which attracted considerable media attention. Vanessa George was a nursery worker jailed in December 2009 for an indeterminate period for sexually abusing children in her care and exchanging images that she took of the abuse with two other people, one of them another woman (Plymouth Safeguarding Children Board, 2010). George, a mother of two, used a mobile phone that she called her 'fun phone' to take pictures of herself abusing children at Little Ted's Nursery in Plymouth and exchanged more than 7,000 texts, photographs and calls with her two co-defendants over a sixth-month period (*The Times*, 2009). The initial contact with one of her co-defendants, Colin Blanchard, was made on a Facebook page called 'Are You Interested?' and was followed by a request for her to send pictures of children with whom she worked. She responded initially by sending pictures of herself changing babies' nappies, but these later included images of real, or simulated, penetration of children with objects. The Court was told that mobile phones were not allowed in the nursery but that the rules had been relaxed because the in-house phone was unreliable. This case in part attracted attention because the person involved was female and the abuse was of very young children. It further challenged common stereotypes of sex offenders because she was married with children and had no previous criminal history. An extract from a (internet) Yahoo Discussion Forum in 2009 captures some of these issues:

> 'When you work in a nursery the last thing you think of is that one of your colleagues is a paedophile. Also it is easily done to do what she did. Nursery nurses who have been police checked (not foolproof as this case proves because she had no previous convictions) are free to take children to the toilet and change nappies. As she had access to a mobile my guess is that's when she did it. The nursery where I worked did not allow any mobile phones on the premises unless they were in your handbag and in a staff room locker' (Yahoo Discussion Forum (2009) at uk.answers.yahoo.com).

Technology facilitated offending cases are not uncommon. In 2009 a music teacher was given a jail sentence within a UK court for having a sexual relationship with a fifteen-year-old pupil that included sending sexualised texts and nude pictures of himself via his mobile phone (Mail Online, 2010). In the United States ABC News America reported in April 2010 the case of a swimming coach who secretly taped teenage girls in two high school pool changing rooms, having directed them to a 'special' shower room where he had hidden a camera inside a locker. Abusive practices relating to images are also not confined to photographs taken of children and young people but also the exposure of young people to images of adults. In October 2010 an American teacher pleaded guilty to sending four pictures of herself with her genitals exposed to a 15-year-old pupil via her mobile phone. She also sent text messages detailing sexual acts that she wanted to perform with him. She was identified not because the student made a disclosure but because he forwarded the images to his friends (*Huffington Post*, 27.7.10).

A simple way of categorising technology-mediated abusive acts in the workplace might discriminate between those that involve the use of technology to commit the abuse against children within the immediate physical environment and acts that exploit opportunities within the workplace to act in ways which are illegal and involve children more remotely. Examples of the former might include the use of digital cameras or mobile phones to take abusive or exploitative images of children whilst the latter might include using a work computer to download illegal material or to groom children for abuse. The next sections outline some of the technology mediated sexual acts increasingly causing concern within organisations.

ABUSIVE IMAGES

The majority of studies concerning children whose sexualised images are available through the internet describe such material as 'child pornography' (Akdeniz, 2008; Lanning, 2008). This has been contested by child advocacy groups such as Save the Children (e.g. Jones and Skogrand, 2005) who favour the term 'abuse images' to avoid minimising the seriousness of the material, in that these are not youthful equivalents of adult pornography but actual images of children being abused. For those who have not viewed such material, it can be difficult to fully understand the nature of the images commonly accessed. A study by Wolak, Finkelhor and Mitchell (2005) of 1,713 arrests for relevant offences in the USA gives some further understanding of the nature of what is being viewed. Nineteen per cent of the arrests involved images of children younger than 3 years; 39% images of children 3–5 years; 83% images of children 6–12 years; 17% had images exclusively of children younger than 13 years and 75% images of children 13–17 years old. 92% had images focusing on genitals or explicit sexual activity and 80% images showing sexual penetration including oral sex. Twenty-one per cent had images depicting bondage, rape or torture. Most of these involved images of children gagged, blindfolded or otherwise subject to sadistic sexual acts. A further account is provided by the Canadian Centre for Child Protection (Bunzeluk, 2009) of 15,662 websites hosting child pornography. When selecting images to assess, each site was viewed by an analyst who chose the image that depicted the most severe abuse against the youngest child. The results from this study indicated that 35.9% of the images depicted sexual assaults against a child, 57.4% depicted children under eight years and 83% of the images were of female children.

Interest in abuse images is far from new, although technological advances, such as photography, has democratised their availability. Edwards (1994) describes the popularity of explicit 'erotic scenes' depicting children in the 1800s and noted that postcards of girl children far outnumbered those of adult 'pin-ups', and resulted in occasional seizures by police. Adler (2001) dates the recognition of child pornography as a societal problem to the late 1970s and this is certainly reflected in the increase of legislation from this time in countries such as the USA (Adler, 2008). The advent of internet technology lowered the cost of the production of these images, dramatically increased their availability and reduced the risk of detection that was associated with the criminalisation of production and possession (Taylor and Quayle, 2003; Adler, 2008). The result, as Middleton, Elliott, Mandeville-Norden and Beech's (2006) observe is that the internet combines 24 hour, 7 day a week access, and affordability with free material of their choice available to knowledgeable users and anonymity, thus 'increasing the user's sense of freedom, pace and ... willingness to experiment' (p. 589).

There is little information about the children whose images have been uploaded onto the internet (Quayle and Jones, 2011) but it is known that image production, exchange and downloading is a serious problem, in terms of the impact that it may have on the child or children in the photograph (Quayle, Lööf, and Palmer, 2008).

The spectrum of such images on the internet includes:

• A child abused by a contact offence and pictures taken of that abuse but not distributed.
• A child abused by a contact offence and pictures taken of that abuse and distributed.
• A child photographed (where there is no contact offence) without distribution.
• A child photographed (where there is no contact offence) with distribution.

A further continuum relates to how much knowledge the child might have of the fact that photographs have been taken. At one end is the child who is sexually abused and who is made aware that this abuse is being photographed. At the other end of the continuum is the child who is unaware that someone is using a hidden camera to take pictures. Until recently taking photographs of children involved risks with both developing and storage with cameras that were large, visible and usually required the film to be taken to a photographic shop or chemist. However with digital technology cameras can be easily hidden and images from devices such as mobile phones without them being seen by anyone else. In 2010 a Birmingham man was convicted of taking pictures of students using a hidden camera placed inside an air freshener (*Prokerala News*, 2010).

SEXTING

Sexting refers to the use of the camera built in to mobile phones to produce and distribute images of oneself, or another, in a sexually provocative or revealing position. Sexting is becoming increasingly common amongst young people with, for example, sexual pictures being sent between girlfriends and boyfriends (Corbett, 2009). Research in the United States suggests that sexting often involves: the exchange of images exclusively between romantic partners; images that have been exchanged between romantic partners which are shared with others outside the relationship, and the exchange of images where at least one person would like to start a romantic relationship (Lenhart, 2009). Images produced for 'sexting' can also be distributed to unintended third parties, often leading to embarrassment and harassment. Moreover, senders are also in danger of being charged with possession and distribution of child pornography, regardless of the fact that they may be minors and the pictures are of themselves (Zhang, 2010).

Whilst such image exchange between young people is problematic, sexting can also take place between adults and children. This may include:

• sexual images of a child sent to the same child;
• sexual images of a child sent to another child;
• sexual images of a known adult sent to a child.

This may be as part of a grooming process or indeed used coercively to secure a child's co-operation by threat of distributing the images more widely.

GROOMING

Grooming refers here to an adult with a sexual interest in children contacting a child and gaining their trust for the purpose of meeting them and engaging in sexual behaviour (Kierkegaard, 2008). As the law changes to try to keep pace with the opportunities that the internet affords for offending activities, so do definitions of illegal behaviours and content In the UK the Sexual Offences Act 2003 created an offence that included grooming, the purpose of which was to identify preparatory behaviour that could be criminalised before the offender had the opportunity to sexually abuse a child. The offence requires an offender to have met or communicated with a child on two or more occasions and subsequently to meet or travel to meet a child with the intention in either case of having sexual contact with a child (Gillespie, 2006). The legislation in part grew out of a series of high-profile cases where an adult had used the internet to 'groom' children for 'offline abuse'.

STALKING

Stalking encompasses a range of behaviours initiated by an individual who engages in a pattern of harassing or threatening behaviour. Originally identified as an 'offline' behaviour it is increasingly identified as an 'online' or cyberspace activity. Alexy, Burgess, Baker and Smoyak (2005) suggest that the ability of an online stalker to instil fear and gain control over a victim reflects the modus operandi of an offline stalker, although it might be argued that the anonymity afforded by the internet and the possibility of engaging in stalking activity by use of information provided by the child impacts on the ease with which this crime is committed. It also is clear that such stalking behaviour may include a range of behaviour from sending sexualised texts via a mobile phone to taking control of another person's computer account.

ADULT PORNOGRAPHY

There is considerable debate as to the harm posed by exposing a child to adult pornographic materials (e.g. Livingstone, 2010), but in the main this is with reference to children being exposed to material that does not target them, as in photographs taken for an adult audience which children come across or access deliberately. Targeting a child by sending adult pornographic materials as an email attachment or exposing them to pornography through an internet web site is an intentional act which might be part of a grooming process in that it serves as a way to engage the child and normalises sexualised material.

MISUSE OF SOCIAL MEDIA

Kaplan and Haenlein (2010) discuss some social media that may have relevance for organisations. These include:

- Blogs – online diaries or personal websites. While initially text-based, increasingly they involve sound (podcasting) and video blogs (vlogs).
- Collaborative projects (such as rankmyteacher.com, Wikipedia and Delicious) allow a community to develop: Wikis (web pages that allow users to modify text-based content), and social bookmarking (users collect, and rate websites or share bookmarks).

- Content communities (such as Youtube and Flickr) allow the sharing of media (documents, videos, audio, images).
- Social networking sites (such as Facebook, Myspace and Twitter) allow to the creation of a personal profile and to interact with other users through chat, sharing photos, applications, and micro-blogging (short 144-character messages that can be linked to the user's geographical location).
- Virtual social worlds (such as Sims and Second Life): here users create avatars to represent themselves and interact in a 3D virtual environment.
- Virtual game worlds (such as World of Warcraft) allow players from across the world to play in online game worlds.

It is apparent that these social media can be used by staff within organisations to compromise the safety of children. A staff member having a profile on a social networking site that identifies their occupation and place of work, and online chat with known and unknown individuals about children within an organisation are examples, as are inappropriate internet use by an employee which leaves content on a computer used by children. For example, there was a media report of a teacher who named a child on Facebook and mocked her for crying when sent to 'sit under the thinking tree'. These comments were seen by the child's parents (*The Metro*, 2010).

THE INDIVIDUAL AND ORGANISATIONAL ABUSE

It would be reassuring to think that employees who present a risk for technology-mediated abusive practices towards children are readily identifiable. However, although commonly described as 'paedophiles', as with others who sexually offend against children they appear to be a diverse group displaying a range of behaviours, which may, or may not, be underpinned by a primary sexual interest in children (e.g. Seto, 2010). Research interest has largely focused on people who use, distribute or produce abusive images of children. There is very little research in relation to online grooming and even less to do with the exchange of text based material, such as fantasy stories or scripts. It is also important to acknowledge that online sexual activity is normative behaviour for many people in the Western World (Döring, 2009), and includes using the internet to access: pornography; sex shops; sex work; sex education; sex contacts and sex subcultures. Such activities may be regarded as having a poor fit with the values needed to work with children, but they are not in themselves illegal and are unlikely be a topic for discussion in a usual job interview.

Early work by Cooper, Putnam, Planchon and Boies (1999) suggested that those who use the Internet for sexual activity can be divided into three broad categories. *Recreational users* for whom the internet is used to entertain or satisfy curiosity, and who experience no problems associated with this; the *sexually compulsive* who have pre-existing problems managing their sexual thoughts and behaviours and might find their symptoms made worse by the internet and *at-risk users*, who have no previous sexual difficulties but find that their online sexual behaviour creates problems in their lives.

Much of the existing research has focused on the individual as a problem and it is worth examining this in the light of what it indicates about organisational issues and new technologies. In their paper on Risk Assessment and Internet sex offenders Hanson and Babchishin (2009) suggest that a meta-analysis of relevant studies would indicate that one in eight convicted offenders are caught for both contact offences as well as internet related sexual offences and that one in two admit to both. They suggest a process model in which *attitudes* (a positive approach to paedophilia, being emotionally close to children, not viewing adult-child sexual activity as wrong and having a negative stake in conformity), *norms* (having deviant internet peers and an absence of prosocial influences), and *perceived control* (knowledge of the internet and increased self-efficacy) contribute to an intention to commit an offence. When this interacts with access to children and an absence of surveillance the likelihood of the commission of an offence is increased. This has similarities with other process models such as that proposed by Quayle and Taylor (2003) and Elliott and Beech (2009) which suggest that there is evidence that internet offenders use various online behaviours (which may or may not include the use of child abuse images) to address immediate problems related to interpersonal and emotional difficulties and that child abuse images are often used to fuel quite specific sexual fantasies. In the case of Vanessa George, newspaper reports suggested that possible motivations for her offences included dissatisfaction with her emotional and sexual life and a pursuit of risk-laden excitement (Harris and Salkeld, 2009).

Traditionally when recruiting staff for organisations child protection has been addressed by screening for, and excluding through disclosure of information, those with a known history of sexual offending. Quite rightly it has been assumed that previous problematic behaviour is a good predictor of future problematic behaviour. However, it is also known that those who commit technology facilitated sexual crimes against children are a heterogeneous group and that many have no previous criminal history (e.g. Seto, 2009). A recent study by Henry, Mandeville-Norden, Hayes and Egan (2010) was designed to see whether men convicted of viewing abuse images on the internet are divisible into the same 'clusters' as men who commit contact offences. Four hundred and twenty-two internet offenders were analysed on three psychometric tests assessing pro-offending attitudes and five measures assessing socio-affective functioning. Three corresponding clusters were obtained which were described as: normal; socially inadequate, and sexually deviant. People within the normal cluster looked similar to a normal population, although scored higher for social desirability than those in the other groups. The inadequate cluster demonstrated socio-affective difficulties, deficits in levels of self-esteem and emotional loneliness. The third cluster was labelled deviant because they had high scores on all three pro-offending measures. The largest cluster (164 men) fell into the normal group.

What can be concluded from existing research is that those who use the internet to commit sexual offences against children are more likely to have high scores on scales which assess 'impression management' (Middleton *et al.*, 2006; Bates and Metcalf, 2007; Henry *et al.*, 2010) and that a proportion of such offenders have socio-affective difficulties, showing problems with self-esteem and emotional loneliness. The work of Laulik, Allam and Sheridan (2007) has also indicated that internet offenders are likely to experience difficulties with interpersonal functioning and two-thirds of a sample of Swiss offenders were found to exhibit problematic internet use (Niveau, 2010).

What conclusions therefore can be drawn from this about safeguarding children in organisational settings? Clearly while screening and vetting procedures have an important role in excluding those who have a history of sexual crimes against children, they are of little help in identifying the majority of people who go on to commit technology facilitated crimes within organisations. Equally, employers are unlikely to have the resources to require employees to complete batteries of psychometric tests, and even if they did so it is likely that the majority who did so would not result in scores indicative of 'deviancy'. It might also be the case that 'impression management' increases the likelihood of people completing questionnaires in such a way to minimise sexual interests that might otherwise be seen to be problematic. However, in the case of Vanessa George, the Serious Case Review and press coverage of the trial suggested that changes were observed in her behaviour such that she had begun to spend more and more time on the computer and that there were changes in her levels of sexual interest within her marital relationship and in her engagement with her children and ordinary household tasks. This was also commented on by other staff and it was noted that, 'Her position of power within the staff group was such that although staff became increasingly concerned about her crude language, discussion of extra-marital relationships and showing indecent images of adults on her phone, they were unable to challenge her' (Plymouth Safeguarding Children Board, 2010). Changes in behaviour patterns in relation to technology use, including increased preoccupation with internet access and discussion of use of the internet for sexually recreational reasons may all be indicators for concern. However, creating safer organisations is unlikely to result solely from monitoring the personality or behavioural characteristics of employees.

SITUATIONAL FACTORS AND TECHNOLOGY MEDIATED ORGANISATIONAL ABUSE

A further approach to child protection focuses on the organisational environment rather than the individual and allows a consideration of situational perspectives on technology facilitated sexual crimes against children. As outlined in Chapter 8 a situational prevention approach suggests that while we all differ in our propensity to commit crimes, most people are capable of committing crime given the right set of circumstances if certain conditions are met (Wortley and Smallbone, 2006). Wortley and Smallbone suggest that the immediate environment can precipitate crime in four basic ways. Firstly by presenting cues that prompt an individual to commit a criminal act. Secondly by exerting a social pressure on the individual to offend. Thirdly by weakening moral constraints permitting potential offenders to commit an offence and finally by producing emotional arousal that provokes a criminal response. In addition, a rational choice perspective (Cornish and Clarke, 1986) suggests that offenders are active, purposeful, decision-makers who undertake cost-benefit analyses of criminal opportunities. Therefore, the immediate environment provides them with information regarding the potential costs, and benefits, of crime about which rational decisions to offend or not are made.

Technological change has clearly brought enormous benefits to all aspects of our lives, including the organisational contexts in which we work. However the internet does have characteristics that, whilst not making it an inevitable arena for crime, may change the expression of crime and facilitate its occurrence in the right circumstances (Taylor and Quayle, 2008). In relation to technology facilitated sexual crimes against children it might be argued that the internet may: alter mood; lessen social risk and inhibitions; enable multiple self-representations; show evidence of group dynamics; validate, justify and offer an exchange medium; challenge old concepts of regulation and disrupt and challenge conventional hierarchies (Quayle, Erooga, Wright, Taylor, and Harbinson, 2006). These might offer clues as to what may facilitate the expression of problematic sexual behaviour given the intention to commit a crime. Furthermore, the internet's 'triple A engine' of Accessibility, Affordability, and assumed Anonymity (Cooper, 1998) allows people to explore a wide range of situations with apparent anonymity and impunity, encouraging risk taking and enabling mood change – again, a more general contextual factor.

Taylor and Quayle (2006) describe how internet crime might be understood in terms of the 'rational choice' theory concepts of search, precriminal situations and opportunity (Cusson, 1993). In this sense the concept of 'search' refers to the individual seeking a suitable precriminal situation that will, contingent on some action, result in the commission of an offence. 'Precriminal situations' are the set of outside circumstances immediately preceding and surrounding the criminal event and making an offence more or less difficult, risky or profitable (Cusson, 1993). The precriminal situation is therefore the situation where the potential to commit an offence is present, depending on the activity and response of the potential offender. One criminogenic quality of the internet, at least with respect to abuse images of children (and other images as well), lies in the extraordinary ease with which an individual in a precriminal situation (a potential offender) can move to become an actual offender, through, for example pointing and clicking on a link on a web page. The same might be said of using a digital camera or camera phone, or clicking 'Send' having written an email or text based message. The sequences of choices and actions made by the offender during the criminal event, including use of available means to reach ends in a precriminal situation, are referred to as criminal tactics. Tactics are shaped by the precriminal situation, and reflect its situational context, and in particular in the situation of primary concern here, the affordance qualities of environmental cues. The possible sexual arousal that accompanies sexual behaviour involving children might also be thought of as a powerful motivational force and influence decision making, including the likelihood of taking risks (Boufford, 2002).

Brantingham and Frederic (1976) identify three kinds of crime prevention initiatives: primary prevention, which focuses on stopping a crime before it occurs; secondary prevention, which is directed at individuals thought to be at a high risk of committing an offence, and tertiary prevention which focuses on known offenders. Within the context of creating safer organisations it might be assumed that the only acceptable initiative is primary prevention, particularly as vetting procedures should have precluded the other two. Conventionally, primary prevention is divided into social preventative measures and situational preventative measures. Social preventative measures address the 'inclination' to offend, and are generally conceptualised in terms of educational initiatives, or in broad social engineering terms, where initiatives tend to be undifferentiated as to target group, and available to all regardless of risk.

Educational programmes promoting safer use of the internet may fall into this category. Finkelhor (2009) has suggested that 'as yet no true evidence-based programs or policies exist in the area of preventing child sexual abuse' (p. 170) but that there is some evidence of the efficacy of school-based educational programmes. This clearly has considerable relevance for some organisations that work directly with children. In the context of internet mediated crime, the majority of such educational programmes target children and encourage the use of reporting buttons when they are exposed to distressing or problematic content or behaviour. These results of such interventions are quite difficult to measure and their impact might be assumed to be long-term. For example, in evaluating the Child Exploitation has and Online Protection (CEOP) educational training package 'ThinkUKnow', Davidson, Martellozzo and Lorenz (2009) found that a high proportion of young people were unable to recall whether or not they had been part of the programme, and that recall of safety messages appeared to fade over time. Situational measures tend to be less general in their approach and more 'crime specific' and address the immediate environment where crime takes place and focus on reducing opportunity to offend and increasing perceived risk.

Cornish and Clarke (2003) in their typology of situational crime reduction techniques identify five broad categories: *increase effort; increase risk; reduce rewards; reduce provocation* and *remove excuses* and Kaufman, Hilliker and Daleiden (2006) have provided such a situational prevention model as a response to reducing the sexual abuse of children. It might be suggested that *increasing effort* might best be addressed through the involvement of the internet industry itself, seen or example in Internet Service Providers using a list of URLs known to be associated with problematic content to block access to certain web sites. A URL is a Uniform Resource Locator which specifies where a resource is available. The best-known example of the use of URLs is for the addresses of web pages on the World Wide Web, which appear at the top bar of the page, such as http://www.ed.ac.uk. For example the UK Office of Government Commerce (2010) has issued a procurement policy note which requires all Government departments to 'ensure that when specifying for internet related services they include a requirement to block access to web pages depicting child sexual abuse'. Currently there are debates as to whether States, rather than organisations, should be blocking content, although Akdeniz (2010) has argued that there could be a breach of Article 10 of the European Convention on Human Rights if blocking measures or filtering tools are used at state level to silence, for example, politically motivated speech on the internet. Article 10 of the European Convention on Human Rights protects the right to freedom of expression.

How therefore might situational crime reduction techniques be more immediately relevant to the organisations? Increasingly, organisations are adopting internet usage policies, management training and software packages to block employees' problematic use of technology. Software can be used to automatically monitor, filter and block content in the hope of reducing misuse by employees (either through wasting time or, for example, accessing sexualised or illegal content) or reducing accidental or intentional exposure of such content to children. Internet filtering software has been adopted by parents, schools, libraries and businesses to protect users' internet access on either private or public computers (Chou, Sinha, and Zhao, 2010). However, there have been few studies that have evaluated how effective these actually are. Hunter (2000) evaluated four popular commercial products (CYBERsitter, CyberPatrol, Net Nanny, and Surf Watch) in the context of objectionable or non-objectionable contents related to language, nudity, sex, and violence. Overinclusive blocking (incorrect blocking of allowed or appropriate content) and underinclusive blocking (incorrect passing of problematic content) error rates were reported. Hunter's evaluation showed that overinclusive blocking and underinclusive blocking error rates were 21% and 25%, respectively, based on the combined decision of the four filtering programmes. It might be concluded from this and other studies that such commercial products may not match the expectations of most organisations in managing content and may also make it difficult to access some relevant content. Chou *et al.* (2010) suggest that organisations might consider using a learning component into internet filters, so that they can learn from successes and failures. They give as an example the Barracuda Spam Firewall which allows a user to classify an email message as 'spam' or 'not spam', and, based on the feedback, adapts its future blocking behaviour. They also suggest a text-mining approach as a more sensitive alternative.

Increasing risk refers to making the individual more likely to be observed or detected when engaging problematically with children. This might be achieved through increasing the sense of external surveillance of employees and increasing external guardianship. One of the factors already noted about the problematic nature of technology facilitated abusive practices is the level of perceived anonymity afforded by the technology itself. Simple strategies such as placing desktop computers in a central and visible location may not preclude problematic behaviour such as accessing content or engaging in online grooming behaviour, but it does increase the inappropriate user's sense of risk. Similarly, having it known that random checks of emails and internet history or level of data transfer are made within the organisation may also increase perceived risk. Regular reminders about policies concerning camera phone use might be posted on walls (a strategy that has been used with other criminal and problematic behaviour), along with access to a handset that works (e.g. a payphone on the wall) to reduce the likelihood of breaches. Organisations working with children might also offer educational sessions to parents as well as staff reinforcing awareness of indicators both in care-givers and children that there may be something wrong.

Reducing rewards is more difficult to manage for some internet facilitated sexual behaviours towards children. For example, taking a photograph of a child, sending photographs to a child or engaging in online grooming or stalking behaviour may be associated with sexual arousal and be implicitly rewarding in themselves. However, Wortley and Smallbone (ibid) have suggested that providing information to children as to how they might formally complain and having regular inspections to see that procedures were being followed might serve to reduce the rewards associated with problematic sexual behaviour. *Reducing provocation* and *removing excuses* might be achieved through having clear compliance policies with regard to technology use that are reinforced by frequent meetings to discuss the same. The use of regular reminders may serve to alert the conscience of employees and undermine the ease of engagement with children in a problematic way. It may also be the case that accepting that there are individuals who are aware that their thoughts or feelings towards children are inappropriate and may lead to the commission of an offence against a child means that proactive interventions may have a place (Beier, Neutze, Mundt, Ahlers, Goecker, Konrad, and Schaefer, 2009). Organisations such as Stop It Now! (www.stopitnow. com) provide posters, handouts, information leaflets and a telephone helpline which 'aims to prevent child sexual abuse by raising awareness and encouraging early recognition and responses to the problem by abusers themselves and those close to them'. One of the problems associated with technology facilitated abusive practices is that prosocial norms may be undermined by engagement with online practices and communities and this may serve to promote offence supportive cognitions (O'Halloran and Quayle, 2010). Information which is visible that challenges abusive practices within organisations might act as a deterrent.

GUIDELINES ON CHILD PROTECTION POLICIES AND PROCEDURE IN RELATION TO TECHNOLOGY

Internet Use Policies (IUP) and Acceptable Use Policies (AUP) are adopted by many organisations to reduce internet use for non-work-related purposes. Young (2010) has suggested that, 'employees who use the internet during work hours, or extensive personal use, cost companies significant losses in job productivity and increase their risk or corporate liability'. It may be that of equal concern is misuse of technology that leaves children vulnerable to sexually abusive and exploitative practices. The response to such threats touches on many of the areas already considered and includes (Figure 6.1):

- screening for internet addiction;
- acceptable internet use policies;
- electronic monitoring of networks;
- filtering that blocked inappropriate websites;
- layered computer security to track employee internet use.

Case and Young (2001) outline a comprehensive theoretical framework to manage employee internet abuse explained as a range or continuum of approaches. The following is a reworking of that original model:

This framework suggests that policies should be the first level of prevention and would exclude some of the problems associated with screening beyond those of existing vetting procedures. The policy focus can take into account new digital technologies that keep pace with change and adds a component of employee training as a more aggressive way to communicate policies,

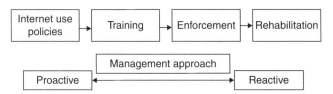

Figure 6.1 Framework for internet management from proactive to reactive approaches (from Young, 2010).

especially to people who are newly hired. A comparison is made to sensitivity training for sexual harassment or diversity training, all of which are designed to increase employee awareness of the issues, reduce the future occurrence and, from an organisational perspective, decrease corporate liability. Li, Zhang, and Sarathy (2010) argue that internet abuse in the workplace occurs in specific organisational contexts and that formal sanctions are important instruments for deterring deviant behaviours. They conclude that employees are more likely to abide by Internet Use Policies when they perceive a high likelihood of being caught for committing abuses of technology (similar to earlier arguments for increasing a sense of external surveillance). Li *et al.*'s (2010) research would suggest that increasing the probability of detection, as opposed to the severity of the sanction, increases compliance. Of relevance to child protection, specifically stating what is accepted and allowed within the organisation and what disciplinary measures will be taken for violations, appear to be central, (discussed further in Chapter 9).

Many organisations have developed guidelines for writing child protection policy and procedures, often derived from the NSPCC Keeping Children Safe Toolkit (Keeping Children Safe Coalition, 2006). Tool One outlines the basic standards for all organisations working in child protection. Tool Two provides guidance and activities to help organisations meet those standards and Tool Three provides flexible training exercises and materials to help organisations train staff to meet the standards. In Tool One organisations are asked to ensure that guidance exists on appropriate use of information technology such as the internet, websites, digital cameras, etc. to ensure that children are not put at risk. In Tool Two it is emphasised that if a staff member is suspected or found with abusive (pornographic) images of children on a computer or suspected of an internet crime, this should be reported to the police. Important aspects of the Toolkit in relation to technology facilitated problems can be summarised as:

- Any checklist for recruitment and selection should take account of what other sort of contact may the person have with children (such as email, letter, telephone and other internet protocols).
- Ensuring that there is a policy set of procedures for taking, using and storing photographs or images of children.
- Agreed procedures for reporting any suspicions or allegations of abuse.
- Have training procedures that give staff information about the use of abusive images of children on the internet and how digital cameras and mobile phones have become an easy way to access children.

BECTA (2008) have also produced guidelines for educators that may be useful in other organisations as part of their child protection guidelines. These have also been used as part of the Guidelines for Parents, Guardians and Educators on Child Online Protection (www.itu.int/cop) and are presented in a modified form in the following table:

		Key areas for consideration	Description
Safety and security as part of child protection strategies	1.	Use a whole establishment approach towards responsibility for e-safety	It is important that even if organisations do not allow the use of a certain technology within the workplace, they educate staff how to behave sensibly and appropriately when using it and educate them about the risks
	2.	Develop an Acceptable Use Policy (AUP)	These should detail the way staff, children and all network users (including parents where appropriate) should use ICT facilities. This includes guidelines on camera phones, web cams, content access, and content transmission (including social network sites)
Rules and policies	3.	Sample AUPs are available both online and via local authorities	It is important to tailor these rules to fit the particular context of your organisation
	4.	Link AUPs with other organisational policies	These should include other child protection guidelines, policies on bullying and sexual harassment as well as copyright, plagiarism and data protection
	5.	Single point of contact	Designate a senior management team manager with responsibility for safe guarding to also be the central point of contact for all e-safety issues
	6.	Need for leadership	The head of the organisation, supported by other senior staff and, where appropriate, the board of governors, should take the lead in embedding the agreed policies into practice
Be inclusive	7.	Maintain awareness amongst staff and where appropriate young people	Ensure that young people related to the organisation are aware of potential risks and how to practice safe, responsible behaviour wherever and whenever they use technology

(Continued)

	8.	Support resiliency	Allow young people within organisations to develop their own protection strategies for whenever adult supervision and technological protection are not available
	9.	Encourage disclosure of harms and responsibility taking	Help young people understand that they are not responsible for the actions that others may force upon them and that there are sanctions that the organisation will impose for inappropriate behaviour
Technological solutions	10.	Audit practice	Ensure technological measures and solutions are regularly reviewed and updated to ensure maintenance of an effective e-child protection policy
Internet safety policy	11.	Educate staff on Internet safety policy	Educate staff on e-safety with regard to their own conduct and that of the children within their care
	12.	Reinforce that personal information about self (in the context of work) and the children under care of the organisation should ever be disclosed in the online environment	Ensure that staff are aware that giving out information concerning the organisation in which they work or the children under their care should never be disclosed in the online environment
	13.	Require staff and young people to adhere to agreed guidelines about access to people and materials online	Have clear policies about the interface between private and work-related internet use such that accessing sexual or illegal content, and engaging in online sexualised chat are not permissible
	14.	Preview or test websites before sending links to other staff or to young people	It is important to check that websites are checked to see that the url does not give access to problematic content

CONCLUSION

Changes in technology use within our society have posed further challenges for organisations with regard to child protection issues. However many of the traditional strategies used to ensure safer organisations have a key role to play in relation to technology use and abuse. Finkelhor (2009) has noted, referring to incidence in North America that, '... in spite of the evidentiary chaos, philosophical disagreement, and meagre evidence base in this policy area, sex crimes against children have declined dramatically since the early 1990s, in concert with overall crime declines and other child welfare improvements. This is undeniably good news, suggesting that something is helping. But it is hard to ascertain whether any of the organized prevention initiatives have contributed to this decline' (p. 168). In the context of the UK, Radford, Corral, Bradley, Fisher, Bassett, Howat and Collishaw (2011) report that there has been a fall in registrations for physical and sexual abuse since the early 1990s. Their data from the NSPCC 'Child abuse and neglect in the UK today' study indicated that in a population survey of retrospective reports by young adults, a comparison of coerced sexual acts under age 16 shows a reduction from 6.8% in 1998 to 5% in 2009. The authors suggest that, 'These results should be interpreted with caution, but they possibly indicate a slight decline in forced or coercive sexual activity since 1998, and a relatively constant level of underage sexual activity, with those significant differences having a low effect size.' (p 11).

It may not be possible for organisations to evidence whether their response to child protection will be the sole determinant for reducing technology-enabled crime within the workplace, but developing, implementing and monitoring strategies are important responses to both current and future problems.

REFERENCES

Adler, A. (2008). All porn all the time. *31 N.Y.U. Rev. L and Soc. Change* 695.

Adler, A. (2001). The perverse law of child pornography. *Columbia Law Review, 209*, 1–101.

Akdeniz, Y. (2008) *Internet Child Pornography and the Law. National and International Responses.* Aldershot: Ashgate.

Akdeniz, Y. (2010). To block or not to block: European approaches to content regulation, and implications for freedom of expression. *Computer Law and Security Review*, 26, 260–272.

Alexy, E. M., Burgess, A. W., Baker, T., and Smoyak, S. A. (2005). Perceptions of cyberstalking among college students. *Brief Treatment and Crisis Intervention, 5*(3), 279–289.

Bates, A. and Metcalf, C. (2007). A psychometric comparison of Internet and non-Internet sex offenders from a community treatment sample. *Journal of Sexual Aggression*, 13(1), 11–20.

BBC News (Monday, 8 March 2010). *Internet access is 'a fundamental right.* Available from http://news.bbc.co.uk/1/hi/technology/8548190.stm.

BECTA (2008). *Harnessing Technology: Next Generation Learning.* Available online at http://publications.becta.org.uk/display.cfm?resID=37348.

Beier, K. M., Neutze, J., Mundt, I. A., Ahlers, C. J., Goecker, D., Konrad, A., and Schaefer, G. A. (2009). Encouraging self-identified pedophiles and hebephiles to seek professional help: first results of the Prevention Project Dunkelfeld (PPD). *Child Abuse and Neglect*, 33, 545–549.

Blanchard, A.L. and Henle, C.A. (2008). Correlates of different forms of cyberloafing: The role of norms and external locus of control. *Computers in Human Behavior* 24, 1067–1084.

Bouffard, J.A. (2002). The influence of emotion on rational decision making in sexual aggression. *Journal of Criminal Justice*, 30, 121–112.

Brantingham and Frederic (1976). A conceptual model of crime prevention. *Crime Delinquency*, 22 (3),284–296.

Bunzeluk, K. (2009). *Child Sexual Abuse Images.* Winnipeg: Canadian Centre for Child Protection.

Byron, T. (2008). *Safer Children in a Digital World.* The Report of the Byron Review. Available online at http://www.dcsf.gov.uk/byronreview/.

Case, K.J. and Young, K. (2001) Employee internet misuse: An epidemic in need of a research framework. Journal of Business and Information Technology,1(1). 30–36.

Chou, C.-H., Sinha, A. P., and Zhao, H. (2008). A text mining approach to Internet abuse detection. *Journal of Information Systems and e-Business Management*, 6(4), 419–439.

Cooper, A., Putnam, D.E., Planchon, L.A., and Boies, S.C. (1999). Online sexual compulsivity: Getting tangled in the net. *Sexual Addiction and Compulsivity*, 6, 79–104.

Cooper, A. (1998). Sexuality and the Internet: Surfing into the new millennium. *CyberPsychology and Behavior*, 1, 187–193.

Corbett, D. (2009). Let's Talk About Sext: The Challenge of Finding the Right Legal Response to the Teenage Practice of 'Sexting'. *Journal of Internet Law*, 3–8.

Cornish, D. B., and Clarke, R. V. (2003). Opportunities, precipitators and criminal decisions: A reply to Wortley's critique of situational crime prevention. In M. J. Smith and D.B.Cornish (Eds.), *Theory for practice in situational crime prevention*. Crime Prevention Studies, Vol. 16. (pp. 41–96) Monsey, N.Y.: Criminal Justice Press.

Cornish, D. B., and Clarke, R. V. (1986). *The Reasoning Criminal*. New York: Springer-Verlag.

Cusson, M. (1993). A strategic analysis of crime: criminal tactics as responses to pre-criminal situations. In Clarke, R.V. and Felson, M. (Eds.) *Routine Activity and Rational Choice. Advances in Criminological Theory*, Volume 5. Transaction Press, New Brunswick.

Evaluation of CEOP ThinkUKnow Internet Safety Exploration of Young People's Internet Safety Knowledge.Available online at http://www.cats rp.org.uk/pdf%20 files/Internet%20safety%20report%204-2010.pdf.

Davidson, J. Martellozzo, E. and Lorenz, M. (2009) Evaluation of CEOP ThinkUKnow Internet Safety Programme and Exploration of Young People's Internet Safety Knowledge Available online at http://www.cats-rp.org.uk/pdf%20files/Internet%20 safety%20report%204-2010.pdf.

Döring, N.M. (2009). The Internet's impact on sexuality: A critical review of 15 years of research. *Computers in Human Behavior, 25*, 1089–1101.

Edwards, S. (1994). Pretty babies: Art, erotica or kiddie porn? *History of Photography, 18*, 38–46.

Elliott, I.A. and Beech, A.R. (2009). Understanding online child pornography use: Applying sexual offense theory to internet offenders. *Aggression and Violent Behavior, 14*, 180–193.

Finkelhor, D. (2009). The prevention of childhood sexual abuse. *The Future of Children*, 19 (2), 169–194.

Gibson, William (1984) *Neuromancer*. New York: Ace Books.

Gillespie, A. (2006) Indecent images, grooming and the law. *Criminal Law Review*, 412–421. Guardian.co.uk (2010). Teachers warn of attacks by parents on networking sites. Available online at http://www.guardian.co.uk/education/2010/mar/28/teachers-social-networking-harassment.

Harris, P. and Salkeld, L. (2009). Price of depravity: Parents' fury as nursery paedophile Vanessa George gets just seven years' jail. Mail Online 16.12.10 Available from http://www.dailymail.co.uk/news/article-1235934/Vanessa-George-jailed-seven-years-chilling-abuse-children-care.html.

Hanson, R.K. and Babchishin, K.M. (2009). How should we advance our knowledge of risk assessment for internet sexual offenders? Paper presented at the Global symposium for examining the relationship between online and offline offenses and preventing the sexual exploitation of children, Chapel Hill, North Carolina, April 5–7.

Henry, O., Mandeville-Norden, M., Hayes, E. and Egan, V. (2010). Do internet-based sexual offenders reduce to normal, inadequate and deviant groups? Journal of Sexual Aggression, 16(1), 33–46.

Huffington Post (2010) Ex-Teacher Melinda Dennehy Pleads GUILTY To 'Sexting' Nude Photos To

Student 07/27/10. Available online at http://www.huffingtonpost.com/2010/07/27/melinda-dennehy-sexting-p_n_660898.html (accessed 20 November 2011).

Hunter, C. (2000). Social impacts: Internet filter effectiveness testing - over- and under inclusive blocking decisions of four popular web filters. *Social Science Computer Review*, 18(2), 214–223.

Internet World Stats (2010). Available online at http://www.internetworldstats.com/stats.htm (accessed 20 November 2011).

Jewkes, Y. and Sharp, K. (2003), ëCrime, deviance and the disembodied self: transcending the dangers of corporealityí, in Y. Jewkes, (ed.), *Dot.Cons: Crime, deviance and identity on the internet*, Cullompton: Willan.

Jones, V. and Skogrand, E. (2005). *Position Paper Regarding Online Images of Sexual Abuse and other Internet related Sexual Exploitation of Children*. Copenhagen: Save the Children Europe Group.

Kaplan., A.M. and Haenlein, M. (2010). Users of the world, unite! The challenges and opportunities of Social Media. *Business Horizons*, 53, 59–68.

Kaufman, K. L., Hilliker, D. R., and Daleiden, E. L. (1996). Subgroup differences in the modus operandi of adolescent sexual offenders. *Child Maltreatment*, 1, 17–24.

Kierkegaard, S, Cybering, online grooming and age play. *Computer Law and Security Report*, 24, 2008, 41–55.

Lanning, K. V. (2008).*Child Pornography*. Paper presented at the Child Pornography Roundtable. National Center for Missing and Exploited Children, Washington DC. February 2008.

Laulik, S., Allam, J., and Sheridan, L. (2007). An investigation into maladaptive personality functioning in Internet sex offenders. *Psychology, Crime and Law*, 13, 523–535.

Lenhart, A. (2009) Teens and Sexting. Available online at *http://www.pewinternet.org/Reports/2009/Teens-and-Sexting.aspx* (accessed 20 November 2011).

Li, H., Zhang, J. and Sarathy, R. (2010), Understanding the Compliance with the Internet Use Policy from the Perspective of Rational Choice Theory, *Decision Support Systems*, 48(4), 635–645.

Livingstone, S. (2010) e-Youth: (future) policy implications: reflections on online risk, harm and vulnerability. In:e-Youth: balancing between opportunities and risks (27–28 May 2010: UCSIA and MIOS University of Antwerp, Antwerp, Belgium

Middleton, D., Elliot, I.A., Mandeville-Norden, R. and Beech, A. (2006). The Pathways Model and Internet Offenders: An Investigation into the Applicability of the Ward and Siegert Pathways Model of Child Sexual Abuse with Internet Offenders. *Psychology, Crime and Law*, 12(6), 589–603.

Niveau, G. (2010). Cyber-pedocriminality: Characteristics of a sample of internet child pornography offenders. *Child Abuse and Neglect*, 34, 570–575.

Keeping Children Safe Coalition (2006). Toolkit. Available online at http://www.nspcc.org.uk/inform/trainingandconsultancy/consultancy/supportingproduct sandresources/keepingchildrensafe_wda47790.html.

O'Halloran, E. and Quayle, E. (2010). A Content Analysis of a 'Boy Love' Support Forum: Revisiting Durkin and Bryant. *Journal of Sexual Aggression*, 16(1), 71–85.

Lenhart (2009) Teens and sexting. Pew Research Centre. Available online at http://www.pewinternet.org/~/media//Files/Reports/2009/PIPTeens and_Sexting.pdf.

Pinheiro, P.S. (2006). *World Report on Violence against Children*. Geneva: United NationsSecretary-General's Study on Violence against Children. Available from http://www.unicef.org/violencestudy/I.%20World%20Report%20on%20 Violence%20against%20Children.pdf.

Plymouth Safeguarding Children Board (2010) Case Review Overview Report Executive Summary in respect of Nursery Z, March (available online at http://www.plymouth.gov.uk/serious_case_review_nursery_z.pdf).

Prokerala News (2010). Available online at http://www.prokerala.com/news/articles/a129106.html.

Quayle,E. and Jones,T. (2011) Sexualized images of children on the internet. *Sex Abuse* March, 23: 7–21.

Quayle, E. and Taylor, M (2003) Model of problematic internet use in people with a sexual interest in children. *CyberPsychology and Behavior*, 6(1), 93–106.

Quayle, E. Lööf, L. and Palmer, T. (2008). *Child Pornography and Sexual Exploitation of Children Online*. (Series editor J. Doerk). ECPAT International: Bangkok.

Quayle, E., Erooga, M., Wright, L., Taylor, M., and Harbinson, D. (2006). *Only Pictures?: Therapeutic work with Internet Sex Offenders*. Dorset: Russell House Publishing.

Radford, L., Corral, S., Bradley, C., Fisher, H., Bassett, C., Howat, N. and Collishaw, S. (2011). *Child abuse and neglect in the UK today*. London: NSPCC.

Seto, M. (2010). Child pornography use or internet solicitation in the diagnosis of pedophilia. *Archives of Sexual Behavior*, 39, 591–593.

Sunday Times (2010) Headmistress resigns after internet storm over Marcusthe slaughtered lamb. 11.2.10. Available online at http://www.thesundaytimes.co.uk/sto/public/sitesearch.do?querystring=Andrea+Charman&sectionId=2&p=sto&bl=&pf=all (accessed 20 November 2011).

Taylor, M. and Quayle, E. (2008). Criminogenic qualities of the Internet in the collection and distribution of Abuse Images of children. *Irish Journal of Psychology*, 29, 1–2, 119–130.

Taylor, M.and Quayle, E. (2006). The Internet and abuse images of children: Search, precriminal situations and opportunity. In R. Wortley and S. Smallbone (Eds.) *Situational prevention of child sexual abuse*. Crime Prevention Studies, Volume 19, Monsey, N.Y: Criminal Justice Press/ Willan Publishing.

Taylor, M and Quayle, E. (2003) *Child Pornography: An Internet Crime*. Brighton: Routledge.

The Metro (2010). Available online at http://www.metro.co.uk/news/815796-teacher-who-used.

UK Office of Government Commerce (2010) Procurement Policy Note – Blocking access to web pages depicting child sexual abuse. Available online at www.ogc.gov.uk.

Weatherbee, T.G. (2010). Counterproductive use of technology at work: Information and communications technologies and cyberdeviancy. *Human Resource Management Review* 20, 35–44.

Wolak, J., Finkelhor, D. and Mitchell, K.J. Child-Pornography Possessors Arrested in Internet-Related Crimes: Findings from the National Juvenile Online Victimization Study. Washington: National Center for Missing and Exploited Children. 2005.

Wortley, R. K., and Smallbone, S. (2006). Applying situational principles to sexual offenses against children. In R.K. Wortley and S. Smallbone (Eds.), Situational prevention of child sexual abuse (pp. 7–36). Morsey, NY: Criminal Justice Press.

Yahoo Discussion Forum 2009. Available online at http://uk.answers.yahoo.com/question/index?qid=20091005181747AA7GPAF (accessed 20 November 2011).

Young, K. (2010). Policies and procedures to manage employee Internet abuse. *Computers in Human Behavior* 26, 1467–1471.

Zhang, X. (2010). Charging children with child pornography e using the legal System to handle the problem of 'sexting'. *Computer Law and Security Review*, 26, 251–259.

7 Safer Recruitment – Guidance for Organisations

Kerry Cleary

INTRODUCTION

> 'Effective recruitment and selection of staff is essential to safeguarding children. Recruitment and the checks that are undertaken as part of this process are the organisation's first chance to make robust efforts to prevent unsuitable individuals from working with children' (Children's Workforce Development Council Recruiting Safely Guidance, 2009).

Following the Bichard Enquiry (2004) into the deaths of Holly Wells and Jessica Chapman in Soham, and the subsequent investigation into the processes which did not prevent Ian Huntley securing a post as a caretaker in Soham Village College, there has been a heightened awareness of the need to ensure that processes for recruiting people to work with children are as robust as possible.

The initial focus of work following the enquiry was on improving the standards of recruitment processes in schools. This led the Department for Children, Schools and Families (DCSF), now the Department for Education (DfE), to create an online and a face to face training programme for school Heads and Governors on safer recruitment. This was subsequently extended to cover the whole of the children's workforce through work carried out by the Children's Workforce Development Council (CWDC).

As discussed in Chapter Three, The Safeguarding Vulnerable Groups Act (2006) and the planned launch of the vetting and barring scheme by the Independent Safeguarding Authority (ISA) in 2010 were seen as further positive steps in building robust recruitment processes. This was to be achieved by ensuring that relevant information about the suitability of individuals for work with children was properly assessed and decisions to bar people from working with children would be taken by experts in the field. At the time of writing the

Creating Safer Organisations: Practical Steps to Prevent the Abuse of Children by Those Working with Them, First Edition. Edited by Marcus Erooga.
© 2012 John Wiley & Sons, Ltd. Published 2012 by John Wiley & Sons, Ltd.

launch of the proposed vetting and barring scheme has been halted in England, Wales and Northern Ireland and the scheme, as well as the criminal records regime underpinning the system, are the subject of review by government as part of the Protection of Freedoms Bill. In Scotland the Protecting Vulnerable Groups Scheme went live in February 2011.

Chapter Three reviewed in detail the principles on which the development of the Safeguarding Vulnerable Groups Act 2006 (SVG) was based and the reasons for review. Information about current arrangements proposed changes can be found at www.homeoffice.gov.uk/crime

The current chapter seeks to put safer recruitment in the context of a 'whole organisational safeguarding' approach including, but by no means limited to, those aspects prescribed by legislation and regulation and to explain its importance and its limitations. It describes a model of safer recruitment which organisations should follow to ensure they are doing everything possible to minimise the risk of unsuitable people having contact with children. It is intended as a practical guide to implementing a safer recruitment process but inevitably cannot be exhaustive and does not intend to replace in-depth safer recruitment training, signposting to which can be found at the CWDC website www.cwdccouncil.org.uk.

The chapter also highlights one example of a more in-depth and researched safer selection tool developed by the NSPCC, known as Value Based Interviewing (VBI). The VBI method and the research which underpins it will be outlined here and offers practical principles for safer interviewing which can be applied in reader's own organisations. Highlighting the importance of clear organisational values and culture the method relates to the ability to assess, during recruitment processes, the alignment of individual and organisational values and culture. Overall it demonstrates the important role selection can play in building and sustaining an organisational safeguarding culture.

Readers will be keen to understand how their own recruitment processes currently compare to the best practice detailed in this chapter. Whilst it is not possible to provide here a comprehensive guide to recruitment, the chapter does outline safeguarding aspects in sufficient detail to be of practical use. A valuable resource for more in-depth information about recruitment related issues is the Chartered Institute of Personnel and Development website www.cipd.org.uk.

DOING THE BASIC THINGS WELL

The Bichard Enquiry identified that basic good recruitment practice had not been followed in the case of the recruitment of Ian Huntley and that had it been that may well have prevented Huntley securing a role in an education setting. 'Doing the basic things well' is a recurring theme through a number of enquiries dating back to the Warner Report, *Choosing with Care* (1992).

Similar to the Bichard Enquiry in that its remit was to consider the broader relevant issues rather then the specifics of the case itself, *Choosing with Care* was established following the enquiry into abuse committed by Frank Beck, Officer-in-Charge of four Leicestershire children's homes and approved foster parent, who had systematically abused children entrusted to his care and was sentenced to seven life sentences in 1991 for 17 offences of physical and sexual abuse of residents (Kirkwood, 1993). In view of the systematic failings which allowed this to happen, Warner made recommendations about appropriate recruitment and selection processes in children homes, still relevant today. Subsequent enquiries, including Sir William Utting's '*People Like Us*' (1994) continued to identify basic failings in organisational recruitment processes.

A review of the literature which included a range of organisational abuse enquiries showed that not just in safer recruitment, but in a wide range of basic good management and best practice areas, organisations across time continually failed to put basic processes in place and then follow them consistently (Erooga, 2009).

Value Based Interviewing, described in more detail below, is a more sophisticated and in depth recruitment method to identify those who may be unsuitable to work with children, but for those organisations which persist in failing to follow basic good practice, for example reference checks exploring gaps in career history, any effort spent on more sophisticated processes will be wasted.

If the basics are both important and basic, the question arises as to why organisations continue to fail to implement them. There could be a number of reasons for this including:

- time pressures to have staff in post and so cutting corners for expediency;
- avoidance of difficult conversations around career gaps or issues raised on references;
- recruiting staff not given adequate training in safer recruitment.

An organisation that wants to make a real difference to its safeguarding culture should start with an audit of basic safer recruitment processes, ensure that basic best practice policies and procedures are in place and check that they are routinely followed.

IMPORTANCE OF VALUES AND EMOTIONAL INTELLIGENCE

In any recruitment process, it is important not only to consider an individual's behaviour but also to understand their underlying motives and values in order to identify whether they are suitable to work with children. For example, an individual might be viewed positively when forming appropriately close relationships with children until their values and motives are explored further and it becomes apparent that the relationships they form with children are more about meeting their own, rather than the child's, needs.

Recommendation 16 of the Warner report supported this approach: 'Employers should use preliminary interviews as a standard part of establishing a fuller picture of the character and attitudes of short listed candidates for all posts in children's homes' (Warner, 1992).

Values can be defined as 'an enduring belief that a specific mode of conduct or end state of existence is personally or socially preferable to an opposite or converse mode of conduct or end state' (Rokeach, 1973). This is significant from a recruitment perspective as it indicates that values, as opposed to behaviour, don't change significantly over time and therefore values identified at the recruitment stage are likely to remain consistent across time.

Emotional Intelligence is also an important concept in safer recruitment. Goleman (1998) defines emotional intelligence as:

'The capacity for recognising our own feelings and those of others, or motivating ourselves, and for managing emotions well in ourselves and in our relationships' (p. 22).

Goleman's framework is based on two key competencies, how we manage ourselves and how we handle relationships. It identifies some of the key competencies which contribute to success in relationships with children including self management and awareness of the impact one is having on others. Selection processes often focus on skills and experience and fail to consider the importance of not only what the individual does but how they do it.

Evidence from 'mock' values based interviews with incarcerated child sex offenders (Erooga, 2009) found some having a good ability to reflect and identify a problem with behaviour, but evidence of learning from past mistakes and changing future behaviour as a consequence was lacking in the majority of cases. They failed to see what was wrong with their behaviour in specific circumstances with a specific child or how they could or should have changed that behaviour. This evidence is very much contextual. Research has shown that some offenders can show high degrees of empathy for children generally but not in relation to their victims (Marshall *et al.*, 2001). It is therefore not possible to generalise about the emotional intelligence (EI) of offenders as a group.

A literature review by Erooga (2009) undertaken as part of the value based interview research project to identify common characteristics professional abusers concluded that whilst there was no single typology of individuals who might abuse in organisations or of organisations where abuse would occur, there were common themes for both.

The study indicated four key areas which were common amongst those who abused children in professional settings and which could helpfully be explored within an interview process:

• Awareness and observation of professional boundaries.
• Appropriateness of relationships with children.

- Commitment to, and evidence of, taking action to protect.
- Self-awareness.

These areas were all heavily value laden and also linked to the concept of emotional intelligence and validated the importance of focussing on values and motives as well as behaviours and skills within the recruitment process.

SAFER RECRUITMENT WITHIN A SAFEGUARDING CULTURE

The safeguarding culture of an organisation is to a large extent defined by the values and actions of senior managers and those in leadership roles and their ability effectively safeguard children. The review referred to above (Erooga, 2009) indicated that there were a number of common features of organisations where abuse had occurred which increased their vulnerability. This was based on the relatively limited amount of literature about organisational abuse but does provide a valuable insight into the importance of culture in organisations.

The review identified that a safeguarding culture has a number of key components:

- An explicit safeguarding culture and ethos with values and behaviours which are both articulated and lived at each level in the organisation.
- Clear policies and procedures which make clear to staff what is expected of them and facilitate the raising of concerns.
- Courageous management who are prepared to act appropriately on concerns and staff who are prepared to challenge and raise concerns.
- Children and young people having a voice and mechanisms for raising their concerns which are taken seriously.

Safer recruitment has a role to play in a number of these areas: it is part of the safeguarding culture; it should use organisational values and behaviours in recruitment processes; it should be used to bring managers and staff into the organisation who model the organisational values and behaviours and who will take action.

Finkelhor's Four Pre-Conditions of Sexual Offending Model (1984) can be adapted to show how organisations can create barriers or inhibitors which make it more difficult for individuals who either target organisations or opportunistic offenders from being able to abuse children in that organisation (Figure 7.1).

The model demonstrates how safer recruitment is only one component of a safeguarding culture but is an important first opportunity to have robust safeguarding practices in place. It will not identify all those who are unsuitable but supported by good induction, training, supervision and clear whistle-blowing processes it will ensure organisations are doing everything possible to ensure unsuitable people do not work with children.

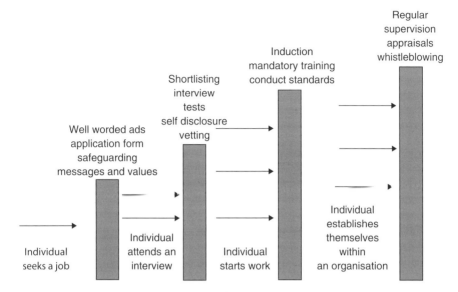

Figure 7.1   Safer recruitment and culture model.

The remainder of this chapter considers in more detail the different components of a safer recruitment model.

A MODEL OF SAFER RECRUITMENT – PICK

As indicated above the guidance and accompanying training from CWDC on safer recruitment is extensive and can provide more detailed guidance than can be contained in this chapter (www.cwdcouncil.org.uk). What this section does is to highlight the key safer recruitment processes which will make the most difference to ensuring that organisations only recruit suitable people to work with children and explains their importance as a tool to assist organisations in making the case for such a comprehensive approach to recruitment (Figure 7.2).

This section can be used like a check list for organisations wishing to review their safer recruitment process.

P – PLAN

Recruiting the right people into an organisation is one of the most important management tasks an organisation undertakes and yet in practice the planning of the recruitment process is often seen as time consuming and given a low priority.

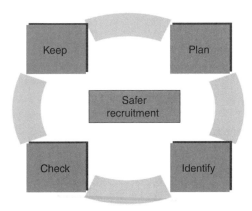

Figure 7.2   The PICK Model of safer recruitment.

Once effective planning has taken place for a specific role it becomes a time saving activity as it ensures that organisations are well placed every time they recruit to identify the most suitable individual for the role. Investing time to get the right person in post will also ensure that it is not necessary to spend considerably more time 6 or 12 months later managing an unsuitable individual out of the organisation.

Planning is also important to ensure that candidates are given as much information in advance about the role and the organisation which will enable them to self select out of the process if they have unsuitable motives for seeking to join the organisation. It also ensures that the recruiters have considered in advance what they require of the individual in the role what behaviours, skills and values they are looking for in that individual and know how they will assess all that during the recruitment process.

DEFINE THE ROLE

Before starting any recruitment, ensure that the job description (JD) and person specification (PS) reflect what is required of the person in the role, make clear the safeguarding responsibilities of the person in the role and are aligned with the organisational values and behaviours. In order to do this time must be spent in advance considering what makes someone effective and suitable for a role. This should then be translated into a clear JD and PS and once this task is completed it should only require minor amendments for future recruitment.

This is particularly important in the safeguarding context as it will send out a clear message to candidates about expected behaviour and conduct.

SETTING CLEAR EXPECTATIONS

Send candidates clear information about the organisation's safeguarding and child protection policy and the vetting requirements of the role so that candidates are clear about the commitment to safeguarding and the safeguarding culture of the organisation.

Again one could hypothesise that organisations which make clear to potential recruits from the outset the organisational commitment to protecting children and what action will be taken against individuals who seek to harm children will be more effective at deterring those with unsuitable motives from applying to join those organisations. Even for those more opportunistic individuals who don't actively target organisations, using the safer recruitment and culture model above creates a barrier by making clear from the outset that inappropriate behaviour will not be tolerated.

TRAINING FOR RECRUITERS

Identifying who will be involved in the recruitment process and ensuring they have had safer recruitment training is essential so that these individuals are clear what they need to assess within the process.

All too often people involved in recruitment processes are not equipped to make impartial and evidence based recruitment decisions. In the absence of formal training and guidance individuals resort to their 'gut feelings' about candidates or recruit candidates in their own image as opposed to the most suitable person for the role. In safeguarding terms training is even more important in ensuring any gaps are identified and explored and any concerning information is properly interrogated and assessed.

DEVELOP ASSESSMENT TOOLS

Develop interview questions and other assessment tools and criteria which assess values, behaviours and motives as well as skills and experience. The majority of organisations recruit using interviews, but these can be poorly designed and based solely on an individual's skills and qualifications, not giving sufficient focus to their attitudes, behaviours and values.

In posts working with children it is critical to assess values, attitudes and motives, as identified by Warner (1992) when he proposed the introduction of preliminary interviewing. A well qualified and experienced individual who has worked with children for a long time can also be unsuitable and a potential risk to those children due to their attitudes and the ways in which they behave.

Crucially, recruitment using values and attitudes must still comply with relevant employment legislation. Advice about specific employment law issues should be sought from an organisational HR department or the CIPD website www.cipd.org.uk.

I – IDENTIFY

Even the best designed and executed selection process cannot guarantee identifying the right person for the role but well planned processes that focus on safeguarding and suitability to work with children are more likely to be successful in doing this than those which are rushed and only consider skills and experience.

SHORTLISTING APPLICATIONS

Sufficient time should be allocated to shortlisting to ensure that all available information can be reviewed and any gaps or inconsistencies identified and then explored with candidates. Those involved in the shortlisting process should understand the role being recruited to and its requirements and should understand the importance of the shortlisting process – a common pitfall is for it to be treated as a simple 'tick box' activity. Equally in cases where there are few applicants and an urgent need to recruit, tempting though it may be, those shortlisting should never compromise standards around suitability to work with children in order to get someone in post. To paraphrase the old adage 'Recruit in haste, regret at leisure'.

ASSESSING CANDIDATES

As a basic minimum selection processes should involve a face to face interview. However, research shows that interviews have a low predictive validity of 0.2–0.3 (Taylor, 2010), meaning they are not a good predictor of how someone will perform once they are in a role. Using a number of different assessment tools such as interview plus role plays, written exercises or tests, often referred to as an assessment centre, has a greater ability to predict performance in post (around 0.4–0.6). This is because candidates get a number of opportunities to demonstrate their abilities and behaviours in different settings and ensures that the evidence collected is not due to chance but observed more than once. It allows the emergence of not only what the candidate wants to present but also what they may not consciously know about themselves or want to present.

The Johari's Window Model (Luft and Ingham, 1955) (Figure 7.3) provides a useful pictorial illustration of these different facets of the human persona. Traditional interviews will see candidates in the open/ free area but this is only one of four facets of persona. In order to get nearer to the true values, motives and attitudes of individuals to assess their suitability to work with children, interviews and other assessments should seek to draw out from candidates the hidden area where concerns may arise, and also the blind area where candidates may be unaware of how they may act in different situations and under different pressures The unknown area is not something that a selection process

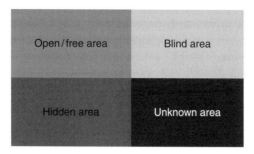

Figure 7.3   Johari window model.

which can be managed within reasonable organisations timescales and pressures could seek to explore as it would involve extensive assessment and interrogation of individuals.

In order to get to this more in depth understanding of an individual's attitudes and values, organisations should ensure that interviews probe attitudes towards, and motivations for, working with children. This does not mean that candidate should be asked questions which are so obvious in terms of having a right answer that the information gained is of little value. Rather through asking candidates to provide evidence of their past behaviour with children in their work and then probing not only what they did but also why they did it and how that impacted on them and the child/ren, a more thorough and effective assessment of values and attitudes can be achieved.

Case Study – Value based interviewing at the NSPCC

Background

In 2004 NSPCC embarked on a project to develop a form of interviewing based on values, behaviours and suitability to work with children. Value Based Interviewing (VBI) as the new interview approach has become known, is a structured approach to interviewing created for roles in organisational settings where the welfare of children and young people are at the centre of their vision and mission.

NSPCC's commitment to the development of VBI arose following the Warner Report 'Choosing with Care' (1992) and a desire to improve the way in which organisations select staff to work in positions of trust with children and young people. The 2004 Bichard Report into the events at Soham again demonstrated to the NSPCC that safer recruitment was fundamental to organisations' ability to safeguard children and deter unsuitable individuals from obtaining positions with organisations that work with children and young people. As well as working closely with the Department for Children, Schools and Families (DCSF) on the development of safer recruitment training for schools, the NSPCC developed and evaluated an approach to interviewing which probes into candidates' values and behaviours in a structured, consistent and job relevant manner to help organisations make better recruitment decisions about the suitability of applicants.

NSPCC had invested time and resource in ensuring the basics of safer recruitment were in place for a number of years prior to the organisational launch of VBI. This was essential as it was recognised that there was little point in having a sophisticated interview approach if reference and criminal record checking processes were not adequate.

The organisation had also undertaken an extensive job analysis exercise to develop a set of values and behaviours which were reflective of the organisation and hence gained ownership by the organisation, and which also provided a robust framework on which to develop interview questions and criteria.

An interview model was then created which looked at the interaction between the organisations values, individual values and how people were expected to behave in their roles. It was based on the theory that values underpin behaviour and so it was desirable not only to understand how someone would behave but why and hence how their behaviour may change in different situations (Figure 7.4).

The VBI model is also based on the same principles that underpin competency based interviews which are predicated on the understanding that past behaviour is the most accurate predictor of future behaviour. A bank of interview questions and assessment criteria were designed to draw out examples of past behaviour in candidates and then using the SOAR probing technique (Situation, Objective, Action taken, Results and reflections) follow up questions would elicit information about candidates behaviour, attitude and values.

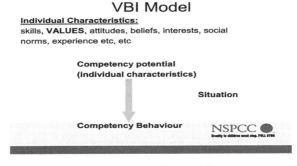

Figure 7.4 The VBI model.

In terms of the Johari Window model VBI allows exploration of both the hidden area by probing beneath what candidates initially present and looking for information about values and attitudes, and also the blind area by asking candidates to reflect on their past behaviour and its impact on others in a way they have not been able to or perhaps wanted to in the past. It is here that value is added to selection processes.

A very practical two day training course was then developed which involved interviewing individuals from temporary staff recruitment agencies who used their own experiences to answer questions in mock interview scenarios.

Between 2005 and 2007 VBI was rolled out in the Children's Services function with a specific focus on the suitability of staff providing direct services to children to work with them. As well as training managers in the new method, managers and candidates were also informed that an evaluation and validation process was being undertaken which would involve looking at how candidates performed at interview and then checking back on how they performed in role once they joined the organisation. This was an important element of the project as its aim was to test whether VBI could accurately predict performance in role, hence building the case for VBI being included in recruitment processes and why the feedback from VBIs should be given due consideration in the selection process.

During the period of the project recruitment data was gathered from over 500 applicants who had a Value Based Interview for positions in Children's Services. This included Value Based Interview ratings, equal opportunities information and selection outcomes (reject/appoint). The performance (specifically behaviours) of 100 successful candidates was monitored during their first 12 months of service. The data analysis included both quantitative (numerical) and qualitative (feedback) items. Extensive feedback was gathered from managers, interviewers and candidates. Data analysis was carried out in partnership with an external consultant to ensure objectivity in the process and selection method validation expertise.

An external trial of VBI was also undertaken with two external organisations to determine whether the VBI model of interviewing was transferable to other contexts and roles outside the NSPCC. The external trials showed that the VBI model could easily be transferred to other settings with minor language and cultural changes to the questions and criteria. Both the external organisations felt VBI added real value to their selection processes and better enabled them to identify those who may be unsuitable work with children.

At the end of the process the validation and evaluation process found that VBI did make a meaningful and real contribution to safer recruitment within the NSPCC and in the external organisations and had a high ability to predict how someone would behave once in post. The research by Erooga

(2009) referred to above supported the importance of VBI as one part of a safeguarding culture.

For organisations considering implementing a more in depth interview process as outlined here some key learning points from the NSPCC experience are:

- Ensure buy in from senior leaders and an overall organisational sponsor for the work
- Base the work on a set of organisational values and behaviours that have been tested for relevance with a number of staff groups and job roles
- Identify people with the right skills to become interviewers and ensure they have the time and continual training to continue to develop their skills
- Brief applicants in advance of interviews on what a values focused interview is and what is expected of them
- Create banks of questions and criteria to ensure consistency of approach
- Ensure the values interview is distinct from but complementary to other selection tools so that it does not duplicate other parts of the process
- Invest the time in the method – short cuts don't work!

C–CHECK

There is still considerable reliance on formal vetting processes, in particular criminal records checks/disclosures by organisations for screening applicants. Obvious though it seems, it is vitally important that all vetting checks are complete before an individual has contact with children.

REFERENCES

In an increasingly litigious society, organisations are becoming more cautious about what they are willing to state explicitly in a reference for a past employee, often only providing minimal factual information about dates of employment, salary and job title of individuals. However, particularly in the safeguarding context, references provide an essential safeguard for organisations as they can identify behaviour and patterns of behaviour which may fall short of those prescribed by regulatory standards or criminal process but which cast doubt on the suitability of an individual to work with children.

References should seek to identify any concerns a previous organisation has about an individual's conduct or suitability, and it can often be what is not said or implied that is valuable in this context.

Some key considerations when making the most effective use of references:

- Pre-written references are not acceptable. They may not be specific to your role or organisational context or more seriously could be fraudulent or the result of a compromise agreement following a disciplinary process and not contain the full information about an individual's conduct

- Ensure that referees are suitable to comment on the individual's suitability to work with children and that at least one is a recent reference.
- Consider carefully the value of personal referees who may be able to give a useful insight into the character of the individual but who are less likely to be able to identify shortcomings in the person in a professional role due to their personal relationship
- Ensure the referee's details match the career history of the individual.
- If there are concerns about what a reference does or doesn't say, follow it up with a phone call to the referee and ask questions about any concerns or things that you think the referee may not have made explicit. Referees may be more willing to be forthcoming on a telephone call than they would be to put down their concerns in writing due to a fear of potential litigation.

For more information about the legality of requesting and providing references, talk to your HR department or go to www.cipd.org.uk

CRIMINAL RECORDS AND ID CHECKS

Ensure ID is thoroughly checked by seeing originals of all ID documents to ensure vetting checks are carried out on the right person. This is to ensure that the individual is not fraudulently using someone else's identity to avoid detection as someone with a criminal or otherwise unsuitable past.

If information does come back on a criminal records disclosure it should be properly risk assessed against the role the individual has applied for. Only if the organisation is satisfied that the person doesn't pose a risk to children should an offer be made. Not all convictions revealed on a criminal records disclosure are necessarily of concern or would preclude an individual from work with children. For guidance on fairly and effectively assessing the relevance of criminal records information go to www.nacro.org.uk

SELF-DISCLOSURES

All successful candidates should be asked to complete a self disclosure form detailing their spent and unspent convictions, any disciplinary processes or investigations or any other relevant information related to their suitability to work with children. This is important as it gives the opportunity to discuss with them in advance any issues that may arise from their references or criminal records checks and to check their integrity in terms of their honest completion of the self disclosure. As the information is self disclosure it cannot be relied on but should be used as a useful cross check with information that comes back from other sources.

K IS FOR KEEP

The research by Erooga (2009) and the adapted Finkelhor model (1984) discussed above demonstrate that recruitment has its limitations, both in terms of what candidates reveal about themselves and the preparation and skill of the organisation to identify those with unsuitable behaviours, values or motives. It is also important to note from the research that contrary to popular belief a proportion of offenders within organisations do not actively target a specific organisation in order to abuse children within it. As well as those who do so there are others who are opportunistic or situational offenders, either unaware of their interest in abusing children or had not considered it and the organisational context until they were working in the organisation (Erooga *et al.*, 2012).

This strengthens the case for keeping a focus on a safeguarding culture, clarifying expectations of behaviour and effectively supervising individuals critical to the safeguarding of children in organisations. A safeguarding culture involves:

- A thorough induction for new recruits to ensure they are clear about expected behaviour and boundaries and what action the organisation will take should any issues arise. This should act as a deterrent to those who may otherwise have seen the organisation as an opportunity to abuse.
- Ongoing training and appraisal to ensure that staff do not act inappropriately with children due to insufficient knowledge or training or lack of clarity around their objectives and what is expected of them.
- Regular supervision and effective management of performance issues, which are critical in sending a message that work with children will be monitored closely and that any issues will be identified early and action taken. As with the discussion about interviews earlier, supervision should not just focus on the tasks an individual is undertaking but also probe into their relationships with clients, their behaviour and the reflection and learning.
- Use of codes of conduct and child protection policies are important as visible signs of the organisations' ongoing commitment to protecting children. It is essential that they are not documents that sit in a folder or on an intranet site and never referred to. Rather they must be integrated into induction, training and supervision and set out a clear and consistent message about expected behaviour in the organisation.
- Highlighting whistleblowing policies regularly to all staff and taking decisive action if any issues are raised. Erooga (2009) found that a common feature of organisations where abuse occurred was colleagues and other individuals who were aware that there were issues around an individual's conduct with children, though not knowledge of abuse taking place, before the abuse was finally made public. Through either fear or a lack of clarity about who to report it to and a lack of belief that action would be taken, they did not act. It is essential that policies are clear, simple, communicated to all staff and are decisively acted on as soon as any issues are raised.

THE BASICS ARE NECESSARY BUT NOT SUFFICIENT

Many of the recruitment processes detailed in this chapter should already be in place in organisations; it is their consistent and robust application to every recruitment process which will help to ensure that individuals do not slip through the net.

Having done all of this correctly, if an individual has never previously harmed a child or never been caught behaving inappropriately, the checks outlined above may not be sufficient to identify them as unsuitable.

As organisations our responsibility is to do everything possible to prevent the abuse of children in our care. As stated at the beginning of this chapter, safer recruitment provides the first tangible opportunity for doing so but must not be relied on as a sufficient safeguard. We must be tireless in the creation of organisational cultures which make clear the unacceptability of abuse of children and demonstrate at every opportunity the seriousness with which issues will be dealt with. Only then will organisations become safer places for children.

REFERENCES

Bichard, M. (2004) *The Bichard Inquiry Report – An independent inquiry arising from the Soham murders*. House of Commons: London, The Stationery Office.

Children's Workforce Development Council (2009) *Recruiting Safely: Safer Recruitment Guidance helping to keep children safe*. Leeds. CWDC.

Erooga, M. (2009) *Towards safer organisations: Adults who pose a risk to children in the workplace and implications for recruitment and selection*. NSPCC, London.

Erooga, M., Allnock, D and Telford, P (2012) *Creating Safer Organisations: Using the perspectives of convicted sex offenders to inform organisational safeguarding of children*. NSPCC, London.

Finkelhor, D. (1984) *Child sexual abuse: New theory and research*. Free Press, New York.

Goleman, D. (1998) *Working with Emotional Intelligence*. Bantam Books.

Kirkwood, A. (1993) *The Leicestershire Inquiry 1992. The Report of the Inquiry into Aspects of the Management of Children's Homes in Leicestershire between 1973 and 1986*. Leicester: Leicestershire County Council.

Luft. J and Ingham, H (1955) 'The Johari window, a graphic model of interpersonal awareness'. *Proceedings of the western training laboratory in group development*. Los Angeles: UCLA.

Marshall, W., Hamilton, K and Fernandez, Y. (2001) Empathy deficits and cognitive distortions in child molesters. *Sexual Abuse: A Journal of Research and Treatment*, 13(2), 123–131.

Rokeach, M. (1973) *The Nature of Human Values*. New York, Free Press.

Taylor, S. (2010) *Resourcing and Talent Management*. CIPD.

Warner, N. (1992) *'Choosing with Care' The Report of the Committee of Inquiry into the Selection, Development and Management of Staff in Children's Homes*, HMSO.

Appendix 1　Safer Recruitment Checklist

Activity	Currently in place Yes/No	Action
PLAN		
1) Ensure Job Descriptions and Person Specifications reflect the boundaries of roles and the responsibilities for safeguarding		
2) Send candidates information about safeguarding standards, organisational culture and values and required vetting checks		
3) Identify and train staff who will be involved in the selection process		
4) Develop internal questions and selection tools in advance of recruitment taking place		
IDENTIFY		
5) Ensure a minimum of 2 people shortlist applications using an agreed criteria and identify any gaps		
6) Assess candidates using a range of selection methods where possible		
7) Probe values and attitudes towards children as part of the interview process		

CHECK		
8) Carry out criminal records checks on all staff working with children		
9) Check the ID documents of every applicant and only accept originals		
10) Take a minimum of 2 references and follow up an concerning or vague references by phone		
11) Ask candidates to declare any criminal convictions or other information relevant to their work with children as part of the application process		
KEEP		
12) During induction of all new staff set clear expectations of acceptable behaviour and the boundaries of their role		
13) Ensure staff have all the relevant training they require to be safe and effective in their role		
14) Carry out regular one to one supervision meetings with all staff and focus on their attitudes, values and behaviours as well as what they do		
15) Ensure clear policies and procedure exist and are accessible, telling staff what to do if they have any concerns about a child or the behaviour of individuals towards a child		
16) Respond quickly and appropriately to any allegations about the behaviour of a member of staff towards a child		

Note. The term 'staff' is used to apply to staff and volunteers.
Note. This checklist is not exhaustive but covers the key activities within a safer recruitment process

8 Prevention Is Better Than Cure: The Value of Situational Prevention In Organisations

Keith L. Kaufman, Hayley Tews, Jessica M. Schuett, and Benjamin R. Kaufman

Each year millions of children and adolescents spend time involved with community based organisations and institutions. These settings provide a broad range of services and social programmes including medical care, education, structured sports and leisure programmes, social activities, and even temporary or permanent foster care. For example, more than 10 million UK children attend state funded schools (British Council, 2010), while in the US close to 50 million children are involved in public elementary and secondary schools (National Center for Education Statistics, 2010). In excess of 833,000 UK children and adolescents required emergency hospitalisations in 2006–2007 (Cochrane, 2008). Further, recent estimates suggest that more than 60,000 English children were under the care of the child protection system (Department of Health, Social Services and Public Safety, 2010). In the US, estimates place more than 463,000 children in the foster care system (Administration for Children and Families, 2009). While less closely tracked, a large portion of children in the US participate in activities and programmes sponsored by 'youth serving and leisure organisations'. Estimates suggest that: 41 million US children participated in various youth sports (CNN, 2006); in excess of four million US youth were involved in programmes offered by Boys & Girls Clubs of America (Boys & Girls Clubs Of American, 2009), and 2.8 million youth took advantage of Boy Scouts of America's activities (Boy Scouts of America, 2009).

While comprehensive estimates of child and adolescent sexual abuse in organisations and institutions are not available, the media regularly reports on child sexual abuse in these settings. Moreover, the limited scientific evidence that is available points to the significant role of child sexual abuse occurring in

Creating Safer Organisations: Practical Steps to Prevent the Abuse of Children by Those Working with Them, First Edition. Edited by Marcus Erooga.
© 2012 John Wiley & Sons, Ltd. Published 2012 by John Wiley & Sons, Ltd.

community based programmes and institutions. In fact, one of the few broad based investigations of child sexual abuse in institutions across England and Wales found that 52% of extra-familial child sexual abuse cases occurred in such settings (Gallagher, 2000). At the same time estimates confirm that a sizable proportion of child sexual abuse victims in the US are offended against by non-familial perpetrators (40% in the US NIS-4 study; Sedlak, Mettenburg, Basena, Petta, McPherson, Greene, and Li, 2010). These findings are echoed in 'Toward Safer Organisations', an excellent comprehensive review of UK and US cases of institutional and programmatic child sexual abuse by the National Society for the Prevention of Cruelty to Children (Erooga, 2009).

Despite strong evidence prevention efforts to date have neglected to address organisational and institutional child sexual abuse. This chapter offers a systematic framework for assessing and addressing child sexual abuse in community based institutions and organisations. More specifically, it reviews efforts in other areas of activity to create safe environments, describes the re-conceptualisation of the Situational Prevention Model for use with child sexual abuse within community organisations and institutions, and outlines a process for applying the approach in community settings to identify risks and to prescribe prevention and risk reduction strategies to address concerns. This process was developed in the USA and the case example is an American one. However, the indications are that it is entirely applicable to a UK and international context.

A FOUNDATION FOR PREVENTION IN ORGANISATIONS AND INSTITUTIONS

Criminology, architecture, and city planning have long wrestled with issues regarding the creation of 'safe spaces' in the community. These fields have developed a number of working theories over the years that have significant implications for the prevention of child sexual abuse in organisations and institutions. Of particular relevance are Rational Choice Theory (Cornish and Clarke, 2002), Routine Activity Theory, (Cohen and Felson, 1979) and Defensible Space Theory (Newman, 1972). This section briefly reviews these theories as a foundation for the prevention of child sexual abuse in organisations and institutions.

RATIONAL CHOICE THEORY

Rational Choice Theory suggests that all offenders are active decision makers and choose to perpetrate crimes as a means to an end (Cornish and Clarke, 2002). They aim to obtain desired benefits (e.g. power and control, money, objects of value, sexual gratification), whilst avoiding consequences (e.g. detection, arrest, injury). It is assumed that offenders are continually performing an internal 'cost-benefit analysis' to determine whether they can meet their goals within tolerable risks, by committing a crime at a particular time and within a given set of circumstances. Since we live in a dynamic world, where situations are always changing, offenders are constantly required to assess the benefits relative to the risks associated with any given situation. As with all decision making, the choices that offenders' make are constrained by the available information, their own perceptions and abilities and the time they have to make a given decision (Cornish and Clarke, 1986). For offenders who commit crimes over time it is likely that they benefit from their own experiences and develop a better sense of how much risk they are willing to tolerate to achieve particular gains (Cornish, 1994). Rational choice theory is a popular criminological framework that has been successfully applied to a variety of criminal behaviours. These include: robbery (Groff, 2007); automotive theft (Rice and Smith, 2002); domestic violence (Rotton and Cohn, 2001); online victimisation of youth (Marcum, Higgins, and Ricketts, 2010); and stalking women (Mustaine and Tewksbury, 1999). Rational choice theory has also been applied to sexual offending directed toward child victims. Proulx and his colleagues (Proulx, Ouimet, and Lachaine, 1995) examined the decision making process of adults who sexually offended against children from the rational choice theory perspective. Their study revealed the choices that an offender was faced with prior to perpetrating a sexual offence. The critical elements that were identified in this process included: (1) Where to look for victims (the 'hunting field'); (2) When to perpetrate the crime; (3) Who to select as a victim (i.e. based on vulnerability, familiarity, and erotic value); (4) What strategy to use as a means of approaching the victim; and (5) Which strategy to employ to involve the victim in abusive acts. In a series of studies, Beauregard and his associates used rational choice theory to explore the 'hunting process' of serial sex offenders (Beauregard, Rossmo, and Proulx, 2007; Beauregard, Proulx, Rossmo, Leclerc, and Allaire, 2007b). Their findings led them to suggest a model with nine key factors which included: routine activities (i.e. victim and offender); where to find victims ('the hunting ground'); selection of victims; approach method; offence location; strategy for luring the victim; attack location choice; strategy for committing the crime; and where to release the victim (Beauregard, Rossmo, and Proulx, 2007a). Their research also revealed three types of offender 'scripts' underlying the hunting process: (1) coercive; (2) manipulative; (3) non-persuasive (Beauregard, Proulx, Rossmo, Leclerc, and Allaire, 2007). Finally, Beauregard and Leclerc (2007) examined the decision making processes of a group of serial sex offenders within a rational choice theory framework. In doing so, they documented the purposeful and premeditated nature of the process associated with many sexual offenders' crimes. Evidence of the deliberate nature of sex offenders' processes was noted during the 'Pre-Crime Phase' (i.e. prior to the onset of offending), during the 'Criminal Event Phase' (i.e. crime perpetration), and at the 'Post-Offence Phase' (i.e. following the sexual offence).

This series of studies supported both the tenets of the rational choice theory and highlighted the importance of environmental and situational factors. These investigations also demonstrate the active nature of sex offenders' decision making process and the variety of associated decision points involved in this process. The dynamic nature of the offence process is also underscored and highlights the extent to which environmental and situation factors play an integral role in the decisions that offenders make regarding whether to and how to perpetrate sexual crimes. For example, situational factors such as the presence of a pedestrian in an isolated part of a park, a teacher's greeting when leading a potential victim away from the school or noticing the presence of a CCTV camera in an unexpected location can all dramatically alter an offender's decision to commit a sexual offence.

ROUTINE ACTIVITY THEORY

Based in criminology, the Routine Activity Theory (routine activity theory), was initially proposed by Larry Cohen and Marcus Felson in 1979 (Cohen and Felson, 1979). Much like rational choice theory, routine activity theory's focuses on the characteristics of the crime and the environment in which it occurred, rather than on individual offender characteristics. The routine activity theory states that three factors must be present for a crime to occur: (1) A suitable crime target or victim; (2) A motivated offender; and (3) A lack of adequate supervision or guardians. The theory suggests that crimes follow regular patterns requiring these three components, rather than simply representing chance occurrences. The suitability of a crime victim or target reflects both availability as well as the 'attractiveness' of a victim or target to a particular offender (Cohen and Felson, 1979). A lack of supervision or guardianship denotes the absence of persons or technology available to prevent or deter the crime from occurring (Meier and Miethe, 1993; Tseloni, Wittebrood, Farrell, and Pease, 2004). Finally, a motivated offender is someone who is willing to commit a crime if a suitable victim or target is available and if supervision or guardianship does not present an obstacle (Mustaine and Tewksbury, 2002).

The research literature has provided considerable support for the routine activity theory as an explanatory framework in a broad range of general criminal behaviours. These include, but are not limited to: stalking (Mustaine and Tewksbury, 1999; Burglary (Tseloni, Wittebrood, Farrell, and Pease, 2004); kidnapping (Marongiu and Clarke, 1993); Suicide (Clarke and Mayhew, 1989); street robbery (Groff, 2007); auto theft (Rice and Smith, 2002); and domestic violence (Mannon, 1997). While few studies have examined the routine activity theory in relation to sexual offending, those that have reported findings consistent with the theory. For example, Schwartz and Pitts (1995) investigated the ability of routine activities to predict sexual aggression on a college campus. They found that specific routine activities (i.e. use of alcohol and drugs) were related to sexual assault for both men and women. In a different study that examined the online victimisation of youth, Marcum, Higgins, and Rickets (2010) explored college students' experiences while they were high school seniors and college freshmen. Consistent with routine activity theory, their results revealed that victimisation increased with greater exposure to motivated offenders and increased victim suitability. Inconsistent with the theory was their finding that greater guardianship was not a significant deterrent to sexual crimes.

DEFENSIBLE SPACE THEORY

The assumption that physical spaces can be 'defensible' against crime has been prominent since the 1960s. Oscar Newman's Defensible Space Theory, influenced by the fields of architecture and city planning, was proposed in 1972 and has been a leading framework in this area. The theory is based upon the notion that the physical arrangement and design of living environments can determine their degree of vulnerability to criminal behaviour. In particular, Newman's defensible space theory suggests that the safety of spaces is dependent on three factors: (1) Territoriality; (2) Natural surveillance; and (3) Image/milieu. Territoriality is considered the central tenant of Newman's theory and refers to the ability of the physical environment to establish 'zones of territorial influence' (Newman, 1972). These zones can be differentiated between 'public', 'private', and semi-private' spaces, which are created through the use of physical and symbolic barriers. Physical barriers are established through the use of such devices as doors, walls, gates, landscaping, fences, and locks, while symbolic barriers can be created through signage and landscaping (Newman, 1972, 1973). Physical and symbolic barriers can work independently or in conjunction with one another to communicate that a space is restricted or private and should not be accessed. Natural surveillance represents the ability of a physical design to allow for, or prohibit, surveillance on the part of residents. For example, orienting housing or apartments so that residents can see the entrances of each other's dwellings would increase natural surveillance. According to Newman (1973) this in turn increases residents' sense of territoriality and their commitment to defending the space. He goes on to suggest that individuals draw conclusions about resident lifestyles based on their perceptions of the physical environment's 'image' and 'milieu'. As such, an area perceived as neglected or run down is more vulnerable to crime than one which is seen as well cared for and under the control of its inhabitants (Newman, 1972). In the former case, it is assumed that inhabitants are not as actively invested in the defence of the space, while in the later case residents are perceived to be committed to maintaining its boundaries. Territoriality appears to be dependent upon the degree of natural surveillance and the image/milieu perception of others who are viewing the property (Reynald and Elffers, 2009).

Newman's (1972) defensible space theory was at the heart of political and policy decisions in the UK and the US related to creating safer housing for their citizens (Cozens, Hillier, and Prescott, 2001). As a foundation for approaches based on the idea of creating 'defensible spaces', these housing initiatives demonstrated reductions in crime and crime related difficulties (Brown, 1999; Armitage, 2000; Clarke and Eck, 2005). At the same time, questions have been raised about the lack of understanding of the processes and mechanisms underlying defensible space theory (Reynald and Elffers, 2009). In fact, defensible space theory has been criticised on a number of fronts. In particular, concerns have been raised about the theory's basic tenets being too vaguely defined to allow for empirical analysis (Taylor *et al.*, 1980; Merry, 1981). Concerns have also been raised about Neman's exclusive focus on physical characteristics of the environment and his lack of attention to the social processes that underlie efforts to create safe spaces (Atlas, 1991; Merry, 1981). Finally, defensible space theory's lack of attention to the 'level of analysis' in considering territoriality has been considered problematic (Ratcliffe, 2003). In other words, while the focus of Newman's initial work was on creating safety in high rise apartment buildings, defensible space theory has often been applied more broadly to housing developments and neighbourhoods which can reflect multiple level of territoriality (e.g. the house, the housing development, the neighbourhood).

Recently, Reynald and Elffers (2009) re-examined Newman's theory, reviewed research that addressed key criticisms, and discussed means of enhancing its utility. In this article, they highlight research that supports the integration of social factors into Newman's concept of territoriality. In particular, they identify the importance of the individual's strong sense of community and social bonds (Brown and Altman, 1983; Taylor *et al.*, 1984), a shared set of needs and a real commitment to meeting these needs (McMillan and Chavis, 1986), as well as a unified set of behaviours and attitudes (Taylor *et al.*, 1984). They go on to discuss the importance of these factors in creating well cared for communities which are under the control of local residents (Chavis and Wandersman, 1990; Schweitzer *et al.*, 1999). Reynald and Elffers (2009) describe the fusion of Altman's (1975) territorial behaviour and privacy theory with defensible space theory as a means of resolving the concerns expressed about Newman's lack of attention to the multiple levels that exist in community settings. The work of Altman and his colleagues (Brown and Altman, 1981) focuses on territoriality as an issue of 'boundary-regulation'. It inherently includes considerations related to environmental (e.g. the proximity and visibility of apartment entrances) and behavioural indicators (e.g. the extent to which residents care for their property). Given this conceptualisation, one would expect that someone intending to commit a property crime would take into consideration these territorial factors at multiple levels, and in a fashion that makes logical sense for evaluating the attractiveness of a particular area for the commission of a crime. In other words, a potential perpetrator may consider factors in a neighbourhood, housing development, and an individual residence before deciding to commit a burglary. At the same time, they would be unlikely to go beyond neighbourhood considerations if those were considered unfavourable or if they decreased the odds of success. To strengthen defensible space theory, therefore, Reynald and Elffers (2009) suggest the importance of considering it in concert with routine activity theory (Roncek, 1981). They argue that both recognise the importance of routine activities in a setting for determining crime opportunities and conclude that with these modifications, defensible space theory represents a more promising approach to enhancing community safety.

APPLYING THE SITUATIONAL PREVENTION MODEL TO CHILD SEXUAL ABUSE

Rational Choice Theory (Cornish and Clarke, 2002), Routine Activity Theory, (Cohen and Felson, 1979), and Defensible Space Theory (Newman, 1972) form the foundation for the Situational Prevention Model (Clarke, 1995). This criminological approach represents a framework for examining the contextual and situational risks that increase the potential for a crime to occur in a given setting (Clarke, 1995; Clarke and Homel, 1997). Drawing from rational choice theory, the model assumes that perpetrators are active decision makers, continually evaluating the likelihood of successfully committing a crime and balancing these odds against the possibility of incurring consequences. situational prevention model also presumes the presence of a motivated offender, an available victim, and the potential for compromised supervision as suggested by routine activity theory. Defensible space theory contributes the assumption that environmental factors, both physical and symbolic, can contribute to the risks of crime occurring in a particular situation. The situational prevention model is a probabilistic model, concerned with factors that either increase or decrease perceived opportunities for a crime to be successfully perpetrated. While initially conceived for application with general forms of criminal activity (e.g. robbery, burglary), Kaufman and his colleagues have adapted the model for use in the prevention of child sexual abuse (Kaufman, Mosher, Carter, and Estes, 2006; Kaufman, Patterson, and Hayes, 2010). This revision tailored the situational prevention model based on what is known about the modus operandi (i.e. patterns of perpetration) of child sexual abuse offenders (Kaufman, Knox, and Valensuela, 2010; Kaufman, Barber, Mosher, and Carter, (2002); Kaufman, et al., 1998). Moreover, it was designed around the recognition that a model focused on contextual and environmental factors, such as the situational prevention model, has the greatest utility for extra-familial child sexual abuse. This adaptation of the situational prevention model (which will be referred to as 'situational prevention model'), was designed to have particular relevance for application in the types of organisations and institutions that have been identified as influential in the lives of children and adolescents.

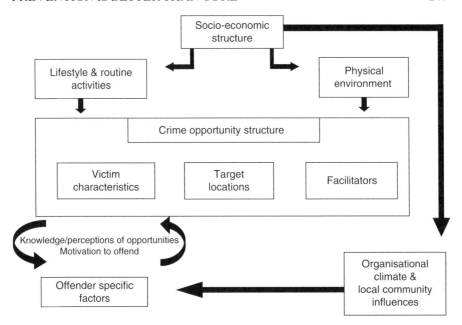

Figure 8.1   The situational prevention model for child and adolescent sexual abuse (Kaufman, 2005).

The core mechanism of the adapted situational prevention model, the 'Crime Opportunity Structure,' is presented in Figure 8.1 (Kaufman, 2005). It relates to the most central elements that an offender considers in deciding whether or not to perpetrate child sexual abuse. These three factors include: (1) Victim Characteristics; (2) Target Locations; and (3) Facilitators (Kaufman *et al.*, 2006):

Victim Characteristics can reflect the physical attributes (e.g. young, preverbal, disabled) as well as the social and emotional characteristics (e.g. lonely, needy) of the child that increases his or her vulnerability to abuse. This category also includes external factors that are directly related to the child (e.g. living in a one parent household, having a cognitively disabled parent).

Target Locations represent specific places within a setting that pose a particularly high risk for the occurrence of abuse. These may include locations that are isolated (e.g. an unused school classroom), difficult to supervise (e.g. an outside playground shielded by tall hedges) or have limited access (e.g. a recreation centre supply closet).

Facilitators denote factors associated with the setting, programme, or organisation that increase the probability that abuse will occur (e.g. poor staff to child ratio, a lack of role clarity for employees, long term employees who are not held to organisational rules). While each of the components of the Crime Opportunity Structure may individually contribute to the probability of a crime occurring, multiple factors across the three dimensions may contribute to risk in a synergistic fashion.

The other components of the model represent the influence of key external factors which may indirectly increase or decrease the probability that child sexual abuse will be perpetrated.

Lifestyle and Routine Activities refer to the overall living situation of individuals associated with the organisation or institution as well as to the day-to-day tasks that these individuals engage in on a regular basis. Lifestyle factors would be exemplified by overcrowded living situations that prompt teens to hang-out for longer hours at the community centre. Examples of Routine Activities include children taking public transportation by themselves or walking alone to school. Concerns of this nature may contribute to various aspects of the Crime Opportunity Structure. For example, a single parent (Victim Characteristic) who is forced to work two jobs (Lifestyle and Routine Activities) may have a child who becomes involved with multiple after-school activities to avoid going home to an empty house. Such a situation combines risk factors and greatly increases the potential for abuse to occur. Similarly, a child's need to leave early for and stay late at school due to a parent's work schedule (Lifestyle and Routine Activities) may increase the odds that he or she plays in the woods behind school (Target Location) without supervision (Facilitator) and as a result, is at greater risk for abuse.

The Physical Environment refers to both the specific physical attributes of the organisation and to the grounds and neighbourhood that forms an environmental context for the setting. For example, the organisation might be situated in an older building complex that has seen many small building additions. This has created a 'maze' of rooms and hallways with a large number of external doors. As a result, the building is hard to supervise and the many exits and entrances are difficult to secure. Such an environment may contribute to the probability of an offence occurring by presenting a number of likely target locations or by making it impossible to hire enough staff to adequately supervise (Facilitators) the children and teens who participate in the organisations' programmes. The fact that an organisation is located in a 'rundown' section of the city may also present particular concerns. Abandoned buildings (potential Target Locations), as an example, could greatly increase risks of abuse for children (Victim Characteristics) who walk home alone after dark (Lifestyle and Routine Activities).

Organisational Climate and Local Community Influences can be defined as factors which directly or indirectly structure and control behaviour in settings. Organisational Climate refers to factors within the agency and can include the impact of the mission statement, policies, procedures, the quality of supervision, and a perceived sense of the agency's commitment to its workers and clientele. Local Community Influences represent the impact of factors external to the organisation that may affect both agency decision making and employee behaviour. These may include city and county regulations, donor and community expectations, and local cultural norms. For example, an organisational climate lacking in strong job or volunteer position descriptions may allow a potential offender to become involved in activities that circumvent typical organisational 'checks and balances' (e.g. covering for a supervisor who otherwise would be monitoring that staff member's behaviour). Further, local norms might encourage socialisation of staff with families of teens participating in organisational programming. This, in turn, may increase the chances of a staff person being alone with a teen off-site or being asked to 'babysit' for a teen and their siblings.

Offender Specific Factors are also relevant when considering the risk of sexual offences against children and teens involved with organisations and institutions. It is important to be aware of the number of known offenders in a particular area, their risk to reoffend, the quality of their ongoing treatment, and how closely they are supervised. It is also critical to keep in mind that offenders' current motivation to offend as well as their knowledge and perceptions of offence opportunities are factors that directly relate to their likelihood of committing a sexual crime.

Finally, it is clear that a particular neighbourhood's *Socio-Economic Structure* will have a profound influence on the other components of the model. It influences the types of physical settings in which organisations are housed (i.e. newly built or remodelled vs. older construction), the resources that drive individual's lifestyle choices and routine activities (e.g. driving a child to private piano lessons vs. a child walking to a group music programme at the community centre), and even the quality of offender supervision (e.g. the ratio of probation/parole staff to offenders who need to be supervised). It may also directly influence elements of the Crime Opportunity Structure. For example, greater financial resources may translate into hiring additional staff for organisational programmes which work with high risk youth (e.g. disabled children – Victim Characteristics), replacing solid classroom doors with more expensive partial glass doors to enhance the ability for supervision (Target Locations), and purchasing security cameras to expand monitoring at a medical facility (Facilitators). The socio-economic structure of a community may also translate into differences in Organisational Climate and Local Community Influences such as hiring policies with more intensive screening or hiring practices that include offering higher salaries to ensure the hiring of employees with broader training and competencies.

The situational prevention model is intended as a conceptual framework to guide policy development and research. At the same time, it was designed to foster community and organisational practices that enhance the safety of children and adolescents. The following sections outline a structured approach to identify organisational risks, link them to prevention and risk reduction strategies, and provides illustrations of situational prevention model applications in the community.

A STRUCTURED APPROACH TO APPLYING THE SITUATIONAL PREVENTION MODEL WITH COMMUNITY ORGANISATIONS AND INSTITUTIONS

Prevention theories abound, yet few offer a direct means of enhancing community safety. The situational prevention model, with its roots in architectural design, safe housing, and efforts to reduce community crime represents an exception, as it is easily translated into a practical prevention strategy. Prevention initiatives have also been sharply criticised for an overemphasis on strategies that seek to change the community one individual or family at a time (Kaufman, 2010). In contrast, the situational prevention model approach represents a mechanism directed at organisations and institutions that are rooted in local communities and are utilised by millions of children, teens, and families nationally (e.g. youth serving organisations, schools, medical centres). Changes made in these national organisations and their local sites happen at the grass roots level and can have far reaching implications. Moreover, rather than an expensive safety audit or site visit conducted by professionals external to the organisation, the situational prevention model approach represents a structured, systematic process that organisations can perform as a self-assessment. Empowering local organisations in this fashion fosters their ability to reassess their setting as needed. This is critical given the dynamic nature of organisations. Over time, programming changes, staff turnover, and buildings are remodelled. With these modifications comes a shift in risks that needs to be addressed. The ability to engage in risk assessment without incurring the high cost of external consultants will prompt organisations to more frequently reassess their setting, improving safety. At the same time, inviting organisational staff to take on a key role in this process helps them develop a 'critical eye' about what constitutes risk, while empowering them to act on behalf of children, teens, and the organisation as a whole. Finally, the situational prevention model approach affords an opportunity to include the local community and its members in a manner that is not possible with external evaluations. Therefore, the goal of utilising the situational prevention model approach in the community is typically two fold. First, to assist local organisations in conducting a tailored assessment of risks that lead to the implementation of prevention and risk reduction strategies. Second, to assess common risks within national organisations and institutions (across local settings) and to direct policy development and to improve national staff training.

THE SITUATIONAL PREVENTION MODEL APPROACH
TO ASSESSING LOCAL ORGANISATIONAL SETTINGS

Introducing the situational prevention model process to staff as well as the organisation's community (i.e. participants and their families, donors, key inform-ants [e.g. local decision makers], residential neighbours) creates a context which will foster the situational prevention model approach's success. Broad based community participation will offer the most comprehensive perspective on organisational risks. It can also encourage community 'buy in', which may increase opportunities for later assistance in addressing identified risks (e.g. donations to support building modifications, help with local policies and regulations).

Creating a tailored situational prevention model assessment involves a six step process which includes: (1) Brainstorming key organisational risks; (2) Obtaining input on risks from staff, volunteers, and the organisation's community; (3) Linking risk to risk reduction and prevention strategies; (4) Prioritising risks to address; (5) Implementing risk reduction and preven-tion strategies; and (6) Ongoing monitoring and reassessment. Each of these steps is described in detail in the section that follows.

(1) Brainstorming Key Organisational Risks This process involves the creation of a primary working group whose task it is to generate an initial list of organ-isational risks. The group should be composed of a cross section of organisa-tional staff including administrators, supervisors, line staff, and volunteers. Preference should be given to the inclusion of staff with greater knowledge of the organisation and those who represent various facets of the agency (e.g. facilities, security, different programme areas). A minimum of two sessions should be allotted to complete this portion of the process. The first meeting should begin with an overview of the situational prevention model approach and its goals. The introduction should briefly mention each of the six steps involved in the situational prevention model approach. It should be made clear to the working group that while the first step in this process is identifying risks, the ultimate goal is to link these risks to prevention and risk reduction strate-gies that create a safer environment. The situational model itself should be reviewed (see Figure 8.1) and each model component should be defined. It is helpful to distribute a copy of the model as well as a list of definitions for each model component. In explaining the model, it is helpful to begin by talking about the 'Crime Opportunity Structure' and then discussing each of the fac-tors that may influence these crime opportunities.

Once a context has been provided, time should be spent generating risk fac-tors related to child/adolescent sexual abuse associated with each model com-ponent (e.g. Victim Characteristics, Target Locations, Lifestyle and Routine Activities). A number of strategies can be used to organise this task. Often it is helpful to ask participants to take a few minutes to generate their own list of risk factors for a particular model component. Once accomplished, group members can share their ideas in a 'round robin' (i.e. participants offer ideas one at a time until all suggestions have been presented to the group) or open discussion format. With a smaller number of participants, it may be most efficient to work through the process as a single group. Larger work groups can be divided into sub-groups to increase efficiency. The facilitator captures the ideas generated on a piece of flip chart paper or on a white board, while a second staff member takes notes on a laptop computer. Suggestions are clarified as needed and the facilitator advocates for combining similar ideas. Ideally, the first session should allow enough time for brainstorming risks related to each of the model components (probably about 2.5 hours). This will ensure that a draft set of risks can be distributed to work group members prior to the second meeting. It should be noted that some organisations may choose to limit time spent addressing Offender Specific Factors and Socio-Economic Structure (given the challenge in impacting these areas) or even decide not to address those areas as part of this process.

The second session should focus on clarifying the wording of identified risks, adding missing risks, and reducing duplication. This will also be an opportunity to explain the next step in the process which involves getting broader organisational and community input to ensure that a comprehensive list of risks have been identified and that the relative impact of each risk is clearly understood. About two hours is likely to be sufficient for this second meeting. Figure 8.2 reflects a list of possible risks associated with a youth serving organisation and offers an illustration of the type of risks that may be generated from initial brainstorming efforts.

(2) Obtaining Input about Risks from Staff, Volunteers and the Organisation's Community The second step in the situational prevention model approach involves soliciting input from organisational staff, volunteers, and members of the organisation's 'community'. In this case, community members refer to: Child and/or adolescent programme participants; Participants' parents; Neighbourhood residents; and Other key informants (e.g. city officials, representatives of funding sources). The goal of this portion of the process is to ensure that all critical risks have been identified and to obtain a sense of how great a concern particular risks present.

For organisational staff and volunteers, soliciting information using a brief questionnaire is likely to produce a good balance between obtaining high quality input and a cost efficient means of gathering the information. Using this strategy involves generating a questionnaire page from the risks identified by the initial work group for each of the situational prevention model components (e.g. Lifestyle and Routine Activities, Victim Characteristics, Facilitators). Figure 8.3 illustrates how items brainstormed by the initial work group could be converted into this brief survey format. The risks presented on this page are taken from the Physical Environment component of the model for the youth serving organisation risk analysis example presented in Figure 8.2.

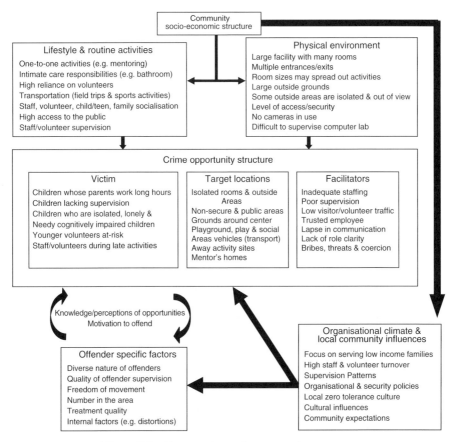

Figure 8.2   Community socio-economic structure.

As can be seen in this sample questionnaire page, Figure 8.3, respondents are asked to indicate both how often these concerns are present and how much of a risk they represent. The questionnaire also provides respondents with the opportunity to suggest risks that were missed by the work group. Of course, the complete questionnaire would begin with an introductory page explaining the larger purpose of the questionnaire and inviting input from staff and volunteers. The introduction should also include a description of the Situational Prevention Model and a definition of each subcomponent for which participants will be suggesting possible risk factors. An important consideration in developing such a questionnaire is whether this information should be gathered anonymously or if respondents should be asked to provide identifying information. On the one hand, collecting the information anonymously may yield more honest answers. On the other hand, collecting information in this manner does not allow for the clarification of ambiguous input.

Instructions: Please complete the following questions to help us identify areas that may increase the safety and security of youth who use our facilities. While we have always made youth safety our first priority, it is important to look for new ways to do more. We would like your help in identifying possible risks related to child sexual abuse. For each possible risk about the **Physical Environment** of our setting listed in Column A, please let us know how often you have been concerned about it (Column B) and how much of a risk it is (Column C) by circling the number that best describes your answer. Feel free to add other risks that you think are important at the bottom of Column A and then answer the questions for each of these risks.

I am a (check one): __Volunteer __Staff member __Program participant __Parent __Community member

Not a risk at all	A small risk	Somewhat of a risk	A big risk
0	1	2	3

Almost never	Less than once a week	More than once a week	About once a day	More than once a day
0	1	2	3	4

Column A Possible areas of risk	Column B How often have you been worried about this risk?	Column C How much of a risk for youth's safety do you think this is?
1) Large facility with many rooms	0 1 2 3 4	0 1 2 3
2) Multiple building entrances/exits	0 1 2 3 4	0 1 2 3
3) Room sizes may spread out activities	0 1 2 3 4	0 1 2 3
4) Large outside grounds	0 1 2 3 4	0 1 2 3
5) Some outside areas are isolated & out of view	0 1 2 3 4	0 1 2 3
6) Level of access/security	0 1 2 3 4	0 1 2 3
7) No cameras in use	0 1 2 3 4	0 1 2 3
8) Difficult to supervise computer lab	0 1 2 3 4	0 1 2 3
9) Other:	0 1 2 3 4	0 1 2 3
10) Other:	0 1 2 3 4	0 1 2 3
11) Other:	0 1 2 3 4	0 1 2 3

Figure 8.3   Questionnaire to expand input on possible organisational risks.

It is worth considering the best mechanism for obtaining 'community' input in this process. Organisations and institutions are critically dependent upon their reputations as safe environments in order to instil confidence in parents who entrust their children and adolescents to their care and other agencies that refer and place youth in their programmes. While the nature of the situational prevention model approach is to identify a comprehensive set of potential risks, it is important to be sensitive to the fact that such a list may be overwhelming for or misunderstood by some community members. First and foremost, it is important to provide an adequate explanation of the process to community participants. This explanation should include recognition that: youth safety has always been a primary goal of the organisation; this process is designed to identify a broad range of *possible* risks; all identified risks will be evaluated and prioritised; and risks will be responded to with risk reduction and prevention strategies based on their associated degree of concern. It is important to impress upon all participants that there is no 100% foolproof approach to ensuring participant safety for any organisation or institution. At the same time, employing active approaches to identify and respond to risks, within the realities of fiscal and practical constraints is likely to enhance organisational safety.

A number of options for soliciting input from community members should be considered. First, with adequate preparation and explanation, some or all community members may be able to provide input via questionnaire. A second option would involve constructing an open-ended questionnaire that would ask respondents to suggest risks related to each of the model component areas. This would offer the benefits of using the survey format and would avoid the possibility of overwhelming parents, youth or other community members with lists of possible risks. A third option would involve holding focus groups comprised of community members in order to generate input. This option offers several advantages that include the ability to create a positive context for the process, being able to request input in a supportive environment, and being available to answer questions, as needed. Disadvantages include the greater time and cost involved in organising and conducting focus groups, as well as the potential for more vocal participants to influence the responses of other group members. Finally, it is possible to use a combination of questionnaires and focus groups. This can be accomplished in two different ways: (1) Very brief focus groups can be paired with requests for the completion of open-ended questionnaires. The group portion of the process would involve introducing the task, obtaining sample risk responses for situational prevention model components, and answering questions. Participants would then be asked to complete an open-ended questionnaire; or (2) The process can be divided with some community members invited to participate in focus groups (e.g. parents), while others would be asked to complete open-ended questionnaires (e.g. local officials).

In completing the second phase, it is important to balance multiple aims. Considerations include: Educating participants as to the goals of the process; Fostering staff, volunteer, and community 'buy in;' Obtaining as comprehensive a set of risks related to the organisation as possible; and Informing participants about how this information will be used to enhance community safety. It is also important to ensure that the input obtained is organised to minimise duplication and to maximise the clarity of the risks identified. This will be critical in order to facilitate the next step in the situational prevention model approach.

(3) Linking Risk to Prevention and Risk Reduction Strategies. Once a comprehensive set of risks are identified, it is important to analyse them in order to determine which can be countered with prevention strategies and which of them should be addressed with risk reduction approaches. Prevention strategies are those that avert sexual abuse by eliminating particular risk factors (often referred to as secondary prevention efforts; Prescott, Plummer, and Davis, 2010). Risk reduction strives to minimise factors related to abuse that cannot be completely eliminated (Kaufman, Hayes, and Knox, 2010). For example, risks for children to be abused in the pool by adolescents during 'free swim' can be *prevented* by changing the schedule so that children and teens do not have 'free swim' at the same time. In contrast, a children's hospital cannot completely prevent risks related to adolescent or adult visitors abusing patients, since the hospital must maintain a visiting policy. Risk reduction is possible, however, and may include: having all visitors (including parents) check in at the lobby desk; requiring visitors to wear a visible pass at all times; colour coding passes to the specific unit that individuals are visiting; and training staff to approach visitors who are out of their designated area and 'offering help'.

An identified risk will be analysed to determine both the approach needed to address the risk, as well as the specific strategy that is reasonable to employ. In the case of some risks, options may be available for either prevention or risk reduction. Even in cases where a prevention strategy makes sense, there may be occasions when logistical and financial realities make that approach less feasible. For example, the placement of six security cameras on the outside of an organisation's building may virtually eliminate risks related to an inability to monitor the facility grounds (prevention). However, the organisation may not be able to afford the equipment or the staff costs of setting up the cameras and monitoring the output. Instead, a compromise is reached in which they opt for installing lights around the grounds at a much lower cost (risk reduction).

Figure 8.4 provides an example of a worksheet designed to assist in linking risks to prevention and risk reduction strategies. The situational prevention model components are listed across the top of this matrix.** The second row down presents one risk factor from each of the situational prevention model components. The third row indicates whether this risk factor is more likely to be prevented or if a risk reduction strategy is more appropriate. The remainder of the left hand column lists a number of different prevention and risk reduction strategies. An 'X' in the matrix represents a prevention/risk reduction strategy that could be used to address the risk factor at the top of the column.

** Note: Two components of the situational prevention model (i.e. Offender Specific Factors and Community Socio-Economic Structure) have not been included in this process due to recognition that most organisations have little ability to impact on these factors. Of course, these can be added for organisations that do have the ability to influence these components.

SPM risk category →	Lifestyle & routine activities	Physical environment	Victim characteristics	Target locations	Facilitators	Organisational climate & local community influences
Organisation specific risk →	High reliance on volunteers	Large outside grounds	Children who are cognitively disabled	Vehicles (transport)	Poor volunteer role clarity	Focus on serving low income families
Prevention or risk reduction →	Risk reduction	Risk reduction or prevention	Risk reduction	Prevention	Prevention	Risk reduction
Prevention/risk reduction strategies ↓						
Employment screening	X					
Staff & volunteer supervision	X		X		X	
Policies/rules	X		X	X	X	
Environmental modification		X	X			
Program modification		X	X	X		X
Modus operandi information	X		X		X	X
Staff/volunteer skills training	X	X	X		X	X
Youth prevention training	X					X

Figure 8.4   Prevention and risk reduction strategies planning worksheet.

For the strategies that are applicable to a specific risk, it is helpful to describe how this strategy would be applied, what costs would be associated with its implementation, and how this risk may relate to particular patterns of perpetration (i.e. modus operandi) and who are the likely offender or victim groups. This process is facilitated by the use of a worksheet similar to the one provided in Figure 8.5. The process illustrated in Figures 8.4 and 8.5 can be conducted for all of the identified risk factors by the organisation's primary work group. The tasks involved in these steps helps position the organisation to prioritise risks in a manner that takes into consideration the practical reality of different types of responses.

(4) Prioritising Risks to Address. In most cases, the question will not be whether to respond to identified risks, but rather which risks should take precedence and how practical realities (e.g. finances) may limit or modify the organisation's response to these risks. It is also important to recognise that many identified risks may reflect a minimal likelihood of contributing to sexual abuse. This would be indicated by lower ratings on staff and volunteer questionnaires or their absence from the input provided by organisational community members. The primary work group should be convened to evaluate the importance of the various identified risks, prioritise them for action, and suggest the prevention and risk reduction strategies that are most likely to succeed, given logistical

(a)

SPM risk category (& organisation specific risk) ➡	Victim characteristics (children with cognitive disabilities)		
Prevention & risk reduction strategies ⬇		Associated costs to consider	Specific offender risk groups & modus operandi considerations
Provide information on modus operandi	Clarify risks related to this population and integrate this into staff/supervisor training.	Minimal administrative time required to do this task.	Consider potential for program participants to offend against each other. Review research on common modus operandi with this group of participants.
Policies/rules	Need to develop specific policies regarding time alone with children & teens with cognitive disabilities.	This will require administrative staff to work on new policies.	Volunteers at greater risk given less intensive screening. Male older teen volunteers at-risk due to bathroom and swimming related dressing responsibilities.
Environmental modification	Move program activities closer to the office where traffic is high and supervision is increased.	No additional costs anticipated.	Add windows to doors and locking closets in the rooms used for this program.
Program modification	Create tailored programs based on existing programs and suggestions from best practice literature.	Hire outside expert assistance to create tailored program. May be able to use volunteer to support this effort.	Expert should have knowledge about sexual abuse modus operandi related to children and adolescents with cognitive disabilities.
Staff & volunteer skills training	Develop staff, volunteer, & supervisor training specific to the needs of and risks presented by this group of participants	Outside expert will need to assist in adding component to our existing training.	Training should take into account risks related to both peer to peer offending and abuse by staff or volunteers.
Staff & volunteer supervision	Provide more intensive & more frequent supervision.	Consider adding one additional supervisor.	More intensive supervision is critical given some participants' inability to understand and communicate about abuse.

Figure 8.5 Prevention and risk reduction details, modus operandi and associated costs worksheet.

(b)

SPM risk category (& organisation specific risk) ➡	Facilitators (poor volunteer role clarity)		
Prevention & risk reduction strategies ⬇		Associated costs to consider	Specific offender risk groups & modus operandi considerations
Provide information on modus operandi	Research information on boundary violations by volunteers to inform the development of policies and supervision.	Minimal administrative time will be required to do this task.	Consider risks presented by volunteer to volunteer and staff to volunteer contacts. Female high school volunteers may be at greater risk of abuse by older volunteers and staff.
Policies / rules	Establish policies that create specific job descriptions for the work that volunteers perform for our agency.	This will require administrative and Human Resource (HR) staff to create new policies. Check with national HR office for models.	Policies should set clear limits to reduce boundary violations with older teen program participants. Policies should also restrict volunteer's ability to have contact with participants outside of the program.
Staff & volunteer skills training	Develop volunteer, staff, and supervisor training around changes in volunteer job descriptions and responsibilities.	Administrative staff working with the national office will be required to update training procedures.	It will be important to differentiate the training needs of each group. Supervisors will need to be particularly vigilant regarding power differences that may put youth or volunteers at-risk.
Staff & volunteer supervision	Create expectations of supervisory staff to support and enforce boundaries related to new job descriptions.	Administrative staff and lead supervisors need to review existing guidelines with an eye toward revisions.	Consideration needs to be given to concerns about volunteers who work with the most vulnerable youth (e.g. young, poor, lacking attention at home) involved in programming.

Figure 8.5   (*cont'd*).

and fiscal realities. To facilitate this process, the following outline can serve as a guide.

The primary work group may find it helpful to begin by prioritising risks within each of the situational prevention model components. Once completed, the group should move on to prioritising risks across the situational prevention model components. At this stage, the group is likely to find clusters of similar or related risks that warrant attention. Looking across components can also suggest ways in which implementing one strategy will resolve a small cluster of risks, or how strategies can be sequenced to get the maximum impact. For example, deciding to transfer programmes that involve transporting children and adolescents (e.g. swimming team, gymnastics team) to another organisation may alleviate organisational risks related to providing adequate supervision. This solution would also alleviate identified risks related to supervision of youth: During early morning team practices; while transporting youth to competitions; during competitions; and after youth arrive back at the facility. During this process, it is also important to clarify how final decisions will be made. Often a working group of this nature is responsible for creating a set of recommendations that will be acted upon by an organisation's management team, director, and/or board of directors. It is helpful to share this process with organisational staff, volunteers, and the community to maintain a 'transparent' process and avoid misunderstandings. Final decisions should specify: (1) Prioritised risks; (2) The strategies selected to address them; (3) The tasks necessary to prepare for and implement each strategy; (4) Who will be responsible for taking the lead on the strategy; and (5) A timeline for completing each phase of strategy.

(5) Implementing Risk Reduction and Prevention Strategies Adequate preparation and planning will facilitate the implementation of risk reduction and prevention strategies. That said, it is important to recognise that implementing multiple strategies at the same time can have unforeseen synergistic effects (i.e. positive or negative). If possible, multiple strategies should be initialised in a staggered fashion with enough time between implementations to allow for an assessment of their impact. This will also allow for any necessary modifications to be made in order to improve the strategies' effectiveness. Evaluation of the implementation phase should also be planned with consideration for the possibility that changes to one programme may have cascading effects which influence other organisational areas. As such, implementation feedback should be solicited from a broad array of agency staff, programme coordinators, volunteers, and community members to ensure that they are kept 'in the loop' and to gain their perspectives on how things are going. It may be particularly advantageous to have the primary work group or some other advisory group coordinate the implementation of prevention and risk reduction strategies. Examining the implementation of prevention and risk reduction strategies relative to existing policies is also a critical part of this step in the process. Modifications in daily practice or procedures should be reflected in policy changes that support such activities. For example, creating new requirements for staff to obtain a supervisor's permission when taking children off site (even if it's for a few minutes to get a bag of crisps at a shop across the street) should be reflected in policy modifications. Finally, organisations should have confidence in the process and commit to new strategies for a reasonable period of time to ensure that they have a fair chance of succeeding. Resistance to change is common, and new strategies need sufficient time to be accepted and integrated. The initial evaluation should be delayed for approximately 4–6 months to allow time to 'work the bugs out,' and to assure a fair assessment of new practices.

(6) Ongoing Monitoring and Reassessment Organisations are highly dynamic entities. Changes in staff, volunteers, programmes, policies, facilities, and efforts to serve new community groups can all result in the development of new risks to agency participants. Establishing a plan for ongoing monitoring and risk reassessment serves as a proactive measure to assure youth's safety. In part, this means creating a programme evaluation plan that will provide ongoing feedback regarding changes implemented as part of the initial situational prevention model assessment. Evaluation can also offer the advantage of obtaining information on programme strengths and areas in need of modification. While it is possible for staff to create and implement their own evaluation plan (c.f. Todal, Davis, and Kaufman, 2010), it is often wise to obtain consultation from a professional with expertise in this area. Local universities and consultation groups are a good place to find assistance. In addition to ongoing evaluation, an organisation should plan for a comprehensive situational prevention model reassessment on a regular basis. How often this is done should be determined based on the number of recent programmatic, staff, building, and policy changes as well as resource considerations. During periods of relative stability, a reassessment about every one to two years seems prudent.

The situational prevention model approach is straightforward, but like any new process it may best be facilitated by an experienced person. A 'train-the-trainer' strategy can be ideal for creating a cadre of organisational staff who can teach others to do a tailored risk assessment of their setting. These trainers can also function as consultants who provide 'real time' support, and as evaluators who can monitor the process to ensure that it remains true to the framework.

IDENTIFYING COMMON RISKS ACROSS NATIONAL ORGANISATIONS AND INSTITUTIONS

Many national organisations and institutions provide a strong foundation for their local chapters and branches which increases the availability of programme resources, policy manuals, and training materials. For example in the US, national organisations such as Boys & Girls Clubs of America, Big Brothers Big Sisters of America, Boy Scouts of America, Girl Scouts of the USA, and a number of youth sports organisations offer support of this nature. Similarly, public institutions including schools, hospitals, foster care programmes and other institutions are structured based on national templates and standards. Faith based organisations can also be thought of in a similar manner. It appears, therefore, that large organisations and institutions could benefit from pooling information to create a system-wide picture of common vulnerabilities or shared risk factors. Information of this nature could then inform decisions and lead to important modifications in national policies and training programmes.

The situational prevention model approach offers a potential mechanism for system-wide risk identification. Using an approach similar to the one described for assessing individual organisations, this approach could offer a means of identifying critical system-wide risks. The situational prevention model approach for systems would begin with a series of local and national focus groups. The aim of these focus groups is to identify a broad array of possible child sexual abuse risks within a particular organisation or institution. Local focus groups offer a good starting point for generating risk factors, while the addition of national input ensures that regional differences, community diversity, and urban-rural differences are well represented. Once a broad sampling of risks are identified for each of the situational prevention model components, these risks can be translated into a questionnaire that can be sent out to a representative national sample of organisational staff and managers. The questionnaire can be developed based on the format provided in Figure 8.3 and could be sent to participants via email or designed for online completion. A cover letter explaining the purpose of the project and its value to the organisation is an important addition to promote higher response rates. A few questions that describe the respondent (e.g. administrative vs. staff, years of experience) and the setting (e.g. urban vs. rural) may aid interpretation of findings. However, it is important to eep in mind that questionnaires that allow anonymous responding have been found to result in better return rates. Once the completed questionnaires are analysed, decisions can be made about the implications of results for policy revisions, training, and tailored assessments of individual sites.

Figure 8.6 provides actual focus group data obtained from teachers representing eight different Oregon middle schools. The results presented represent a summary of the most highly rated risks identified for each situational prevention model category. While these results represent preliminary data from a small group of participants, they do identify a number of significant concerns that could greatly increase the vulnerability of student's sexual abuse. These findings also underscore the value of this approach for identifying organisational risks. Additional focus groups are planned with the hope of generating a representative set of risk items that can be translated into a questionnaire for completion by a national sample of teachers.

A more broad based application of this approach is underway as part of a collaboration between the first author and the Boys & Girls Clubs of America. This initiative, funded by the 'Vision of Hope Grant' (Pennsylvania Coalition Against Rape, 2011), will allow for the collection of system-wide *potential* risks from a sample of club directors who are a part of the more than 4,000 clubs around the USA. This information will be available to Boys & Girls Clubs of America to inform their future development of training materials and policy suggestions for their local affiliates. This collaboration represents a proactive stance on the part of Boys & Girls Clubs of America to support new prevention strategies which build upon its multifaceted safety efforts and reflects a commitment to seeking new ways to promote youth safety.

Lifestyle & routine activities
Lack of supervision before & after school
Public access on a daily basis
Not sure who belongs & who doesn't
Waiting for & taking the bus to & from school

Physical environment
Multiple access points to buildings with many unlocked doors
Unused buildings & rooms
Large building
Difficult to supervise outside grounds (e.g. Woods, fields)

Victim characteristics
Too trusting–Naïve
Disabled & Special needs
Implications of low socio-economic status (e.g. parents have multiple jobs)
A lot of time unsupervised
Children looking for an adult connection

Target locations
'Shortcuts' on the way to & from school
Unlocked rooms (that are lockable)
'Student only' areas (e.g. Staircases & halls)
Classrooms–empty or after hours
Locker rooms
Backstage

Facilitators
Lack of policies or lack of policy enforcement
A lot of 'non-teachers' in the building & inabilitity to monitor them
Lack of background checks for volunteers, vendors, & construction workers
Poor funding leading to reduced staffing (e.g. Poor student-teacher ratio)
Closed doors common
Unsupervised use of technology
After-school programs

Organisational climate & local community influences
Confidentiality of problem incidents interferes with the ability to keep the setting safe
Public building–Suggest open access
Lack of routine background checks
Poor role clarity for staff, volunteers, & teachers
Administrative staff being overwhelmed leads to poor supervision
Lax after-school policies & enforcement
Online child abuse training for teachers and staff is inadequate

Figure 8.6   School risks Brainstormed by local middle school teachers.

SITUATIONAL PREVENTION MODEL CHILDREN'S HOSPITAL CONSULTATION – A CASE STUDY

The situational prevention model approach proved to be a useful tool during consultation to a large metropolitan children's hospital that discovered a long-term employee had sexually abused children under his care over a number of years. This employee was very well regarded and his offences were against victims who were unable to report due to severe physical and cognitive disabilities. The lead author was asked to serve on a small consulting team to assess existing risks within the hospital setting and recommend prevention and risk reduction strategies to address these concerns in an effort to create a safer environment. As part of the consultation, he was asked to use the situational prevention model approach to facilitate the process of risk identification. Brainstorming with members of the hospital's management team and obtaining questionnaire input from hospital employees were elements of the assessment.

Figure 8.7 presents the results of this process and outlines the risks of greatest concern that were identified. Hospital administrators used this information in conjunction with other input to establish priorities and implement a comprehensive set of prevention and risk reduction strategies. While this proved to be a good test of the situational prevention model, it was also an excellent opportunity to work with an organisation truly committed to the welfare of its patients, their families, its staff, and the community. At each decision point in the process, the hospital management team was thoughtful, inclusive in garnering input, and strived to make the best decisions, even when they involved difficult choices. This highlights the advantage of working with organisations, whose strong values and commitment to best practice, serve to maximise the positive impact of the process. It is critical to remember that the situational prevention model approach is designed to assist in the identification of risks and appropriate responses, it remains the purview of the host organisation to decide how this information is put into practice.

THE BOYS & GIRLS CLUB CHILD SEXUAL ABUSE PREVENTION SELF-ASSESSMENT INITIATIVE

The Vision of Hope Grant (Pennsylvania Coalition Against Rape, 2011) also provides funding for refining the six step Situational Prevention Approach (Kaufman, 2010) as a self-assessment tool for Boys & Girls Clubs across the USA to use as a means of identifying potential child sexual abuse risks and addressing them through prevention and risk reduction strategies. The goal of the project is to put a 'no cost' (or very low cost) self-assessment tool in the hands of local Boys & Girls Clubs as a mean of enhancing their ability to assess and respond to potential risks on an ongoing basis. Development of an implementation manual to tailor use of the Situational Prevention Approach in Boys & Girls Clubs is underway and will involve piloting the approach in three USA cities (i.e. Portland, Oregon; Pittsburgh, Pennsylvania; and Philadelphia, Pennsylvania). The approach will also facilitate connections between local clubs and Rape Crisis Centre staff with prevention expertise. This will contribute to the generation of richer prevention strategies as part of the approach as

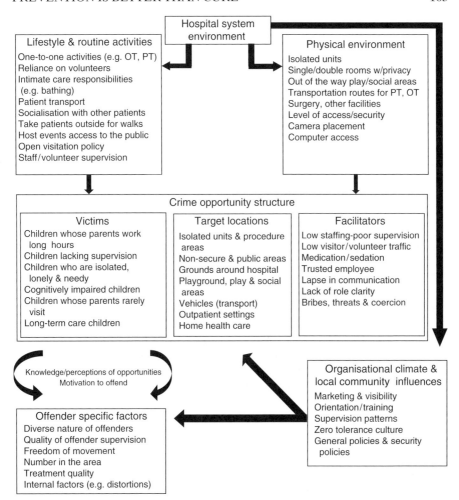

Figure 8.7   Risks brainstormed for children's hospital consultation (Kaufmann, 2006).

well as offer opportunities for long-term collaboration between the clubs and rape crisis centre staff. While the focus is on identifying and addressing potential risks, there is also the hope that participating in this process will increase club staffs members' capacity to recognise concerns early on and empower them to act to seek a resolution. The Vice President for Club Safety and Design of Boys & Girls Clubs of America refers to this as enhancing 'capable guardianship' and stresses the importance of strategies that encouraging club staffs' proactive involvement to enhance youth's safety (Nichols, 2011). To date, the Situational Prevention Approach has been very well received by local clubs. Determining its efficacy will, however, require the completion of future evaluation studies.

CONCLUSIONS

The Situational Prevention Model is strongly rooted in approaches that have been used in the design of safe housing and to enhance community safety for over 40 years. This chapter presents a revision of this model and explores its application to community based organisations and institutions, re-conceptualising it for use in the prevention of child and adolescent sexual abuse in community settings. While application of the situational prevention model is in its infancy, it seems to offer a cost-effective, systematic approach that local organisations can use for self assessment. At the same time, the model can be implemented to assist national organisations and institutions identify risks that require modifications in their programming, policies, and training efforts to enhance the safety of their community settings. Early application of the model with individual organisations showed considerable utility and has led to its refinement as a self-assessment prevention approach for use with a large national youth serving organisation (i.e. Boys & Girls Clubs of America). The potential for its application in other areas (e.g. health care settings, schools, faith based organisations, other youth serving organisations) is reflected in recent inquires by administrators representing these domains. The situational prevention model approach seems promising, however, its ultimate utility will be determined based upon evaluation results from local organisational assessments and research exploring its contribution to the effectiveness of national organisation programming, policy, and training efforts.

All images in chapter 8, © Keith L. Kaufman.

REFERENCES

Administration for Children and Families. (2009). Trends in foster care and adoption. Retrieved from http://www.acf.hhs.gov/programs/cb/stats_research/afcars/trends.htm.

Altman, I. (1975). *The Environment and Social Behaviour*. Monterey, CA: Brooks/Cole.

Armitage, R. (2000). *An evaluation of Secured by Design within West Yorkshire*. Home Office.

Briefing Note 7/00. London: Crown Copyright.

Atlas, R. (1991). The other side of defensible space. *Security Management*, 63–66.

Beauregard, E. and Leclerc, B. (2007). An application of the rational choice approach to the offending process of sex offenders: A closer look at the decision making. *Sexual Abuse: A Journal of Research and Treatment*, *19*, 115–133.

Beauregard, E., Rossmo, K., and Proulx, J. (2007). A descriptive model of the hunting process of serial sex offenders: A rational choice perspective. *Journal of Family Violence*, *22*(6), 449–463.

Beauregard, E., Proulx, J., Rossmo, K., Leclerc, B., and Allaire, J. (2007b). Script analysis of hunting process of serial sex offenders. Criminal Justice and Behaviour, 34(8), 1069–1084.

Boys & Girls Clubs of America. (2009). *Annual Report*. Retrieved from http://www. bgca.org/whoweare/Documents/2009_BGCA_Annual_Report-lowres.pdf.

Boy Scouts of America. (2009). *Annual Report*. Retrieved fromhttp://www.scouting.org/ filestore/annualreport/pageflip.htm.

British Council (2010) Retrieved from http://www.britishcouncil.org/usa-education-uk-system-k-12-education.htm.

Brown, B., and Altman, I. (1981). Territoriality and residential crime. In P. J. Brantingham and P.L. Brantingham (Eds.), *Environmental criminology* (pp. 56–76). Beverly Hills, CA: Sage.

Brown, B., and Altman, I. (1983). Territoriality, defensible space and residential burglary: An environmental analysis. *Journal of Environmental Psychology, 3*, 203–220.

Brown, J. (1999). An evaluation of the Secured by Design initiative in Gwent, South Wales. MSc, Scarman Centre for the Study of Public Order. University of Leicester.

Chavis, D., and Wandersman, A. (1990). Sense of community in the urban environment: A catalyst for participation and community development. *American Journal of Community Psychology, 18*(1), 55–81. DOI: 10.1007/BF00922689.

Clarke, R., and Mayhew, P. (2002). Crime as opportunity: A note on domestic gas suicide in Britain and the Netherlands. *British Journal of Criminology, 29*(1), 35–46.

Clarke, R. (1995). Situational crime prevention. In M. Tonry and D. Farrington (Eds.), *Building a safer society: Strategic approaches to crime prevention Crime and Justice: An Annual Review of Research*, Vol. 19, (pp. 91–150). Chicago: University of Chicago Press.

Clarke, R., and Homel, R. (1997). A Revised Classification of Situational Crime Prevention Techniques. In S. P Lab (Ed.), *Crime Prevention at a Crossroads*. Cincinnati, OH: Anderson Publishing.

Clarke, R. and Eck, J. (2005). *Crime Analysis for Problem Solvers: In 60 Small Steps*. Washington, D.C.: Office of Community Oriented Policing.

CNN. (2006). Youth sports drawing more than ever. Retrieved from http://articles.cnn. com/2006-07-03/us/rise.kids.sports_1_youth-sports-tennis-lessons-kids?_s=PM:US.

Cochrane, H. (2008). Trends in Children and Young People's Care: Emergency Admission Statistics, 1996/97-2006/07, England. Department of Health. Prepared by Chief Nursing Officer's Directorate. Retrieved from http://www.dh.gov.uk/prod_consum_dh/groups/dh_digitalassets/@dh/@en/documents/digitalasset/dh_083711.pdf.

Cohen, L. and Felson, M. (1979). Social change and crime rate trends: a routine activity approach. *American Sociological Review, 44*, 588–608.

Cornish, D., and Clarke, R. (1986). Introduction. In D. B. Cornish and R. V. Clarke (Eds.), *The Reasoning Criminal: Rational choice perspectives on offending* (pp. 1–13). New York: Springer-Verlag.

Cornish, D. (1994). The procedural analysis of offending and its relevance for situational prevention. In R. V. Clarke (Ed.), *Crime Prevention Studies*, Vol. 3, (pp.151–196). Monsey, N.Y.: Criminal Justice Press.

Cornish, D. B., and Clarke, R. V. (2002). Analyzing organized crimes. In A. R. Piquero and S. G. Tibbetts (Eds.), *Rational Choice and Criminal Behaviour: Recent research and future challenges* (pp. 41–63). New York: Routledge.

Cozens, P., Hillier, D., and Prescott, G. (2001). Crime and the design of residential property – exploring the theoretical background - Part 1. *Property Management, 19*(2), 136–164.

Department of Health, Social Services, and Public Safety. (2010). *Child Protection*. Retrieved from http://www.dhsspsni.gov.uk/index/hss/child_care/child_protection.htm.

Erooga, M. (2009) Towards safer organisations: Adults who pose a risk to children in the workplace and implications for recruitment and selection, NSPCC, London.

Gallagher, B. (2000). The extent and nature of known cases of institutional child sexual abuse. *British Journal of Social Work*, *30*(6), 795–817.

Groff, E. (2007). Simulation for theory testing and experimentation: An example using routine activity theory and street robbery. *Journal of Quantitative Criminology*, *23*(2), 75–103.

Kaufman, K. L., Holmberg, J., Orts, K., McCrady, F., Rotzien, A., Daleiden, E. (1998). Factors influencing sexual offenders' modus operandi: An examination of victim–offender relatedness and age. *Child Maltreatment*, 3, 349–361.

Kaufman, K., Barber, M., Mosher, H., and Carter, M. (2002). Reconceptualizing child sexual abuse as a public health concern. In P. A. Schewe (Ed.), *Preventing violence in relationships: Interventions across the life span* (pp. 27–54). Washington, D.C.: American Psychological Association.

Kaufman, K. (October, 2005). *Understanding the revised Situational Prevention Model*. Graduate Student Seminar. Portland State University, Portland, Oregon.

Kaufman, K., Mosher, H., Carter, M., and Estes, L. (2006). An empirically based situational prevention model for child sexual abuse. In R. Wortley and S. Smallbone (Eds.), *Situational Prevention of Child Sexual Abuse. Crime Prevention Studies*, Vol. 19, (pp.101–144). Monsey, N.Y.: Criminal Justice Press.

Kaufman, K., and Patterson, L. (2010). Using sex offenders' modus operandi to plan more effective prevention programs. In K. L. Kaufman (Ed.) *The Prevention of Sexual Violence: A Practitioner's Sourcebook*. Holyoke, MA: NEARI Press.

Kaufman, K., Hayes, A., and Knox, L. A. (2010). The Situational Prevention Model: Creating safer environments for children and adolescents. In K. L. Kaufman (Ed.) *The Prevention of Sexual Violence: A Practitioner's Sourcebook*. Holyoke, MA: NEARI Press.

Kaufman, K. (2010). Future directions for the prevention of sexual violence. In K. L. Kaufman (Ed.) *The Prevention of Sexual Violence: A Practitioner's Sourcebook*. Holyoke, MA: NEARI.

Mannon, J. (1997). Domestic and intimate violence: An application of routine activities theory. *Aggression and Violent Behaviour, 2*(1), 9–24.

Marcum, C., Higgins, G., Ricketts, M. (2010). Potential factors of online victimization of youth: An examination of adolescent online behaviours utilizing routine activity theory. *Deviant, 31*, 381–410.

Marongiu, P., and Clarke, R. (1993). Ransom kidnapping in Sardinia, sub cultural theory and rational choice. In R. Clarke and M. Felson (Eds.), *Routine Activity and Rational Choice*. (pp. 179–199). Piscataway, NJ: Transaction Publishers.

McMillan, D., and Chavis, D. (1986). Sense of community: A definition and theory. *Journal of Community Psychology, 14*, 6–23.

Meier, R., and Miethe, T. (1993). Understanding theories of criminal victimization. In M. Tonry (Ed.) *Crime and Justice: An annual review of research*. Chicago, IL: University of Chicago Press.

Merry, S. E. (1981). Defensible space undefended: Social factors in crime control through environmental design. *Urban Affairs Quarterly, 16*, 397–422.

Mustaine, E., and Tewksbury, R. (2002). Sexual assault of college women: A feminist interpretation of a routine activities analysis. *Criminal Justice Review, 21*(1), 89–123. Doi: 10.1177/073401680202700106.

Mustaine, E., and Tewksbury, R. (1999). A routine activity theory explanation for women's stalking victimizations. *Violence Against Women, 5*(1), 43–62.

National Center for Education Statistics (2010). The Condition of Education 2010. Retrieved from http://nces.ed.gov/pubsearch/pubsinfo.asp?pubid=2010028.

Newman, O. (1973). *A design guide for improving residential security*. National Institute of Law Enforcement and Criminal Justice. Washington, D.C.: US.

Newman, O. (1972). *Defensible Space*. New York: Macmillan.

Nichols, L. (personal communication August 31, 2011) *Boys & Girls Clubs of America*, Vice President For Safety and Design. Atlanta, Georgia, USA.

Pennsylvania Coalition Against Rape (2011). *Vision of Hope Grant*. Harrisburg: Pennsylvania.

Prescott, D., Plummer, C., and Davis, G. (2010). Recognition, response, and resolution: Historical responses to rape and child molestation. In K. L. Kaufman (Ed.) *The Prevention of Sexual Violence: A Practitioner's Sourcebook*. Holyoke, MA: NEARI.

Proulx, J., Ouimet, M., and Lachaine, N. (1995). Criminologie de l'acte pedophilie [Criminology in action and pedophilia]. *Revue Internationale de Criminologie et de Police Technique, 48*, 294–310.

Ratcliffe, J. H. (2003). Suburb boundaries and residential burglars. *Trends and Issues in Crime and Criminal Justice, Australian Institute of Criminology, 246*, 1–6.

Rice, K., and Smith, W. (2002). Socioecological models of automotive theft: Integrating routine activity and social disorganization approaches. *Journal of Research in Crime and Delinquency, 39*(3), 304–336.

Roncek, D. W. (1981). Dangerous places: Crime and residential environment. *Social Forces, 60*, 74–96.

Rotton, J., and Cohn, E. (2001). Temperature, routine activities, and domestic violence: A reanalysis. *Violence and Victims, 16*(2), 203–215.

Reynald, D. and Elffers, H. (2009). The future of Newman's defensible space theory. *European Journal of Criminology, 6*(1), 25–46.

Schweitzer, J. H., Woo Kim, J., and Mackin, J. R. (1999). The impact of the built environment on crime and fear of crime in urban neighborhoods. *Urban Technology, 6*, 59–73.

Sedlak, A. J., Mettenburg, J., Basena, M., Petta, I., McPherson, K., Greene, A., and Li, S. (2010). Fourth National Incidence Study of Child Abuse and Neglect (NIS–4): Report to Congress. Washington, DC: U.S. Department of Health and Human Services, Administration for Children and Families.

Taylor, R. B., Gottfredson, S. D., and Brower, S. (1980). The defensibility of defensible space: A critical review. In T. Hirschi and M. Gottfredson (eds) *Understanding crime*. Beverly Hills, CA: SAGE Publications.

Todal, J., Davis, M. and Kaufman, K. (2010). Rape education prevention: Using program evaluation to identify and answer important questions. In K. L. Kaufman (Ed.) *The Prevention of Sexual Violence: A Practitioner's Sourcebook*. Holyoke, MA: NEARI.

Tseloni, A., Wittebrood, K., Farrell, G., and Pease, K. (2004). Burglary victimization in England and Wales, the United States and the Netherlands. *The British Journal of Criminology, 44*(1), 66–91.

9 Avoiding and Managing Allegations Against Staff

Jo Green

INTRODUCTION

The circumstances surrounding the murders of Holly Wells and Jessica Chapman in Soham in July 2001 have been well documented. It is widely known that Ian Huntley was appointed as caretaker for a community college despite there having been information about allegations against him of sexual offences made by several young people that was not shared at the time of his appointment (North East Lincolnshire Area Child Protection Committee, 2004).

This tragic example of the need for information sharing to inform recruitment decisions and the subsequent establishment of the Independent Safeguarding Authority, recommended by Sir Michael Bichard (Bichard, 2004) as the central means of gathering information about adults who work with children has led to much and often polarised public debate. Opinion since the time of the murders in 2001 has shifted from a public outcry that people who wish to abuse children were all too easily employed in child care/education settings and that 'something should be done' to an increasingly widespread view that the proposed vetting of all adults who work with children, is disproportionate, bureaucratically burdensome and an infringement of civil liberties. (Rogers, 2009) This view was accepted by the UK coalition government and led to a review of the proposed vetting and barring arrangements (Department for Education, Department of Health, Home Office, 2011).

Whilst opposing views understandably existed about the extent of vetting that should be undertaken when selecting adults who will have contact with children there is no valid argument that negates the responsibility of

Creating Safer Organisations: Practical Steps to Prevent the Abuse of Children by Those Working with Them, First Edition. Edited by Marcus Erooga.
© 2012 John Wiley & Sons, Ltd. Published 2012 by John Wiley & Sons, Ltd.

organisations to remain open to the possibility that an adult who has been considered 'safe' may later behave in a way that makes it necessary to further consider their suitability to work with children. As discussed in earlier chapters, no system of vetting, nor any process of recruitment or selection that includes testing the values, beliefs and attitudes towards children held by the candidate, either directly or indirectly through testimony of others, can guarantee that the practice of that candidate will always be safe.

An organisation which recognises this fundamental principle will ensure that all adults working with children understand that the nature of their work places them in a position of trust and so brings particular responsibilities. Such an organisation will have implemented a policy that specifies and clarifies to staff those behaviours which constitute safe practice and those behaviours which should or must be avoided. In recognising that the adoption of such a code of conduct helps organisations to keep children safe by assisting adults to monitor their own practice and that of others within the organisation a national network of Safeguarding Advisers established by the Department for Children Schools and Families (DCSF) produced guidance in 2009 on safe practice for staff working with children. The guidance provides clarity to employers and staff about what behaviour is illegal, unsafe or inappropriate (DCSF, 2009).

Concerns about an individual adult's behaviour may arise directly as a result of an allegation made by a child or children, or indirectly through the observation of colleagues or others of potentially inappropriate behaviour. In all cases, allegations of inappropriate behaviour which *may* constitute abuse must be thoroughly investigated in line with national guidance on the management of allegations against staff (DCSF, 2010).

This chapter considers the difficulties frequently encountered by employers when making judgments about what constitutes inappropriate behaviour. It explores how the professional judgments of those with expertise in child protection should be taken into account when an allegation is being investigated. An issue central to this discussion is the dichotomy between the need to give paramouncy to the welfare of children and the need to ensure that the careers of workers are not wrongly tarnished or ultimately ruined and practical examples are provided of how fairness to adults and the protection of children can be combined through a process which is underpinned by transparency, information sharing, multi-agency working and rigorous assessment resulting in a professional judgment that can properly withstand scrutiny.

THE INCIDENCE OF ALLEGATIONS

There is little empirical evidence about the number of allegations made against members of the children's workforce but the subject has been the topic of regular lobbying by teachers' unions who are understandably concerned about the number of allegations made against their members that are subsequently proven to be unfounded, yet result in damaged careers. In evidence to the House of Commons Select Committee which published its report in July 2009, two teachers' unions offered statistics for consideration.

The National Association of School Masters and Union of Women Teachers (NASUWT, 2009), the largest of the teachers' unions, stated that allegations of abuse rose from 44 in 1991 to between 161 and 193 in each year from 1998 to 2007, but noted that these figures only included cases when the union was required to instruct solicitors to act on their member's behalf in relation to a police interview.

The National Union of Teachers (NUT, 2009) stated that a figure of 200 allegations made against their members each year remained a steady figure, but again it was noted that this figure related only to those cases in which solicitors were instructed by the union. The Committee was presented with statistics by the National Society for the Prevention of Cruelty to Children (NSPCC) that evidenced ChildLine had received 68,758 calls about abuse and bullying during 2007–08. For 1,491 of the children counselled, a teacher was identified as the alleged perpetrator of the abuse. (NSPCC, 2009) There is, however, no way of identifying how many of these 1,491 cases progressed to allegations being made which led to an investigation by the teachers' employers.

The DCSF(2009) submitted evidence that related to the wider children's workforce and supplied figures from a one-off survey for the period from 1 April to 30 September 2007 indicating that there had been 4,069 allegations referred to local authority designated officers (LADO) for consideration during the six-month period.

This data, coming as it does from varying sources and relating to differing thresholds of behaviour is of limited value in providing evidence of whether a significant minority of adults working with children have behaved towards them in a way which has caused them harm or whether differing perceptions of behaviour have led to allegations which, as the teachers' professional organisations believe, have been malicious or unfounded; it also gives no indication of whether individual organisations, such as schools, have recognised and responded to inappropriate behaviour where it has been alleged.

The Parliamentary Committee, however, identified an underlying issue for its inquiry and asked 'whether the rigour of the precautionary approach adopted in order to safeguard children is becoming disproportionate to the cost to those whose careers in working with children in schools may be destroyed on the basis of unfounded allegations' (Children, Schools and Families Committee, 2009).

The precautionary approach referred to by the Select Committee is the response to uncertainty when faced with risk. The practice of responding to even apparently less serious allegations has developed over time in part as a response to evidence that some adult behaviour initially raises little or no concern and progresses as the behaviour goes unchecked ending only when a child is harmed. This approach has clearly raised concern among those who have been subject to an investigation which ultimately proves to be unfounded. In such cases, the adult will often argue that the investigation has caused a 'no smoke without fire' reaction and that future career opportunities are put at risk. However, an investigation which thoroughly examines the nature and context of the allegation can provide the adult with evidence that there was no 'fire' with rumour and speculation being laid to rest.

It is therefore the 'rigour of the precautionary approach', this chapter suggests, which is necessary to ensure the safety and wellbeing of children and the concomitant integrity of the reputations and careers of those who work with them.

BEHAVIOUR THAT GIVES RISE TO ALLEGATIONS

Given the range of relevant professional roles it is essential that all employers set clear personal and professional boundaries for their staff and are explicit about which behaviours are inappropriate, unacceptable or illegal. In many cases this will be within a framework already defined by the appropriate professional body. Adults can then expect alleged behaviour that falls outside of these boundaries to be challenged and investigated and children who may have differing perceptions of what is acceptable and unacceptable behaviour of adults are provided with a safe environment.

The process for managing allegations against adults who work with children is outlined in national guidance (Department for Children Schools and Families, 2010, Appendix 5).and contains the process which should be adhered to when an allegation is made that an adult has:

- behaved in a way that has harmed, or may have harmed, a child;
- possibly committed a criminal offence against, or related to, a child; or
- behaved towards a child or children in a way that may indicate s/he is unsuitable to work with children.

The almost daily contact with children which many adults who work with children have arguably leaves them potentially vulnerable to allegations which fall into one of these categories.

If an adult has harmed, or may have harmed a child the child protection process enables clear decision-making in relation to any harm that a child may have suffered, and to establish whether children have, or are at risk of, suffering as a result of adult behaviour that falls within the remit of the investigation.

When the behaviour or incident that has led to an allegation is a potential criminal offence (e.g. when sexual contact is alleged), there is also a clear process to ensure that a defined purpose is achieved, i.e. that the Police and

Crown Prosecution Service can establish whether there is a criminal case to answer and, if so, to present the evidence in a judicial process.

An allegation which reaches either, or both, of these two criteria is less open to differing interpretations than the third criteria that an adult has behaved in a way which may indicate s/he is *unsuitable to work with children*. This criterion has caused much discussion and debate among employers and child protection officers since it was introduced within guidance in 2006 relating as it does to allegations about behaviour which may be deemed inappropriate. What constitutes appropriate or inappropriate behaviour will vary depending on the context and nature of the work undertaken. For example, if a teacher uses corporal punishment this is a undisputedly a criminal act but if a teacher uses physical restraint to protect a child from harming himself or others, and in so doing causes an injury to the child, judgments will need to be made about whether the action was reasonable, appropriate, proportionate, and within the guidelines for the use of physical intervention. (DCSF, 2010) Similarly, if there is evidence that a social worker has used their position of trust to initiate a sexual relationship with a child, a child protection investigation will lead to criminal action being taken. However when advising, assisting and befriending a young person, as is integral to the social work role, if it appears that the adult has created an atmosphere of intimacy which leads to concern about the nature of the relationship, judgments will need to be made about whether that worker's practice was appropriate.

PROCEDURAL FAIRNESS WITHIN A PRECAUTIONARY APPROACH

Managers within organisations are responsible for ensuring their workforce is safe. Individual managers are likely to make differing interpretations about an adult's behaviour based on their own beliefs, values and professional expertise. However, to ensure that procedural fairness prevails it is crucial that objective standards are applied. The application of a process which adheres to the principles of natural justice is essential to ensuring that the concerns of the Commons Select Committee about *the effect of the precautionary approach* are not realised.

Procedural fairness when responding to an allegation that an adult's behaviour may indicate that the person is unsuitable to work with children can be achieved by adherence to the following principles:

- The welfare of the child is paramount.
- All organisations that work with children have a duty to safeguard and promote the welfare of children.
- Organisations that provide services to children should ensure that adults understand what behaviour will be expected of them.

- Adults about whom there are concerns should be treated fairly, honestly, with common sense and good judgement and should be provided with support.
- Allegations should be managed efficiently and as quickly as possible, avoiding unnecessary delay.
- The welfare of the adult should be protected to guard against possibly unfounded allegations.

With these principles in mind, the behaviour of an adult working with children should be considered as causing concern if the individual has:

- contravened any safe practice guidance given by their organisation or regulatory body;
- exploited or abused a position of power;
- acted in an irresponsible manner which a reasonable person would find alarming or questionable given the nature of work undertaken;
- demonstrated a failure to understand or appreciate how their actions or those of others could adversely impact upon the safety and well being of a child;
- demonstrated an inability to make sound professional judgements which safeguard the welfare of children;
- failed to appropriately follow policy or procedures relating to safeguarding and promoting the welfare of children;
- failed to understand or recognise the need for clear personal and professional boundaries in their work;
- behaved in a way in their personal life which could put children at risk of harm;
- become the subject of criminal proceedings not relating to a child;
- become subject to enquiries under local child protection procedures;
- behaved in a way which seriously undermines the trust and confidence placed in them by their employer.

Procedural fairness begins with an organisation being clear about expectations of staff behaviour and an acceptance of personal responsibility on the part of each individual who has contact with children. When this clarity is established at the outset, in a written code of conduct or similar guidance which all employees are made aware of and expected to adhere to, employer and employee will know and understand those behaviours which are acceptable and those which are not. Any breach of the organisation's code or guidance can therefore be deemed misconduct, or gross misconduct, depending on the nature of the behaviour with consequences at a level appropriate to the full circumstances, as illustrated in this example:
In circumstances where no code of conduct exists, or where it exists but is open to ambiguous interpretation, the process for making judgements will be far more difficult.

Mrs Adams, the manager of an Early Years Setting was informed by a supervisory member of her staff that one of the workers, Mrs Booth was seen to pull a three-year old boy down from a table on which he was standing. She was observed shouting at the child, and having secured him in a standing position on the floor, to hold his shoulders and shake him while she reprimanded him for his poor behaviour.

Mrs Adams asked to see Mrs Booth immediately and asked her about the incident.

Mrs Booth acknowledged that she had momentarily lost her temper with the child who had been previously misbehaving before climbing onto the table and stamping his feet.

At the time of the interview the child was observed happily playing and appeared unharmed.

During the interview Mrs Booth fully acknowledged that she had acted outside the agreed code of conduct that had been issued to all staff and about which training had been regularly received.

Mrs Booth's behaviour had never before given cause for concern during the 4 years that she had worked at the nursery.
Following agreed procedures and having advised Mrs Booth she would do so, the manager of the nursery sought advice from the Local Authority Designated Officer (LADO) and it was agreed that there were no apparent child protection issues to be addressed and that Mrs Adams should seek advice from the nursery's HR provider.

It was subsequently agreed that Mrs Booth should be issued with a written warning relating to misconduct which would remain on her personnel file for a period of one year.

Mrs Adams spoke with the child's mother about the incident. The boy's mother confirmed that her child was unharmed but had mentioned to her that he had been naughty at nursery school and Mrs Booth had been cross with him. The parent was satisfied that the manager was dealing with the matter under the robust procedures employed by the nursery.

This course of action was considered most appropriate because whilst there had been a breach of acceptable behaviour it appeared to be an isolated incident, not part of any pattern of behaviour, and no lasting harm had come to the child. By using a formal disciplinary route, there would remain to the benefit of Mrs Booth's continuing career a clear record of how the matter was investigated and the judgements taken. In terms of future safeguarding, the record would indicate a possible pattern of behaviour should any further concerns arise and may indicate that Mrs Booth was not suitable to continue in her post.

Not all cases will be so clear cut and in many it will be necessary for the behaviour of the adult to be considered from a multi-agency perspective by those with expertise in child protection and whose judgements will be based on knowledge, skills, experience and messages from research about behaviour that poses a risk to children.

It is within this arena that differing views may arise and this is frequently most apparent when considering behaviour which could be regarded by those with experience of inappropriate behaviour of adults towards children as 'grooming' but which may equally be regarded by others as demonstrating an ability to form close relationships with children.

An organisation which has not provided staff with unambiguous guidance about expected or acceptable behaviour is an organisation where neither children nor adults are adequately protected. This is illustrated, in the case study below, one where 'the rigour of the precautionary approach' could have prevented the difficulties which ensued.

Whilst a precautionary approach is necessary in order to fully consider any concern about an adult's behaviour toward children it is equally necessary to employ an approach that demonstrates procedural fairness – and keeps children safe.

Kelly Brown had been regularly attending after school rehearsals with the school orchestra for the end of year concert when many of the students were to leave school. Kelly had been undecided about whether to continue in the 6th form. Her parents wanted her to do so but recently Kelly had been offered a job in a local music shop and was keen to accept the position and leave school.

She told her parents that she had discussed her options with her music teacher, Richard White, who had agreed that the opportunity was too good to be missed and she was now determined to accept the position and leave school. She had told the owner of the music shop that she would take the job.

Kelly's mother drove her daughter to school one morning as usual and then noticed that she had left her mobile phone in the car. By the time she reached her office, the phone alerted her to the receipt of a text message. Believing that Kelly was using a friend's phone to tell her mum that she had left her own phone in the car, she read the message:

CU tonite after rehearsals – you get the prize for best student!

That evening Mrs Brown spoke with her daughter about the text message. Kelly explained that Mr White had been helpful to her and her two friends, Shakira and Grace, discussing their options for their future careers. He had spent extra time with them all after orchestra practice. She said that he was a great teacher who had encouraged them by offering extra help with difficult parts of the performance. He had said he would give a prize to whichever of the three he decided deserved it by being the most improved. The prize was to accompany him to one of the proms concerts in the summer holidays.

Mr and Mrs Brown were concerned that Mr White appeared to have shown a particular interest in their daughter and the following morning arranged to see the Headteacher.

After hearing Mr And Mrs Brown's concerns the Head sought to reassure them that Mr White was an experienced and exemplary teacher. He was well thought of, especially in regard to his ability to gain the trust and confidence of young people, thereby encouraging them to achieve their musical potential.

Mr Brown was not satisfied. He expected the Head to take action against Mr White on the basis that he had made contact of a personal nature with his daughter. He told the Head that if the school did not do so, he would report the matter to the Police.

The Head advised Mr and Mrs Brown that he would consult with colleagues in the Local Authority and would report back to them on what, if any, action was deemed appropriate.

An initial consultation with the Local Authority Designated Officer (LADO) based on the information about Mr White's actions led to advice that a multi-agency meeting should be held during which the Head's professional opinion of Mr White would be considered alongside the views of the Police and colleagues from children's services.

Based on the available information the multi-agency group considered Mr White's actions not to constitute a potential criminal offence, nor had his actions caused any apparent harm to Kelly Brown. However, both the child protection professional and the Police Officer present had concerns that Mr White had acted in a manner which required further consideration in that he had formed, or attempted to form, a personal relationship with a pupil and that his intentions in so doing remained unclear.

Procedural fairness following a multi-agency initial consideration of an allegation which does not meet the threshold for Police or Children's Services involvement relies on sound professional judgements being made. Making such judgements about an individual's behaviour is a difficult and complex process. Integrating the following tenets into their decision-making process will assist the employing organisation's senior staff in reaching decisions about what action to take:

• Consult appropriately.
• Record and document carefully and promptly.
• Acknowledge any lack of expertise or information and seek advice or guidance as needed.

- Keep an open mind until a conclusion is reached.
- Know and act in accordance with the law or get advice if needed.
- Know and apply appropriate procedures.
- Take into account appropriate guidance.
- Take account of all relevant factors.
- Give each factor appropriate weight.
- Apply the duty of care to children and adults.

By continuing the case study of Mr White it can be seen how these rules should be applied to the decision making process in order to determine what action should be taken.

Having consulted appropriately, the Head was able to acknowledge that his own views of Mr White's behaviour were based solely on his professional appraisal of his skills at engaging and interacting with young people and that the views of Police and Child Protection colleagues experienced in the patterns of behaviour of adults who seek to form inappropriate relationships with children should also be considered. In view of the advice received the Head agreed with colleagues that an investigation should be undertaken by the school. The scope of the investigation was agreed as:

- Obtaining from Kelly a full account of the circumstances leading up to receiving the text message from Mr White and her understanding of appropriate and inappropriate behaviour.
- Obtaining statements from Shakira and Grace about their understanding of the prize to be awarded to one of the three girls and their understanding of appropriate and inappropriate behaviour.
- Obtaining from Mr White a full and written account of the circumstances leading up to the sending of the text message to Kelly Brown and his understanding of appropriate and inappropriate behaviour.
- Establishing whether on the basis of the information gained from the investigation there was a case for Mr White to answer.

STATEMENT BY KELLY BROWN – YEAR 11

When I started in year 10 I joined the school orchestra because Mr White was trying to replace those people who had recently left school at the end of year 11. I've always loved playing and I was doing GCSE music. Mr White said that by joining the orchestra I would increase my chances of getting a good grade. At the end of year 10 the orchestra played during the end of year concert for parents. Mum and Dad were really pleased with the progress I'd made and Mr White was too. We had practiced after school once a week and the performance was really good.

In September when I was in Year 11 Shakira, Grace and me talked to Mr White about our chances of going into the 6th form. Shakira and Grace said they were sure they wanted to do music as one of their A levels. They both want to go on to university but I didn't think I wanted to mainly because I knew that I wouldn't get good enough grades in all my GCSEs. Shakira and Grace are both cleverer than me but Mr White said I should aim high too.

Mum and Dad thought that I was spending too much time practicing and not enough time on my other subjects and we had a few arguments about that. But Mr White was always offering to give me extra time to practice in the music room and I enjoyed spending lunch times and sometimes after school in there with Mr White and so did Shakira and Grace. I was never there on my own. I don't think there was anything wrong in that – everyone knew we were doing it. My form tutor knew because she told me it would be best if I kept my clarinet in the music room so that Mr White could keep it locked in there until he opened up the room at lunch time or after school.

We were practicing once a week with the rest of the orchestra but it was just Shakira, Grace and me who did extra practice.

It was good fun. We all enjoyed it but when Mr White said that he would set up a competition between us to see which one of us was best that took some of the fun out of it because we all wanted the prize of going to a concert with Mr White in the summer holidays.

On Saturdays I work at Smithson's music shop. They sell all musical instruments, sheet music, and everything really. I enjoy it and Mr Smithson takes on students quite a lot. Some are in their gap year; some are reading music at university. I've learnt a lot through working there and Mr Smithson talked to me about working there full time after my GCSEs – the money's not bad and I thought it would be a good idea. I could join the city orchestra. My grade predictions apart from music wouldn't get me in to the 6th form and I don't really like studying that much. I talked about it a lot with Mr White. He said it would be too good an opportunity for me to miss. Mum and Dad were a bit disappointed but I know that they understand I struggle sometimes with academic work so they were ok about it. Shakira and Grace are definitely going to do their A levels – they are predicted good grades in their GCSEs.

Mr White thought that me leaving school would be quite a good idea because I would be working and jobs like this one don't come round too often. So last Saturday I told Mr Smithson that I would like to accept the job. He was pleased too. I told Mr White yesterday and told Mum and Dad last night. They were ok about it. And I told them that I had talked to MrWhite about it and they didn't seem bothered about that so I don't know why they're making a fuss now except that Mr White sent me that text message.

I was so pleased that I was going to get to go to the proms. Now all that's been ruined and I really don't know why they're making a fuss – it's so embarrassing, especially as Mr White has been so kind to me and to Shakira and Grace. I don't know if they know I won the prize.

STATEMENT BY GRACE ROBERTS – YEAR 11

I joined the orchestra in year 10. So did Kelly and Shakira. We'd been friends since year 7 though probably Shakira and I have become closer friends recently because we both know that we want to go to University to read music. Kelly is going to leave school at the end of the year. She's been offered a job at Smithson's. She works there on Saturdays and it's a great opportunity but I still think it would have been good if she stayed on at school with us. She thinks that she won't do well enough in her GCSEs and I know that she finds some of her other subjects difficult but honestly she's really talented at music. I think her mum and dad are ok about her leaving. Perhaps she'll take up her studies later – I know she'll keep on with the clarinet after she's left school.

She practices more than Shakira and I do. But we've all given up our lunch times and stayed behind after school more recently as the end of year concert is getting closer. We've all improved – Mr White is so encouraging and helps us with our breathing and the way we stand, and things like that.

He said that he'd treat one of us to a night out at the Royal Albert Hall in appreciation of our commitment and all the time we've given up. He only had two tickets booked so he said he'd take whichever one of us had improved the most. It was always going to be Kelly I think. She does a fantastic solo piece on her clarinet. Anyway, yesterday he told us that he was arranging for Kelly to go and hoped we weren't disappointed. He said that she's worked extra hard and that because she's leaving school at the end of the year it was ok for him to take her whereas if Shakira and me stay on we couldn't really go. It wouldn't be right.

STATEMENT BY SHAKIRA BAKARA – YEAR 11

Kelly, Grace and I are members of the school orchestra. We all joined in year 10. I play the violin and Grace plays the flute. We both also play the piano. Kelly plays the clarinet in the orchestra but doesn't play any other musical instrument. We were the only three new members of the orchestra. We replaced those who left at the end of their year 11. The orchestra is made up from pupils in years 10 and 11 and the sixth formers.

All three of us have talked about our future and our music studies. Grace and I both want to read music at university. Kelly doesn't want to do this but

Grace and I have tried to persuade her to come into the 6th form with us. She thinks she's not clever enough but we think she is. I know she does sometimes struggle with balancing her work across all subjects. But she's really talented at music. She should take it forward. I know that she has asked for Mr White's opinion. She told us that he had said he understood and that if she wanted to leave school that was her decision. I was a bit surprised at that because mostly the teachers try to encourage you to stay on at school.

Kelly, Grace and I have done extra practice for the end of year concert. We were the newest members of the orchestra and there are some quite difficult pieces. We've given up our lunchtimes quite often and stayed after school sometimes. We always stay with the rest of the orchestra once a week, but we did extra. We all enjoy it actually mainly because Mr White is such a good teacher. He encourages us.

He said that he had two tickets for a Proms concert in the summer holidays and that one of us could go with him. At first I thought he was joking but it seemed he wasn't because he told Grace and me yesterday that he was going to take Kelly because she had decided to leave school in July whereas we were going to stay on. He said that it wouldn't be right for either of us to go with him but it was ok if Kelly wasn't at the school. That made sense to me. And anyway to be honest Kelly is just terrific on her clarinet; she's worked hard and deserves the prize.

STATEMENT OF MR RICHARD WHITE – MUSIC TEACHER

The Headteacher asked to see me yesterday morning. He told me that the parents of Kelly Brown had complained because I had sent their daughter a text message about winning a prize.

I told the Headteacher what I'm telling you now and what I've already told my Union rep who's here with me.

Three new members of the orchestra joined at the beginning of Year 10. I needed replacements for three year 11 students who had left at the end of the year. By the end of Year 10 these three girls were accomplished members of the orchestra. It was clear that one of them in particular had great talent – that was Kelly Brown. The other two, Shakira and Grace were very able girls – good all rounders with a particular interest in music, but Kelly struggled with her academic subjects so for her to outshine others in the orchestra was good for her self esteem. I've been a music teacher for many years – I can spot talent and Kelly has talent. That's my job, to encourage all the students and particularly those for whom music is an area where they can excel if they are struggling with other aspects of the curriculum.

Most of the orchestra stay on for the 6th Form and at the end of last year no members left so it has been a stable group for two years now. We practice after school once a week during the spring and summer term in preparation for the concert which takes place in July to mark the end of the academic year. Last year's concert was very good, but because the group has been all together now for two years I have really high expectations of how this year's will be reviewed.

Kelly plays the clarinet – her two friends play the violin and the flute. As I've said Kelly is very talented so I wrote a particularly difficult solo part into this year's concert for her to play. She needed extra help with it of course. But it's not sensible for me to focus on one student with regard to providing extra tuition so all three girls used to come together some lunch times, and stay after school on some occasions and practice together.

Naturally I've had some discussions with them about their futures. All Year 11 students want to talk about that. It's obvious that Shakira and Grace will thrive in the academic atmosphere of the 6th form but Kelly is quite self-aware and had real doubts about her ability to study at A level. At music she would sail through, but she's not an academic and is unlikely to gain sufficiently good grades in her other subjects. She'll definitely get an A grade at music though. This was discussed with her parents earlier in the year. They were thrilled to hear of how well she was expected to do at music and I know they would like her to continue her studies.

Kelly spoke to me recently following an after school practice. She said that she had been discussing everything with her parents in light of the fact that she had been offered a full-time job at Smithson's. I told her that I thought that was a fantastic opportunity to remain linked to her music and that in these difficult times, it was good to secure a job. I suggested that she could always return to studies at a later date.

A few weeks ago I had told all three girls that I had two tickets to a proms concert in the summer and that I would give one of the tickets away to whichever one of them had made the most progress because of their practicing. It was obviously Kelly, but I didn't want to discourage or disappoint the other two so I explained to them that as Kelly was leaving school it was more appropriate that I offered the ticket to her.

I had no intention of taking any of the girls to the concert, I was merely offering up a spare ticket.

They have interpreted my intentions wrongly.

I did send Kelly a text message. I wanted to tell the other two before telling her so that I could gauge their reaction. They seemed fine about it and I didn't want them to tell her before I did which is why I contacted her by phone.

I'm not aware of any rule that states members of staff can't use text messaging as a means of getting in touch with pupils. In fact I regularly use it as a means of confirming times of orchestra practice and students text me if they are unexpectedly unable to attend. I think that's only courteous.

The extra practice sessions I provide for the orchestra is known throughout the school. It's a regular after school activity.

> The lunch times sessions I gave to these three girls are not so formal, but all the staff know that I've been doing it. No problem with it has ever been raised by anyone. Until now that is. I'm angry that you are investigating this.

In this scenario there are inevitably differing opinions about Mr White's actions. One is that he is a committed teacher who has demonstrated willingness to provide extra tuition to pupils, to encourage them to fulfil their potential and to offer encouragement and reward. He has not breached any code of conduct by his actions and his behaviour is reasonable, even laudable.

An alternate view is that Mr White's acted outside professional boundaries and despite there being no code of conduct, demonstrated little more than a lack of 'common sense'.

A further possible view is that Mr White's behaviour is characteristic of adults who deliberately seek or create opportunities to abuse children or young people.

Would the adoption of a precautionary approach as identified by the Commons Select Committee lead to Mr White's career being ruined, or will it lead to children being protected from someone who is unsuitable to work with them?

The basis for reaching a conclusion as to whether Mr White has a case of misconduct to answer is an analysis of the available information. In doing so the following questions should be considered in order to distinguish which, if any, of Mr White's actions were those that were within professional guidelines, or generally believed to be acceptable by others in the profession, or would be considered as deviating from acceptable practice.

Whilst the reader does not have to reach a decision about Mr White, the professionals involved in such a case would have to do so based on professional judgement. An organisation striving to become a safe organisation will readily engage in the multi-agency process which follows concerns about an adult's behaviour being raised. Such a process provides the rigour that is necessary for an organisation to assert that it is safe, but this reactive approach to concerns when they arise is only one characteristic of a safe organisation.

THE ADULT – MR WHITE

Is it reasonable for a teacher to provide extra opportunities for practice or tuition?

Was there any discussion with a manager and is there any record of that?

Were the extra practice sessions agreed and authorised by a manager?

Were the pupils' parents informed of the extra sessions other than by the pupils themselves?

Why were only three girls selected to benefit from these additional sessions?

Was it reasonable to offer a reward to one of the three girls as a means of encouragement?

Why was the gift of a ticket to a concert chosen as the reward?

What was Mr White's intention for use of the remaining ticket?

Apart from her obvious talent, why was Kelly Brown chosen as the winner of the reward?

What was the significance of Kelly's decision to leave school and how did this impact on Mr White's decision to award the prize to her?

Why was it within the music teacher's role to advise a pupil on the merits of leaving school to take up employment?

What is the significance of Mr White's statement that he was angry about the investigation into his actions and his denial of any wrongdoing?

Why does Mr White compare sending a personal text message to a pupil with using text messaging to arrange or re-arrange scheduled lessons?

THE YOUNG PEOPLE

What is the significance of Kelly Brown feeling concerned about her parents bringing the matter to the attention of the Headteacher for investigation?

What is the significance of one of the friends stating that she was surprised at the advice given to Kelly by Mr White?

Why did all the young people perceive Mr White's offer of a ticket to the concert to include accompanying him on the evening in question?

Why did Kelly never receive extra help alone for the solo piece she had been chosen to play?

Kelly is believed to be of lower academic ability than the other two girls – is this a significant factor in Mr White's choice of recipient for the prize?

THE HEADTEACHER

Why does the Head consider Mr White to have a particular talent for gaining the trust and confidence of young people?

How would he have viewed Mr White's actions had they been brought to his attention by someone other than the pupil's parents?

What weight did the headteacher apply to Mr Brown's assertion that he would bring the matter to the attention of the Police if the Headteacher did not take action against Mr White?

MR AND MRS BROWN

Why were Mr and Mrs Brown not reassured by the Headteacher's professional opinion of Mr White?

CHARACTERISTICS OF A SAFE ORGANISATION

A safe organisation will ensure that its recruitment, induction and supervisory processes place high importance on establishing and maintaining an adult workforce that recognises it has a unique opportunity to interact with children and young people in ways that are both affirming and inspiring yet allow no room for the work that is carried out to be a vehicle for abuse. Such an organisation will also assist children in recognising which behaviours are safe and which are not. These processes support an organisation's work force in understanding what behaviour may call into question an adults suitability to continue to work with children and young people together with an acceptance that any concerns which arise they will be thoroughly and fairly considered.

Characteristically, the organisation will:

- ensure its recruitment procedures are robust and in line with national guidance on each occasion an adult is recruited and selected to work with children;
- provide written guidance on the behaviour expected of all adults in the organisation;
- expect all adults to agree with and abide by the guidance;
- provide induction training for newly recruited adults and regular training thereafter;
- ensure that adults are subject to supervision, providing advice and further guidance if necessary;
- ensure that all adults understood how to access whistle blowing procedures;
- act promptly and robustly on any concerns that do arise;
- Work closely within a multi-disciplinary colleagues, accepting advice as appropriate
- understand the difference between behaviour which might lead to a criminal conviction and that which falls outside the organisation's code or conduct or guidance;
- be prepared to follow disciplinary procedures appropriately;
- ensure that procedures are demonstrably fair.

Such an organisation will be adopting a precautionary approach which recognises that children must be protected from those who are unsuitable to work with them and in so doing establishes clear boundaries for behaviour and clear processes for responding to behaviour that oversteps those boundaries. Such an organisation is protective of both children and adults alike.

REFERENCES

Bichard M. (2004) The Bichard Inquiry Report, London: The Stationery Office. Available at www.**bichardinquiry**.org.uk/10663/report.pdf (accessed 24 February 2011).

Children, Schools and Families Committee (2009) Fifth Report: Allegations against School Staff. Available at http://www.publications.parliament.uk/pa/cm200809/cmselect/cmchilsch/695/69502.htm (Accessed 20 February 2011).

Department for Children, Schools and Families (2010) Working Together to Safeguard Children. Available at http://www.education.gov.uk/publications/standard/publicationdetail/page1/DCSF-00305-2010 (accessed 20 February 2011).

Department for Children, Schools and Families (2010) Guidance for Safer Working Practice for Adults Working With Children and Young People. Available at http://webarchive.nationalarchives.gov.uk/20100202100434/dcsf.gov.uk/everychildmatters/resources-and-practice/ig00311/ (Accessed 20 February 2011).

Department for Children, Schools and Families (2010) The use of force to control or restrain pupils: Guidance for schools in England. Available at http://www.scie-socialcareonline.org.uk/profile.asp?guid=1c413171-04f1-4710-b829-9cc948ce7d7d (accessed 20 February 2011).

Department of Education, Department of Health, Home Office (2011) Vetting and Barring Scheme Remodelling Review. Report and Recommendations [pdf]. Available at www.**homeoffice**.gov.uk/publications/crime/vbs-report?view=Binary (accessed 24 February 2011).

North East Lincolnshire Area Child Protection Committee, (2004) Report of Sir Christopher Kelly [pdf] Available at http://www.nelincs.gov.uk/children-and-families/childrens-social-care/local-safeguarding-childrens-board/serious-case-reviews/serious-case-review-ian-huntley/ (accessed 24 February 2011).

Rogers, B. (2009) Why child protection has gone too far. *Prospect Magazine*. Issue 169, Available at http://www.prospectmagazine.co.uk/issue/169/ (accessed 20 February 2011).

Index

Page numbers in *italics* refer to figures, those in **bold** refer to tables.

*Creating Safer Organisations: Practical Steps to Prevent the Abuse of Children by Those Working
with Them*, First Edition. Edited by Marcus Erooga.
© 2012 John Wiley & Sons, Ltd. Published 2012 by John Wiley & Sons, Ltd.